Intergenerational Justice

Routledge Studies in Contemporary Philosophy

1. Email and Ethics
Style and Ethical Relations in Computer-Mediated Communication
Emma Rooksby

2. Causation and Laws of Nature
Max Kistler

3. Internalism and Epistemology
The Architecture of Reason
Timothy McGrew and Lydia McGrew

4. Einstein, Relativity and Absolute Simultaneity
Edited by William Lane Craig and Quentin Smith

5. Epistemology Modalized
Kelly Becker

6. Truth and Speech Acts
Studies in the Philosophy of Language
Dirk Greimann & Geo Siegwart

7. Fiction, Narrative, and Knowledge
A Sense of the World
Edited by John Gibson, Wolfgang Huemer, and Luca Pocci

8. A Pragmatist Philosophy of Democracy
Communities of Inquiry
Robert B. Talisse

9. Aesthetics and Material Beauty
Aesthetics Naturalized
Jennifer A. McMahon

10. Aesthetic Experience
Edited by Richard Shusterman and Adele Tomlin

11. Real Essentialism
David S. Oderberg

12. Practical Identity and Narrative Agency
Edited by Catriona Mackenzie and Kim Atkins

13. Metaphysics and the Representational Fallacy
Heather Dyke

14. Narrative Identity and Moral Identity
A Practical Perspective
Kim Atkins

15. Intergenerational Justice
Rights and Responsibilities in an Intergenerational Polity
Janna Thompson

Intergenerational Justice

Rights and Responsibilities in an Intergenerational Polity

Janna Thompson

Routledge
Taylor & Francis Group
New York   London

First published 2009
by Routledge
711 Third Ave, New York, NY 10017

Simultaneously published in the UK
by Routledge
2 Park Square, Milton Park, Abingdon, Oxon OX14 4RN

Routledge is an imprint of the Taylor & Francis Group, an informa business

First issued in paperback 2013

© 2009 Taylor & Francis

Typeset in Sabon by IBT Global.

All rights reserved. No part of this book may be reprinted or reproduced or utilised in any form or by any electronic, mechanical, or other means, now known or hereafter invented, including photocopying and recording, or in any information storage or retrieval system, without permission in writing from the publishers.

Trademark Notice: Product or corporate names may be trademarks or registered trademarks, and are used only for identification and explanation without intent to infringe.

Library of Congress Cataloging in Publication Data
Thompson, Janna, 1942–
  Intergenerational justice : rights and responsibilities in an intergenerational polity / Janna Thompson.
    p. cm.—(Routledge studies in contemporary philosophy ; 13)
  Includes bibliographical references and index.
  1. Reparations for historical injustices. 2. Intergenerational relations.
  3. Restorative justice. I. Title.
  JC578.T47 2009
  320.01'1—dc22

ISBN13: 978-0-415-99628-0 (hbk)
ISBN13: 978-0-203-87868-2 (ebk)
ISBN13: 978-0-415-84522-9 (pbk)

Contents

1 Introduction: Towards a Theory of Justice for an Intergenerational Polity ... 1

2 Justice, Non-Identity and Intergenerational Relationships ... 14

3 Partnership, Reciprocity and Identity ... 28

4 Lifetime-Transcending Interests ... 39

5 Lifetime-Transcending Interests and Duties to Past People ... 55

6 Taking Responsibility for the Past ... 73

7 Just Inheritance in an Intergenerational Polity ... 85

8 Generational Rights and Duties ... 101

9 Fair Shares ... 113

10 Creating Future Generations ... 128

11 Sustainability and Future Generations ... 145

12 Intergenerational Global Justice ... 160

Notes ... 175
Bibliography ... 179
Index ... 187

1 Introduction
Towards a Theory of Justice for an Intergenerational Polity

A polity is an intergenerational community. Citizens are born into a pre-existing society that, in most cases, will continue to exist, perhaps for many generations, after they are dead. They obey laws and act in the framework of institutions that were brought into being by past generations and their government makes laws and commitments that will affect the lives and relationships of future generations. They are the heirs of a legacy that is the work of many generations and they will in turn provide an inheritance for their successors. Citizens are predisposed to understand themselves and their political actions in a historical framework that connects the deeds of past generations to their own deeds and to aspirations for the future of their society. 'We the people' is a historical continuum that reaches into the indefinite future. It implies the existence and persistence of intergenerational relationships that include past, as well as present and future, members.

How these relationships should be understood, what entitlements and obligations they generate, is the subject matter for a theory of intergenerational justice. This book presents a theory of intergenerational justice focusing on relationships in a polity. 'A *polity* is a political society that persists through time and across generations: an organised entity capable of acting as an agent and taking responsibility for its actions.' The predominant polities of this world are nation-states, but the term can also be used to describe semi-independent, politically organised communities (for example, indigenous nations), trans-national federations or an imagined future world-state. The polities I have in mind in this study are liberal democracies, but in polities that are not liberal democracies members are likely to be motivated by similar moral concerns and political considerations. One of the theses that I will argue for is that intergenerational entitlements and obligations arise out of interests that all individuals are likely to possess.

Almost no one doubts that intergenerational responsibilities exist, but how they should be conceived and determined are puzzles for philosophers, and sometimes for citizens and policymakers. Some of the issues are similar to those that come up when people reason about their duties to contemporaries. For example, those who discuss intergenerational justice must consider what responsibilities they have to people who existed or will exist in countries outside their borders. But the subject of intergenerational justice creates puzzles of its own. A theory of intergenerational justice must come to grips with issues that are conceptual, political, ontological and moral.

WHAT IS A GENERATION?

The obvious conceptual question is, 'What belongs to the subject matter of intergenerational justice'? To most philosophers, intergenerational justice is about the duties that present citizens owe to the young and to unborn generations. John Rawls, for example, thinks of justice between the generations as consisting of duties that citizens owe to their descendants (1999a: 251–8). This conception divides justice into two parts: synchronic and diachronic. *Synchronic justice* is justice between contemporaries, or between those contemporaries who are full participants in the political relationships of their society. *Diachronic justice* has to do with relationships between these contemporaries and future citizens.

There are several problems with this way of conceiving of the subject matter of intergenerational justice. One of them is that it has nothing to say about duties in respect to past generations and their deeds. Most of us believe that such duties exist. Many citizens believe that they have duties to remember and honour the dead—for example, to remember those who died defending their country. Many assume that they have historical obligations in respect to the deeds of predecessors—for example, to keep the commitments that they made or to make recompense for their past wrongs. These conceptions of duty are about relationships between the generations: they tell us what members of each generation ought to be prepared to do for the sake of their predecessors. Whether these duties exist and, if so, how they should be understood and what they require are also topics for a theory of intergenerational justice.

Another problem with the division of labour between synchronic and diachronic justice is that it makes it impossible to conceive of relationships between contemporaries as involving issues of intergenerational justice. That there are such issues is suggested by debates about how the burdens of caring for an ageing population should be shared by members of a society. Younger generations, who in many countries are faced with the prospect of having to support a much larger generation of ageing baby-boomers, are predisposed to question the fairness of an arrangement that may require them to make more sacrifices to support the old than previous generations were required to bear (Thomson 1991). This issue is one among many that members of a society raise about the relative benefits and burdens of co-temporal generations. Is it just that members of younger generations have to pay relatively more for a tertiary education than did their elders? Is it right that they have to service national debts that their elders incurred? These do not seem to be questions that can be answered by a synchronic theory of justice. They require a consideration of how benefits and burdens should be distributed among people who belong to different but interacting generations. They raise issues of intergenerational justice.

The recognition that issues of intergenerational justice also exist among contemporaries invites us to view a political society from a diachronic perspective. As members of each generation pass through life they acquire obligations and entitlements in respect to the members of preceding and succeeding generations. People are born into a previously existing society and acquire a legacy of entitlements and obligations from the past. The elders in their family and society assume responsibility for nurturing them and giving them an education. When they grow up they acquire in their turn responsibilities for younger and unborn generations, and as I shall argue, for discharging the historical obligations of their community or society. They fulfil duties of care to the elderly of their family and society and make justified demands on their successors (as I will also argue); in their old age their support becomes the responsibility of members of younger generations who will also be responsible for fulfilling duties in respect to their interests and deeds after they are dead. Intergenerational justice, broadly understood, is about the nature and justification of these obligations and entitlements and how the benefits and burdens that they entail should be distributed among the generations of a society.

INTERGENERATIONAL JUSTICE AND POLITICAL PHILOSOPHY

According to this broad conception of intergenerational justice, intergenerational entitlements and responsibilities are central to relationships in a political society. They have to do with how members of a society deal with the basic facts of human existence, concerns that transcend individual lives and needs and interests that must be satisfied if a society is to persist and flourish through time. However, political philosophers have not generally treated these concerns as central. In modern political philosophy intergenerational justice generally makes its appearance as an addendum to theories of synchronic justice.

One reason for this treatment has to do with the nature of modern political theory. Theories of justice, right or political responsibility centre on the interests and relationships of co-temporal adult individuals. They concentrate on determining the bargains or agreements that would be endorsed by these individuals, the rights that they can claim or on the responsibilities that arise from their collective political actions. Such accounts cannot easily encompass intergenerational relationships. We cannot make bargains or agreements with the dead or the unborn; it is difficult to understand how dead or future people can have rights or participate in a just process, or how ideas about contracts and collective responsibility apply to them. Philosophers who want to extend their theories to encompass diachronic relationships have to battle against the difficulties created by concepts and approaches that were not designed for these tasks.

This study is based on the proposition that intergenerational justice ought to be regarded as a central concern of a political society. The environmental issues that have become so prominent since the 1970s provide an obvious reason why intergenerational concerns should be central to reasoning about justice and responsibility in a political society. These issues make us aware that our activities can blight the future of our children and the lives of future generations. They warn us that policies and ideals that have been accepted for generations could be having detrimental effects on the environment that future people will inherit. They require us to make intergenerational concerns central to all policy-making. Implicit or explicit in definitions of 'sustainability' or 'sustainable development' is a conception of intergenerational justice.

Another reason why it is a mistake to marginalise relationships between the generations is that they are not marginal for most people. Citizens commonly locate themselves in a history that concerns itself with the deeds of past citizens. They take pride in their nation's achievements and feel shame for its failures or misdeeds. They regard themselves as inheritors of a valued political tradition that they want to maintain for their successors. A modern nation is, according to Benedict Anderson, a 'deep horizontal comradeship' in which members define themselves by reference to a heritage and history and aim to determine their common destiny through political means (1983: 16). Being a member of a nation, says Yael Tamir, requires individuals to keep faith with its history (1993: 29).

The nation is not the only historical community of identification that a polity supports or makes possible. Some citizens identify more strongly with their family or some other social group: a tribe, a local community or an ethnic or religious group. Individuals are likely to have multiple identities. But whatever their allegiances, in forming their ideas about themselves and their world they are locating themselves in histories that go back before the time of their birth and stretch forward into the future beyond their lifetime. According to Annette Baier, individuals are essentially second persons:

> Persons are essentially successors, heirs to other persons who formed and cared for them, and their personality is revealed both in their relations to others and in their response to their own recognized genesis (1985: 85).

She does not mean merely that we depend physically and psychologically on our parents and others who raise us, but that our identity is bound up with the heritage we receive from our cultural and familial predecessors: 'We acquire a sense of ourselves as occupying a place in a historical and social order of persons, each of whom has a personal history interwoven with the history of a community' (90).

Individuals locate and identify themselves in relation to a past that existed before their birth. They also have desires and interests concerning a future that will, or could, exist after their lifetimes. They care about the future well-being of their children, the future of their community and the fate of their projects or their ideals. They want their successors to protect the things that they care about, and sometimes they are motivated to make demands of those who will survive them. I will argue that such 'lifetime-transcending interests' play an important role in the lives and aspirations of individuals, and that they are the basis of practices that enable citizens and members of communities to make moral demands of their successors and which, in turn, give these individuals obligations in respect to their predecessors.

POLITICAL ISSUES IN AN INTERGENERATIONAL POLITY

If it is accepted that a political society ought to be conceived as intergenerational, then we need to give an account of what binds the generations together in relationships of entitlement and obligation. According to contractual accounts, the duties that citizens owe to each other as members of a polity arise out of their consenting participation in relationships that they have formed with each other. This is clearly not an adequate basis for a theory of intergenerational justice. An appeal to mutual consent is not, at least in any obvious way, applicable to relationships between the generations.

That intergenerational bonds exist is nevertheless axiomatic in ordinary political discourse. A polity as an organized collective with a government and officials to carry out decisions is assumed to be an agent and is often described as having some of the characteristics of a person. It decides, acts and is expected to take responsibility for its actions. Since a polity is intergenerational, it seems natural to think of it as having an identity that persists through the generations: a historical past and continuing future. As an agent it is assumed to have responsibilities in respect to both its past and future. This conception of the polity, if taken seriously, leads to some familiar issues about identity through time. Can we say that the United States before the Civil War was the same polity as it was post-Civil War, or as it is now? If its present government is supposed to take responsibility for actions committed in the historical past—for example, if it is expected to pay reparations for slavery—then this seems an obvious question to ask. But it is not clear how we should answer it.

More fundamental is the question of how we conceive of the relationship between the polity as an intergenerational agent and the concerns of its citizens. The Hegelian idea that the state is the true agent of politics and history, with the implication that the wills of its members should be subjected to the aims of the state, is rejected almost unanimously by contemporary political philosophers. Citizens are not required to make sacrifices just so their state can act as a responsible intergenerational agent in national and international politics. If the polity is supposed to behave as a responsible intergenerational agent—for example, to keep its long-term commitments or to make reparation for past injustices—then its having such obligations must be explained by the interests of individuals, whether its own members or people elsewhere in the world. In other words, we need to explain why citizens should accept the obligation of ensuring that their polity satisfies the conditions for being a responsible intergenerational agent. We return to the question of what, if anything, binds the generations in relationships of entitlement and obligation. Let us consider two radically different answers to this question.

According to the first, intergenerational bonds do not exist, or exist at best in a way that does not generate much in the way of obligations. Thomas Paine declared that '[e]very age and generation must be as free to act for itself, *in all cases,* as the ages and generations which preceded it' (1971: 63). Thomas Jefferson agreed: 'One generation is to another as one independent nation to another', he said, thus insisting on the right of citizens of each generation to re-make their institutions, commitments and policies according to their own interests and values (1907: 456). Following this line of thought, Jefferson, at one time, suggested that the constitution ought to be renegotiated in every generation, thus allowing younger generations a chance to construct a political society according to their interests and needs (1907: 459).[1]

Paine and Jefferson thought it wrong that the freedom of democratic citizens to govern themselves should be limited by decisions over which they could exercise no control—whether made in another country or by people of the past. But if we take literally Jefferson's idea that generations are politically independent, then past generations or their deeds cannot be a source of obligations for existing citizens. Citizens can only be expected to take collective responsibility for their own political decisions. An implication of this position is that states cannot be expected to act as morally responsible intergenerational agents that keep their commitments and make recompense for their past misdeeds. Future citizens are entitled to reject commitments made by their forebears and to deny responsibility for their deeds. Moreover, if we understand the position to require that each generation takes responsibility only for itself (as the idea of the periodic social contract might suggest), then it is difficult to explain why individuals, as citizens of a political society, should accept obligations to their successors (or indeed how people who come after can be regarded as successors).

Jefferson, himself the framer of constitutions, was not consistent in his insistence that present citizens should not attempt to bind their successors. And his statement that 'the earth belongs in usufruct to the living' suggests that present people have obligations to future generations (1907: 456). Nevertheless, the radical position that he and Paine sometimes took is a natural consequence of the synchronic perspective. Citizens have political obligations to each other that arise from their endorsement of a social contract and their participation in democratic decision-making. The relationship that gives them these obligations does not hold between them and non-existent generations. The obvious question is whether a political relationship in which the diachronic dimension is missing would be in the interest of citizens. I will argue in this book that it is not: that citizens, as well as outsiders, have interests that can only be satisfied in a society in which each generation takes responsibility for the affairs of its predecessors and accepts obligations to its political successors.

The other extreme—the view that Paine is arguing against—emphasises the diachronic. According to Edmund Burke, a society:

> ... is a partnership in every virtue and in all perfection. As the ends of such a partnership cannot be obtained in many generations, it becomes a partnership not only between those who are living, but between those who are living, those who are dead, and those who are to be born (1968: 194–5).

The relationship between the generations, according to this idea, is a form of cooperation that gives present generations obligations in respect to past as well as future generations. He calls this partnership contractual, but it is not the result of a voluntary agreement. Individuals are born into the obligations and entitlements that the partnership entails, and a morally sound person values his role in the partnership and accepts, as a matter of course, the associated duties and the limitations that they impose on his freedom.

The idea that we have intergenerational duties that follow from membership in a community has been taken up in recent times by those described as communitarians and by those who advocate nationalist or patriotic conceptions of duty. Alasdair MacIntyre says:

> I am someone's son or daughter, someone else's cousin or uncle ... I belong to this clan, that tribe, this nation. Hence what is good for me has to be the good for one who inhabits these roles. As such I inherit from the past of my family, my city, my tribe, my nation, a variety of debts, inheritances, rightful expectations and obligations. These constitute the given of my life, my moral starting point (1981: 220).

In his eyes the past looms large. Like Burke, he indicates that our duties to present and future people are based on historical precedent. Little room is left for individual or collective self-determination of presently existing people. But just for this reason many people find such accounts unappealing, especially those who, like Paine and Jefferson, are not prepared to accept that their duties as citizens are historically given.

There seems to be ample room for alternative conceptions between an idea of a political relationship which is determinedly synchronic and one which is overwhelmingly diachronic. One such idea is Rawls's account of intergenerational relationships in a political society. His view, which leans in the direction of Jefferson and Paine, presents a political society as requiring cooperation between the generations to establish and maintain institutions of justice. Each generation has a duty to do its fair share and each, under ideal conditions, obtains its rightful share. Rawls presents this outcome as a hypothetical agreement reached in a contract that takes into account the interests of all generations (1999a: 225). This contract does not limit the freedom of present people to determine the nature of their political institutions, but it gives them a duty to provide for future citizens what they believe their forebears ought to have provided for them.

Whether Rawls reaches the right conclusion is something that needs to be discussed. But his approach also raises questions about whether intergenerational cooperation, as he understands it, provides a sufficient basis for intergenerational obligations. What kind of account is needed is a central question for this study.

ONTOLOGICAL ISSUES

Whether Rawls's theory or any account of intergenerational justice is adequate depends on its ability to surmount or avoid difficult ontological problems. Future people do not yet exist; past generations exist no longer. In both cases their non-existence makes it difficult to explain why we have duties to them. We wrong others, according to many accounts, by violating their rights or by setting back their interests. Since nothing we can do will gratify the dead or displease them, it is difficult to understand how their interests can be set back. Nor do they seem to satisfy requirements for having rights. Carl Wellman, for example, disqualifies the dead as right bearers because they are no longer agents (1995: 146–57). Other philosophers have questioned whether sense can be made of duties to the dead, however they are conceived, and this scepticism might seem like a good reason for leaving them out of the picture.

That we can act in ways which will make things worse or better for unborn generations is uncontroversial. However, their non-existence poses problems of a different kind. Most accounts of morality and right assume that we owe duties to persons whose identities can be specified. But the identities of future people are indeterminate. Ruth Macklin holds that future people cannot have rights because rights, she says, can only be ascribed to identifiable persons (1981: 152). Richard T. De George argues that future people can't have rights because as indeterminate persons, they cannot be said to have interests: 'future generations or future individuals or groups should correctly be said to have a right only to what is available when they come into existence, and hence when their possible future rights become actual and present' (1981: 160). But this means that we cannot now violate the rights of the unborn. Wilfred Beckerman and Joanna Pasek draw the conclusion that there is no such thing as intergenerational justice (2001: 14).

We not only determine what conditions future generations will experience, we also create the generations who will experience them. Which individuals will exist in the future will depend on the activities we engage in, individually and collectively. These facts of life-making raise a much-discussed philosophical difficulty sometimes called the 'non-identity problem'.[2] Suppose that we pursue a policy that many environmentalists regard as irresponsible: we do nothing effective to prevent the build up of greenhouse gases. Suppose also that because of our inaction, an irreversible train of events is set in motion which results, after 100 years have passed, in a world that is impoverished by environmental damage and social disruption. Since that disruption would have had a large effect on who is born, the individuals who are in existence after the 100 years have passed will mostly have different identities from the individuals who would have existed if we had acted more responsibly. Because of our behaviour these individuals suffer from many deprivations. But it seems that they cannot claim to have been harmed by our irresponsibility (at least so long as they find their lives worth living), since if we had acted differently, they wouldn't have come into existence. Few philosophers want to conclude that the problem of non-identity means that we don't really have duties to, or in respect to, future people. The challenge is to explain how we can wrong future people while avoiding the difficulty.

The non-identity problem is usually understood as a problem about the identity of individuals. But it is important to note that there is also a non-identity problem in respect to groups. Suppose that our reason for thinking that we have a duty to future people depends on their being future members of our community. Some philosophers, as we will see, recommend this conception of duty as a way of avoiding the non-identity problem in respect to individuals. But suppose also that because of our environmental depredations our community no longer exists in 100 years' time. Those who are born after that date cannot complain that we have failed in our duty to them. By divesting the world of our community, it seems that we have also divested ourselves of duties to future members of our community.

A theory of intergenerational justice must circumvent or overcome both non-identity problems and other ontological problems that arise concerning the existence of past and future generations. In Chapters 2 and 3, I will show how this can be done in the context of a theory about intergenerational justice in a political society.

MORAL ISSUES IN AN INTERGENERATIONAL POLITY

A theory of justice requires a moral basis. The basic premise of almost all modern moral and political theories is that all individuals deserve equal respect. Doctrines of human rights, deontological theories that demand that we treat individuals as ends, consequentialist theories which count each individual equally in a calculus which aims at maximising a good are based on this assumption. Distance in space is no reason for disqualifying individuals as equal objects of moral concern. And it seems that distance in time should also make no moral difference. Some of the problems with the analogy between distance in space and distance in time have already been discussed. The status of the dead is unclear, and even if we are willing to believe that we have duties to dead individuals, it is not obvious that their interests should be regarded as equal to the interests of the living. The non-existence of more distant future generations poses conceptual and ontological problems. But the analogy between space and time also brings to our attention additional problems about the scope of our moral concern.

How far into the future (or the past) should this concern extend? Traditional theories of intergenerational justice tell us that we have duties to our immediate successors. But environmentalists point out that some of our activities—storing nuclear waste, for example—could have detrimental effects on generations that are much more distant. Even so, if our duties to others, and the requirement that we treat them as equals, depend on their having certain qualities or the capacity to have certain interests, then it seems possible to doubt that we have duties to people of the distant future. M.P. Golding thinks that we owe nothing to a future being who has become 'Programmed Man, fabricated to order, with his finger constantly on the Delgado button that stimulates the pleasure centre of the brain' (1972: 99). And if duties to future generations depend on their relationship to us—on their being members of our polity, family or community—then we can assume that people of the very distant future are beyond the scope of our responsibilities. Many people reject such limitations. 'Whoever is living in our territory in five centuries time,' says Joel Feinberg, 'will have interests that we can affect, for better or worse' (1974: 65). But if we think that distant future people ought to be objects of moral concern, then the question is not merely what we should do for them, but how we should include them in our theories.

We do things that will have an effect on future people. We also create the people who will be affected. Our people-making powers point to another disanalogy between distance in space and distance in time which has implications for moral reasoning. One of these implications is the non-identity problem. But there are other more familiar and practical moral difficulties: those that centre on the issue of population and population control. Creating too many people could lead to environmental and social disaster; having too few could create burdens for some generations. In an intergenerational political society it seems inevitable that children will be regarded as a social resource that can exist in too small or too large a quantity. But to treat the production of people as something that can be subjected to social control seems to violate basic ideas about respect for people and their rights. A theory of intergenerational justice has to confront an apparent contradiction between synchronic and diachronic justice; between being just to present people and being just to people of the future.

A theory of intergenerational justice should also have something to say about our increasing ability to determine the characteristics of future people through use of genetic technology. Do considerations of intergenerational justice put limits on how this technology should be used? Could it require us to use it in a particular way?

BEING INTERGENERATIONALLY JUST

The previous discussion shows that those who concern themselves with intergenerational justice must engage in a considerable amount of conceptual labour before they can even begin to propound a particular view about what is intergenerationally just. But few people doubt that intergenerational duties exist. And many would agree with Rawls that justice between generations has to do with each generation giving and getting its fair share. But what should they give and get, and what counts as a fair share?

The entitlements of past generations, I will argue, are best determined by considering what the members of a generation can reasonably demand of their successors. The controversial issue in this case is whether they can reasonably demand anything at all. Duties to the young and future generations could be determined, as Rawls says, by considering what the members of a generation think they are entitled to obtain from their predecessors. According to his view, what each generation should aim to establish and maintain for its successors are institutions of justice. Some find this too little; others wonder whether it is too much. Those predisposed to a Jeffersonian view might insist that we should concentrate on transferring capital, thus leaving future generations free to establish the institutions that they want. In the spirit of Burke, others are likely to insist that we should maintain for our successors the traditions and values that we have inherited from the past. Environmentalists believe that natural values should be preserved, and many citizens assume that they have a duty to maintain for posterity goods of particular significance to their nation.

There is a similar lack of certainty about what counts as a fair share. It seems natural to suppose that a fair share of benefits and burdens for each generation ought to be an equal share relative to wealth. But on reflection it is obvious that this idea of equity cannot be realised. Rawls does not apply his principle of distributive justice to relations between the generations on the grounds that it is impossible to compensate past generations (1999a: 254). But the limitation that temporal location places on our actions is not the only problem with the idea that shares should be equalized. Exchanges of resources between the generations are not completely impossible—particularly between overlapping generations. And older generations, anticipating that their successors will be wealthy, could attempt to get a more equal share by borrowing from the future. Jefferson fulminates against the practice of making younger generations pay for the enjoyments of their elders and many people share his disapproval (Peter 2002). In debates about the problems created by demographic change, the costs that older generations might impose on the young are a main issue. But a question that needs to be answered is whether, and why, such redistributions of wealth count as unjust.

A SURVEY

These, in brief, are some of the issues that a theory of intergenerational justice must confront. In this book I will defend the view that citizens of a polity have duties to and in respect to past generations, and I will argue that each generation has a duty to ensure, so far as it can, that the burdens their successors must bear to maintain institutions of justice, fulfil duties of intergenerational justice and perpetuate other things of value will not be greater than its own. But a large part of this study is devoted to a discussion of how intergenerational justice ought to be conceived and to meeting the challenges faced by any conception of intergenerational obligations and entitlements.

The theory that is advanced in the following chapters is predicated on two basic theses. The first, already mentioned, is that intergenerational relationships are central to a political society. A polity is by nature intergenerational. It has intergenerational responsibilities. It has institutions that are essentially intergenerational. Intergenerational relationships exist among contemporaries as well as between past, present and future generations. And most important, its citizens are motivated by intergenerational concerns. The second thesis is that duties in respect to the past, responsibilities and entitlements of co-existing generations and duties to future generations are interconnected parts of a theory of intergenerational justice. A theory ought to be able to show how all of these responsibilities and entitlements are related.

The relation, I will argue, is grounded on the conception of citizens as persons who have future directed interests that include not only an interest in their future well-being, but also interests that transcend their lifetime. I will demonstrate that these lifetime-transcending interests play a central role in human life, and that they can justify the existence of entitlements and obligations in respect to the past, as well as to younger generations and future people. The first requirement of a just political society is that it should accommodate or underwrite the satisfaction of central interests of its citizens. A polity that answers to the lifetime-transcending interests of its citizens is an intergenerational polity that acts as a responsible agent through time by keeping its long-term commitments, taking responsibility for its past and ensuring that obligations to future people, both inside and outside of its borders, are satisfied.

In Chapters 2 and 3, I set the stage for a theory of the intergenerational polity by considering what strategies we should use for avoiding both of the non-identity problems. A theory which makes entitlements depend on duties that are intrinsic to intergenerational relationships is, I suggest, a way of avoiding the first non-identity problem. To avoid the second non-identity problem it is necessary to explain why individuals should accept duties to perpetuate these relationships. In Chapter 4, I introduce lifetime-transcending interests as an answer to this problem, explaining why they are so important to the lives and identities of individuals. Chapter 5 explains how duties to the dead can be derived from demands that individuals can legitimately impose on their successors for the sake of their lifetime-transcending interests, and Chapter 6 discusses the duties that individuals, as members of polities, owe to their predecessors and their responsibilities in respect to deeds and commitments of the past. This chapter establishes that polities themselves have intergenerational responsibilities.

Subsequent chapters take up the more traditional subject of intergenerational justice: what members of each generation owe to their successors. Chapter 7 focuses on the issue of what ought to be maintained through the generations, and Chapter 8 considers how relationships between overlapping generations contribute to our conception of intergenerational justice. Chapter 9 answers the question of what each generation ought to regard as its fair share in the maintenance of just relationships. Chapter 10 confronts problems associated with people-making and population. Chapters 11 and 12 consider whether a theory that centres on justice in an intergenerational polity can meet challenges posed by environmentalists and cosmopolitans.

The topics of these chapters are united by the themes described above. As individuals and citizens, we have interests directed towards a future that transcends our lifetime. We are predisposed to see ourselves as participants in relationships of cooperation that extend through time and unite members of past and future generations. These relationships bring with them obligations and entitlements. They are the foundation for a theory of the intergenerational polity and for the view of intergenerational justice that will be presented in this study.

2 Justice, Non-Identity and Intergenerational Relationships

A theory of justice gives agents, as individuals or members of a polity, obligations and entitlements. To establish that we have obligations of justice to past or future people it is necessary to determine that they have, or could have, claims on us or entitlements that we can violate. Suppose that we act in ways that make it impossible for future people to maintain just institutions or their political relationships. As we have seen, there are two main ways that we can deny that these future people will be treated unjustly. One is by pointing out that the individuals who come into existence would not have existed at all if we had not acted as we did. This is what I have called the *first* non-identity problem. The second is to claim that by pursuing policies that bring to an end the cooperative relationship between the generations, we divest ourselves of any duties that might be owed to people as participants in that relationship. This is the *second*—the collective—non-identity problem. In the next two chapters I will discuss how these problems can be circumvented and what kind of theory of intergenerational justice is most likely to avoid both of them. This chapter shows that many theories that manage to surmount the first identity problem, including Rawls's view of justice between generations, are in danger of succumbing to the second. In the following chapter I will indicate the direction that we should take in order to avoid both problems.

CONTRACTUAL DUTIES

The first non-identity problem results from an intuitively plausible conception of what it means for an action to wrong someone: that it harms her by making her worse off than she would have been if the action had not been taken. If the action in question led to the existence of the person, then it cannot have made her worse off unless her life is not worth living. The problem might be avoided if we can define a plausible conception of doing wrong to someone that does not involve the counterfactual comparison. There may be a number of ways of doing this, but I will examine a proposal that seems particularly suited to the position that I will advocate.[1]

Using Thomas Scanlon's idea that our duties to others result from acknowledging that they are entitled to make claims on us by appealing to principles that no one can reasonably reject (1998: 4), Rahul Kumar argues that we can have duties to people whose existence is contingent on our actions. Like Scanlon, Kumar holds that to do wrong to others is to fail to fulfil legitimate expectations toward them (2003: 107). Legitimate expectations, he argues, can arise from a status that individuals possess or because they have a position in a relationship. To determine whether the expectation is fulfilled, it is not necessary to compare the present position of a person with the position he would be in if the failure had not occurred. It is enough to establish whether the agent responsible for fulfilling the expectation has in fact fulfilled it. It is a legitimate moral expectation, Kumar points out, that those responsible for a child's welfare should not let it suffer a serious harm or disability when this can be prevented (116). A caretaker has this obligation to anyone who is, or will be, her child. The duty applies to a type, characterised simply as 'child of X', but it attributes entitlements to the individual who turns out to be an instance of this type. So if the caretaker fails to fulfil her responsibility, her child, whoever it is, has not received its entitlement and can claim to have been wronged. How the child came into existence is irrelevant.

Kumar applies his interpretation of the contractual approach to the well-known example discussed by Parfit (1976: 100–1). Suppose a woman (call her Julia) is taking a medicine which she knows will cause a serious birth defect in any child that she conceives during this period. Julia could choose to wait for a few months until the effects of the medicine wear off and she can conceive a normal child. However, she chooses to conceive during the danger period and gives birth to a handicapped child, Florence. Florence would not have existed if Julia had not acted as she did. However, Kumar believes that Florence can claim to have been wronged. Julia as a prospective mother failed to fulfil her duty to the person who satisfies the description 'Julia's child'. Florence has been wronged because Julia violated her obligation as a caretaker, not because Florence is worse off than she would have been if Julia had waited to conceive.

The problem with Kumar's solution to the problem posed by Parfit is that it may not be logically possible for Florence to exist without the handicap. Suppose that the medicine Julia takes produces the handicap by affecting the genetic constitution of the ovum. If we accept that a person's identity depends on her genetic constitution, then Florence cannot claim that *she* has been wronged by Julia's behaviour. If she did not have the handicap, she would not be who she is. There is no possible world where she exists without the handicap, and her ability to *imagine* herself without it is not sufficient to make sense of her claim.[2] If this is so, and a 'genetic identity proviso' is added to the account of X's contractual obligations to those who satisfy the description 'child of X', then we have to conclude that Kumar fails to establish that Florence has been wronged by her mother. If Julia has a motherly obligation, then it is, as Parfit believes, to bring into the world a child who does not suffer from such a disability.

This discussion brings up difficult questions about identity. Does a person's identity really depend on her genetic constitution? But it is important to note that the genetic identity proviso, even if accepted, does not prevent the contractual approach from sidestepping the problem of non-identity in cases of many other kinds—including those with which theories of intergenerational justice are most concerned.

APPLICATIONS OF THE CONTRACT THEORY

Stan and Janet are a feckless and often-unemployed couple who don't bother to use contraception, and as a result, they have a family of eleven children. The size of this impoverished family means that none of the children has a good chance in life. But if Stan and Janet had acted more responsibly and used contraception, not all of the children would have come into existence. Perhaps none of them would exist. Nevertheless, Stan and Janet, as parents, had a duty to ensure—so far as possible—that any child they had would get a good start in life. This duty is owed to whoever turns out to be a child of theirs, and according to the contractual account, they are answerable to each and every one. Each child is entitled to complain that his or her parents wronged them by failing to fulfil the responsibility, and the likelihood that the child wouldn't have existed if Stan and Janet had been more responsible is no reason, according to Kumar's account, for denying that the entitlement exists. In this case, the genetic identity proviso does not stand in the way of making such a claim. There is no logical absurdity in each child saying that he or she has been wronged by the irresponsibility of the parents.

The contractual account can plausibly explain why we think that claims of other kinds are valid. Consider, for example, a story similar to one told by Smolkin (1994: 316). An asbestos mining company pays high wages and attracts many job seekers to a settlement next to the mine, including a man and a woman from different parts of the country who gain employment, meet and get married. In time they bring a child into the world. What the company knows, but its employees do not, is that asbestos poses a serious health risk for workers and their families. Years later, when the child grows up, he develops a cancer which is known to be the result of asbestos exposure. By this time the dangers of asbestos and the company's negligence are well known and he claims compensation for the wrong that it has done to him. The child would never have existed if the mining company had not attracted his parents to the settlement by engaging in its harm-creating activities. Nevertheless, it seems reasonable to hold the company responsible for wronging this person (as well as other wrongs).

Justice, Non-Identity and Intergenerational Relationships 17

That a company has a duty of care to its workers and their families (as well as other stakeholders, where relevant) is a principle that no reasonable person is likely to reject. So if it violates this principle, then it has wronged those individuals who suffer or who are put at risk. This duty is owed to whoever satisfies the description of being an employee of X or being a child of an employee of X. How those who satisfy this description came to be in the position where they could be wronged is irrelevant. In this case the genetic identity proviso will not give us any trouble in reaching this conclusion. The child's identity, as distinct from its existence, does not depend on the company's activities. There is a logically possible world in which he exists and the company did nothing wrong.

An entitlement possessed by someone who may come to exist in the future can also exist because of the act of someone now dead. Suppose that Jim wanted his family line to continue and was disappointed that his children were so uncooperative. So he stipulated in his will that his first grandchild, should there ever be such a person, would receive a large sum of money. As a result, some of his children are motivated to start a family. Assuming that the right of bequest and inheritance can be defended, at least within limits, and assuming that we have no legal or moral objection to the provision of Jim's will, then whoever turns out to satisfy the description 'first grandchild of Jim' has an entitlement to inherit. The obligation to ensure that this entitlement is fulfilled falls on the members of Jim's society—particularly on the executor of his will. And if someone prevents the child from receiving his legitimate entitlement, acting before or after its conception and birth, then it can later claim to have been wronged.

It is important to note that being wronged because of a failure to fulfil such duties is not only compatible with being brought into existence by effects of the wrong action, but it is also compatible with a person not having his interests set back in any way other than failing to obtain his entitlement. It could be that a legacy from a rich uncle saves Janet and Stan's children from deprivation; it could be that all of the children of the mining company's employees luckily avoid being exposed to asbestos; it might turn out that Jim's grandchild does not want the legacy. But nevertheless, by not exercising their responsibility, Janet and Stan and the executives of the mining company wronged those whom they were responsible for. And if Jim's grandchild is prevented from obtaining the legacy, then this child will be wronged. In judging that a person's entitlements have been violated by the actions of those who had such a duty, it is sufficient to compare his situation with the one that should be enjoyed by anyone to whom the obligation is owed—that is, a situation in which an injury, or the threat of injury, caused by negligence or irresponsibility does not exist.

The responsibilities featured in the previous examples arise from agents' relationships to those to whom they owe duties. The relationship creates the responsibility, and understanding the nature of the relationship and why it exists suffices to justify the principle that grounds the entitlements and to specify the obligations that it entails. The non-identity problem is avoided because a future person will be able to claim an entitlement in virtue of his relationship to those who have the obligation arising from the relationship. Given that this is so, questions arise about the general application of Kumar's approach. Does it give us duties of justice to all future people? And if so, on what basis?

The duties owed by parents to their children, employers to employees and their families and executors to those who make and receive bequests are obvious grounds for claims of future people. But it is not so obvious that our present actions will give unrelated future people—especially distant future people—any claims against us. What is it about our relation to them that gives us duties? Is it merely that they are human beings whose living conditions can be affected by what we do? Golding, as we have seen, denies that we have duties to those who have no connection to us, and John Passmore similarly believes that our duties extend only as far as our loving concern for our immediate descendants (1974: 91). But even if we believe that all future people have legitimate expectations, it is not clear what their entitlements are and what we can be held responsible for. Perhaps it would be better to conceive of our responsibility as analogous to Julia's duty—to avoid bringing about a world in which the people who exist have suboptimal lives. If we want a theory of intergenerational justice that gives us well-defined duties to future individuals—persons who will have claims on us—then it seems preferable to begin by focusing on obligations that arise from relationships with those whom we count as descendants or successors, and then to investigate whether these obligations can encompass more distant and less closely related future people.

This consideration provides a general justification for focusing on relationships between the generations in a political society. A polity is a collective which has often been conceived as contractual. It is supposed to give citizens obligations to each other that arise from their political relationship. It seems reasonable to suppose that their contractual obligations include obligations to future citizens and that an account of these duties can be given that is analogous to those relational obligations discussed by Kumar. This focus does not preclude the possibility of a theory of justice that embraces all of humanity—past, present and future—but such an objective may be better approached by beginning with intergenerational relationships which have moral implications that are widely accepted and easier to specify.

OBLIGATIONS TO FUTURE MEMBERS OF A POLITY

Relationships in a political society are the starting point for Rawls in his two accounts of justice between the generations in *A Theory of Justice*

(1972) and *Political Liberalism* (1996). In *A Theory of Justice*, Rawls supposes that members of a society, who are assumed to value their cooperative relationships, have the task of determining the principles of justice for their society. Rawls assumes that the individuals who make the contract are rational but disinterested: they are not related to each other by love, sympathy, duty or the common acceptance of an idea of the good. But their decision is made in the original position behind a veil of ignorance which hides from each individual information about his or her identity: his race, class, gender, religious affiliation and idea of the good. The veil of ignorance requires individuals to make judgments which they can accept, no matter what their position in society turns out to be. However, the contractors know that they are contemporaries and the impartiality that is imposed on them cannot guarantee that they will not ignore, or make judgments unfavourable to, future (and past) generations.

When Rawls turns his attention to justice between generations he incorporates the interests of future citizens, not by putting them in the original position, but by changing his assumptions about the identity and interests of the contractors. They are now conceived to be 'fathers of families' who are assumed to care about their descendants and can thus be depended on to represent the interests of their family lines in the making of the contract.

> The parties are thought of as representing continuing lines of claims, as being so to speak deputies for a kind of everlasting moral agent or institution. They need not take into account its entire life span in perpetuity, but their goodwill stretches over at least two generations (1972: 128).

Rawls argues that these individuals, predisposed as they are to accept duties to their descendants, would subscribe to what he describes as a 'just savings principle'.

This principle is predicated on the care that existing people have for their descendants—a relationship which predisposes them to accept obligations to future members of their society. The contractors accept the just savings principle and the duties it entails because of this relationship, and it is assumed that each succeeding generation will accept these duties in its turn for the same reason. The principle that gives the contractors obligations to members of future generations also gives these future citizens entitlements which they will possess however they come into existence. Non-identity is not a problem for Rawls.[3]

However, the caring relationship between parents and their descendants is a problem for Rawls's theory because by using it as a motivation for the acceptance of a principle of justice, he departs from his initial assumption that the contractors are disinterested individuals who have no essential relationship to each other. He privileges those who have a particular idea of the good, namely those who care about their descendants. D. Clayton Hubin suggests that the assumption of disinterest could be saved if individuals in the original position make the plausible psychological assumption that people in their society generally care about some future persons(1976: 81). But a psychological state, however universal, seems a weak basis for intergenerational obligations. Brian Barry objects to accounts that make obligations to future generations rest on sentiment: 'For both Rawls and Hubin the limits of caring are the limits of justice, so there is no injustice where there are no sentiments; and it is presumably not unjust to lack sentiments of concern for future generations' (1978: 238).

We might answer Barry's criticism by pointing out that the relationship between fathers (and mothers) of families and their descendents is not merely one of sentiment. Parents have duties to look out for and promote the present and future well-being of their children and grandchildren and to ensure that they can become autonomous individuals and equal citizens. We have already had reason to note the existence of such duties of care. People who have these duties will presumably want the institutions of their political society to ensure that their responsibilities can be fulfilled, and perhaps to provide some collective means of fulfilling them. Maintaining institutions of justice through the generations is an obvious way of ensuring the autonomy and future well-being of children and grandchildren. Rawls does not present the matter in this way because he wants to derive all duties from the contract made in the original position. But this is not a necessary requirement of a theory of justice for a political society. It is plausible to suppose that some duties of justice are predicated on moral motivations, on the concern of individual members of a society to maintain their capacity to fulfil obligations of other kinds. In any case, moral motivations are intrinsic to a theory that gives fathers of families the task of representing family lines. Representatives presumably have a duty to look after the interests of those they represent—duties that are logically prior to those derived from the political contract. And it seems reasonable that representatives of family lines acquire their duties as representatives because they have duties of care in respect to their children and grandchildren.

Acknowledging that representatives have duties does not undermine Rawls's main purpose: to show that the obligations that individuals owe each other as members of a political society can be presented as if they were derived from a social contract. It may even strengthen their motivations to accept principles of just cooperation. But the problem remains that representatives of family lines are motivated by their special relationships, and it is not clear why those who have no intention of having a family should make sacrifices so that others can better carry out their familial responsibilities.

This difficulty is symptomatic of a more general problem that the Rawlsian version of social contract theory shares with classical accounts. The contractors in all of these theories appear in two guises. They are independent individuals, who are assumed to be self-interested or disinterested, and they are heads of families, who are supposed to represent the interests of people who must be included as members of society, even though they do not count as citizens. In classical theories, it was assumed that women, as well as children and unborn generations, were represented by heads of families, and Rawls harkens back to this tradition, probably without sexist intentions, when he speaks of contractors as being 'fathers of families'.

The dual role of the contractors creates a number of problems. For one thing, it raises the question of whether contract theory can provide a consistent view of justice. What if the contractors as representatives favour different principles from those they would agree to as disinterested individuals, or give them a different priority?[4] Rawls believes that it makes no difference to the outcome whether the contractors are conceived to be disinterested individuals or heads of families. But even if this is so (given the highly abstract principles that come out of the original position), representatives of family lines are likely to want these principles to be interpreted in a way that is conducive to the well-being of their families.

The dual identity of the contractors thus indicates the presence of a fundamental theoretical and practical problem: how the family, or more basically, the responsibilities traditionally associated with the family—which include, above all, generational responsibilities like the nurturing of children—should be dealt with by a political society and a theory of justice. These are not matters that are likely to be resolved by the twists and turns of those who have attempted to reformulate the contractual approach of *A Theory of Justice*. We will have reason to revisit the issue in later chapters.

GENERATIONAL PERSPECTIVES

To overcome the problems of an account of obligations to future generations that relies on the sympathies of present people, several reformulations within a Rawlsian framework seem possible. One suggestion by some of Rawls's critics is to include individuals of all generations in the original position (Richards 1983: 134). Another—the position eventually adopted by Rawls—is to stipulate that contractors are of the same (existing) generation, but do not know anything about their temporal location in a sequence of generations.[5] Which alternative should be preferred depends on what the contractors are supposed to be doing. They could regard their objective as analogous to the task of those who make the social contract for contemporaries, to formulate a principle of justice which members of all generations will be prepared to accept, whenever they come into existence. Or they might see themselves as prescribing a principle that they think all generations ought to accept, but which future generations, when they come into existence, may not endorse.

The first interpretation encounters the scepticism of Terence Ball, who claims that there is no trans-historical conception of justice (1985). Our successors, he says, are likely to have ideas about justice which are different from ours, perhaps different in ways that would lead them to make a different choice of principles under the veil of ignorance or to refuse to accept Rawls's method for determining principles of justice. They may no longer believe, for example, that individuals have equal entitlements. Contrary to what Ball suggests, scepticism about the existence of trans-historical agreement on principles would not preclude the possibility of reaching any conclusions about intergenerational justice. Our imagined contractors might decide that each generation ought to concentrate on saving capital for its successors. Whatever its views about justice, each generation will require the means to implement them.

However, it seems doubtful that a trans-historical view of intergenerational justice is what we really want. Some of our predecessors believed that 'primitive' peoples and non-whites were their inferiors and did not deserve the same entitlements as white Europeans, Australians or Americans. We now think that they were wrong. If we have reason to believe that our successors will be fascists, we are not obliged to cater to their conception of justice.

What this consideration suggests is that a theory of intergenerational justice should not be thought of as something that all generations, whenever they exist, will find reason to accept. It is a theory about what we think, from our perspective, that all generations ought to accept—and this is a different matter. It should be noted that this interpretation is compatible with Scanlon's conception of contract. Contract, in his view, is a metaphor for the understandings that count as 'moral', with the force and meaning that this description implies. What we count as a moral claim depends on the principles that *we* think cannot be reasonably rejected. Principles of intergenerational justice, like other moral principles, are determined by our view of what we and others cannot reasonably reject. We do not know what principles future members of our society will find acceptable but that does not prevent us from making intergenerational prescriptions.[6] We should thus choose the second interpretation of generational participation in the original position. The contractors belong to the same generation but they do not know their position in the sequence of the generations, and thus they have to suppose that any principle they endorse will apply to them. This interpretation is the one chosen by Rawls when he returns to the topic of justice between generations in *Political Liberalism*.

COOPERATION BETWEEN THE GENERATIONS

In *Political Liberalism* (1996: 273–5) Rawls abandons the idea that the contractors are heads of families and the motivational assumption that goes with it. They are simply individuals who know that they are members of a generation in an intergenerational society, but the veil of ignorance prevents them from knowing their position in the sequence of generations. The contract that establishes principles of justice between the generations is analogous to the contract that establishes principles that hold between contemporaries. Agreement does not depend on ties of sentiment or on a common idea of the good, but rather on the benefits that the parties obtain from a cooperative relationship governed by institutions that embody the principles of justice. Since under the conditions of ideal theory each generation can assume that all generations can be depended on to fulfil their obligations, there is no need for any further motivation. Rawls says that a single individual under the veil of ignorance is in the position to determine principles that all should endorse, and similarly, one generation under the conditions imposed by the original position will arrive at the principle that, from its perspective, should govern the relationship between the generations. The contractors endorse the relationship and their role in maintaining it by accepting the principles, and by consenting to the contract they consent to the obligations that it entails.

In the framework of the relationship that is established or endorsed by the contract, each generation, according to Rawls, accepts an obligation to do its share to save for the purpose of establishing and maintaining institutions of justice. Its successors are, so to speak, the rightful inheritors of these savings and institutions. According to the principle accepted by the contractors, they have a claim to this inheritance, and if their predecessors fail to fulfil their obligation to provide it, then their entitlements as heirs are violated. The particular identities of these successors and the causal factors that brought them into existence are irrelevant to their claims. Rawls avoids the first non-identity problem in this, as well as his earlier, version of the intergenerational contract.

As in the case of the contract that governs the relationship between contemporaries, the contractors assume that they are endorsing principles for an ideal situation in which everyone fulfils their obligations. The generation that endorses the principle of justice between the generations is supposed to assume that its predecessors have fulfilled their obligations and that it will receive the benefits to which it is entitled. When the veil of ignorance is lifted and the contractors emerge into the real world, they might discover that their forebears have not acted according to the principle. This is not supposed to be a reason for failing to fulfil their obligations to their successors. In the real world, individuals and groups often fail to be just. The role of a theory of justice is to provide the standards that members of the polity ought to live up to and by which their actions can be judged.

However, Brian Barry thinks that circumstances in the real world can put into doubt the existence of a relationship of cooperation between generations (1979: 71). His objection can be put as follows. Suppose that we emerge from the veil of ignorance and find that previous generations have not acted according to requirements that we regard as just. There are two conclusions that we could reach. The first is that past generations have wrongly failed to live up to the principles that ought to govern relations between the generations. The second is that relations of cooperation between the generations do not exist, and that there are no intergenerational obligations to live up to. Barry thinks that there is more reason to draw the second conclusion. The legacy of thoughtless environmental destruction left by our forebears suggests that they did not believe in the existence of intergenerational obligations. Barry's judgment seems too swift. Previous generations were probably not aware of the harm that they were doing or assumed that they were fulfilling their intergenerational duty by creating wealth. But his doubts bring to our attention questions concerning the existence and nature of intergenerational cooperation.

The relationship between members of a political society that gives them obligations to each other is supposed to be a relationship that produces benefits that all members have a reason to want and which can only be brought about by political cooperation, the terms of which these citizens have reason to endorse. A theory of justice is supposed to tell us what these terms are. Citizens who are contemporaries can judge whether their fellows accept the relationship and its terms by their participation in political acts, their responses to the challenges faced by their polity or by their acquiescence in the rules of their society. They can signal to each other their acceptance of the terms.[7] But generations of citizens who do not overlap, or scarcely overlap, do not jointly participate in making political decisions, and cannot signal to each other that they regard themselves as part of a common enterprise. If our successors inherit our institutions and our wealth as a matter of course, then why should they suppose that we acted to fulfil the requirements of an intergenerational relationship? Why should they suppose that this relationship exists?

As a matter of fact, people often do labour for the sake of their descendants and are sometimes prepared to make great sacrifices for their sake. There are many ways in which people demonstrate a sense of responsibility for younger and future generations. But their concern is generally focused on younger or unborn members of their family or communities to which they regard themselves as having special duties. Or they are citizens who identify with their political society and want to perpetuate its ideals or institutions. Rawls does not want to presuppose any of these motivations. But if the existence in the real world of intergenerational relationships of cooperation depends on such sentiments or ideas of duty, then it may be a mistake to jettison them in favour of an account that is suitable only for ideal circumstances.[8]

THE SECOND NON-IDENTITY PROBLEM

Let us pose a more basic question about the relationship that generates intergenerational responsibilities. To whom are we supposed to owe intergenerational duties? In *A Theory of Justice*, citizens have duties based on their relationship with their *descendants*; that is, younger and future members of their family lines. The familial relationship exists independently of the political one. In Rawls's later account, the duties of citizens are to their political *successors*; that is, their political relationship is the only one that counts. There are two ways of understanding who will count as our political successors. We might simply think of them as the people who come after us, and who thus take over our institutions, territory and accumulated wealth. Our duties to future generations so conceived are simply duties to individuals whose status as objects of moral concern gives them the right to live under just institutions.

Roger Paden recommends that we understand Rawls in this way (1997: 44). He argues that the requirement to save for the sake of establishing and maintaining just institutions follows from a natural duty owed to others as human persons to promote just institutions, and he thinks that nothing more is needed to establish this principle apart from the sense of justice which participants in the original position are assumed to have. We do not have to presuppose social relationships of cooperation. Paden is, in effect, treating Rawls as if he were in agreement with the view of Jefferson, as described in Chapter 1. If the generations are related to each other like the citizens of different countries, then the duties that a generation owes to its successors are simply the duties that it owes to individuals whose well-being it can affect.

Apart from other difficulties that it might encounter, this interpretation comes up against the obstacle of non-identity. If we pursue a policy that makes it likely that future inhabitants of our territory will not benefit from having just institutions, and these policies also bring into existence people who would not have existed if we had adopted a different, less destructive policy, then how can these people claim that we have violated their entitlements (provided they find their lives worth living even without satisfactory institutions of justice)? In particular, how can we be accused of failing to fulfil duties of justice?[9] In any case, Paden's account does not answer to the common idea that we owe duties to our successors because they have a special relationship to us as future members of our polity.

The second view of who counts as our successors is the one that I have attributed to Rawls: our political successors are those with whom we cooperate to establish and maintain just institutions. Our obligations, and the entitlements of future citizens, arise from this relationship of cooperation. As we have seen, this account raises questions about the nature of the relationship and how members of a political society can determine whether it really exists. But the more basic difficulty is what I described as the 'second non-identity problem'. If the relationship that counts depends on political cooperation, then a necessary, if not a sufficient, condition for regarding a generation as belonging to a political society is its participation in the common endeavour of establishing and maintaining just institutions. The actions and policies of present generations can determine whether future people are in the position to continue the task of saving for or maintaining these institutions. This means that present people could divest themselves of duties of justice to political successors by acting in a way that ensures that they do not have successors—by acting in ways that ensure that future people will not be able to maintain the relationship of cooperation.

It might be thought that this problem is solved, at least in the original position, by the conditions that Rawls imposes on his contract makers. If the contractors do not know what generation they belong to, then they will have to consider the possibility that they might belong to the generation that suffers from the policies of its predecessors. Since they will want to avoid this outcome they will choose a principle of justice that does not allow any generation to inflict harm on successors that could be destructive of their political relationship. The problem is that if eligibility as a contract maker depends on counting as a member of a political society, and this depends on being in the position to participate in establishing and maintaining institutions of justice, then there is no point in contractors supposing that they might belong to a deprived generation. This possibility is ruled out by the terms of participation in contract making. So they are free to accept a principle that allows them to engage in destructive acts if they think that this will bring them greater benefits.

Rawls says that the generation under the veil of ignorance will agree to the principle that it wants all previous generations to agree to. If we think that they ought to have saved or maintained institutions for us, then we ought to accept a similar duty to our successors (1996: 273–4). But this requirement only holds if those who come after count as our successors. Generations overlap, and it might be argued that a principle that takes this into account must rule out irresponsible behaviour. The older members of society have duties to younger members and they must also take into account that these younger members will have duties to members who are now unborn. But this consideration does not prevent us from running down our institutions so that younger people of our society, though able to maintain institutions of justice during their lifetimes, will not have the means either to save or to provide the institutions as a heritage to those who are younger still. Since the existence of a duty depends on the ability of people to perform it, our behaviour will not prevent our immediate successors from fulfilling obligations of intergenerational justice (they won't have any). We are, to be sure, putting them in a terrible position, but all political societies come to an end eventually, we might reason, so why not sooner rather than later?

What prevents reasoning like this in the earlier version of Rawls's theory is the assumption that people care about their descendants (who are assumed to be future members of the society), want them to enjoy just institutions and are predisposed to accept a duty to provide them. The above discussion suggests that appealing to such motivations is difficult to avoid if we want to explain why intergenerational obligations exist. To do so is to violate the basic requirement of impartiality and the presumption of disinterest—as Rawls's critics have pointed out. But the best strategy may be to abandon these assumptions: to allow that citizens of a political society have non-contractual relationships that predispose or require them to accept obligations to each other. In Chapter 3, we will explore theories that base intergenerational obligations on such relationships.

3 Partnership, Reciprocity and Identity

The people who engage in Rawls's contractual exercise in *Political Liberalism* are assumed to be disinterested. They have no attachments to members of past or future generations that can affect the outcome of their deliberations. They have no moral preconceptions about their duties to future citizens. Given that this is so, it is difficult to explain why they should care about the continued existence of their political society. But under the veil of ignorance Rawls's contractors have been stripped of characteristics and concerns that tend to favour the acceptance of duties to future generations. In reality many people are predisposed to believe that they have duties to their successors. They often care about the well-being of their descendants, as Rawls supposes in *A Theory of Justice*. They may also value the institutions or ideals of their polity and want them to survive; or value other communities or goods that their polity protects. Like Burke, they may perceive themselves to be in a relationship of cooperation with past and future generations that brings with it obligations and entitlements. A closer look at these common values and ideas of duty could provide us with a better, more realistic approach to a theory of intergenerational justice for a political society.

An approach through the interests, values and commitments of members of a society is, in fact, true to the spirit of Rawls's endeavour. The requirements of Rawls's theory of justice are predicated on the assumption that citizens value their relationships of cooperation and are predisposed to accept duties to, and to make sacrifices for, each other. The device of the social contract is merely a means for determining what principles they ought to accept given their relationship to each other. My criticisms of Rawls's later theory of justice between generations could be understood as providing reasons for rejecting that device when theorising about duties between the generations and focusing instead on the values and relationships that underwrite the sense of responsibility that most citizens feel for their successors and, in some cases, in respect to their predecessors.

Two sources for this sense of responsibility feature in the philosophical literature. The first is the identification of many people with their nation, their polity or with the ideals for which it stands. The second is the widespread conviction that members of a polity are in relationships of intergenerational cooperation which give them obligations to future people and, perhaps, to people of the past. These two approaches have much in common. Those who identify with their nation or polity are likely to conceive of themselves as participating in a common endeavour, and those who participate in a common endeavour—at least one that they regard as important—are likely to identify with its objective. But those who make identification the centre of their explanations aim to show how moral and political responsibilities arise out of the nature of the self or its commitments; and those who stress cooperation believe that duties arise directly from relationships. In this chapter, I will explore both of these approaches, noting their strengths and weaknesses, and will show how this examination leads us in a more promising theoretical direction.

COOPERATION AND OBLIGATION

The idea that members of different, including non-overlapping, generations are in mutually beneficial relationships of cooperation has sometimes been dismissed as an obvious falsity. 'What have future generations done for me?' is the common way of ridiculing this idea. Backwards causation can be ruled out of consideration, but it is not at all implausible to suppose that the generations of a polity or of other intergenerational associations can be in a relationship that is beneficial to each. Nevertheless, the mere fact that generations do things that benefit their successors does not generate obligations or entitlements. We have to explain why a relationship that exists, or could exist, between generations of a polity counts as a connection that gives rise to responsibilities. If we take as our criteria for such a connection synchronic standards that require consent of all parties, mutual reciprocity or sanctions for non-performance, then of course we will fail to find it. But there may be alternative conceptions more appropriate for diachronic relationships. Let us look at some possibilities.

Burke, as we have seen, claims that members of a polity are participants in an intergenerational partnership which brings with it obligations which he describes as 'contractual'. This idea, or something like it, has been invoked by many others. In the Gettysburg Address, Abraham Lincoln adjured his audience to take up their share of the responsibility for carrying on a political tradition for which the 'founding fathers' of the Republic and those who died in the Battle of Gettysburg made sacrifices (1863). Behind Rawls's discussion of intergenerational justice is the idea—not adequately captured by reasoning behind the veil of ignorance—that generations ought to regard themselves as partners in building and maintaining their institutions of justice.

The obvious question about a partnership between generations is what it entails in the way of obligations, and to whom these obligations are owed. Burke clearly believes that they are owed to ancestors as well as descendants: 'People will never look forward to posterity, who never look backward to their ancestors' (1968: 119). Lincoln implies that the Confederates, by seceding from the Republic that their forefathers had founded, had betrayed a trust. On the other hand, Rawls finds no reason to appeal to the past in order to give citizens duties in respect to the future. It seems sufficient that people are predisposed to accept duties to their descendants and that they value their institutions of justice.

What the partnership between generations should seek to maintain or accomplish is also far from clear. Burke argued that members of polities should not abandon, for the sake of revolutionary ideals, the institutions, forms of government and customs that their predecessors had built up over many generations. But this is the position that Paine and Jefferson rebelled against when they insisted that each generation should be free to determine its own political destiny without being weighed down by obligations that come from the past.

If each generation is free of obligations to ancestors, then how can we conceive of a partnership between generations? In *A Theory of Justice*, Rawls asks us to consider what we think our forebears ought to have done for us when we consider what we ought to do for our descendants. This formulation does not require that we build on or preserve the actual inheritance that we have received from the past. The past does not in any way tie our hands or the hands of succeeding generations. The partnership, in other words, could be more conceptual than real, and this is the basis for Barry's doubts about its actual existence.

Is the notion of an intergenerational partnership useful at all? A liberal in the tradition of Jefferson might argue as follows: 'If an institution or custom that we inherit from the past is good then we have sufficient reason to maintain it. If it is not good, we have no reason to maintain it. The sacrifices and efforts of past people have no moral relevance. They do not give us obligations.' This view would not preclude the belief that we have obligations to our successors, but it implies that these duties cannot be located in requirements imposed by a partnership between the generations. This way of reasoning is reinforced if we take as a paradigm of partnership an association that allows prospective members to refuse, or at least dispute, the objective and terms of participation. An intergenerational partnership must be conceived differently, but how this should be done has not yet been explained.

RECIPROCITY AND GRATITUDE

The relationship that confers obligations on each generation might be better conceived as a relationship of benefitter to benefactor. We have a duty to reciprocate for benefits that we obtain from others, argues Lawrence Becker (1986: 229ff). Many of the benefits we have received come from past generations. We cannot reciprocate by providing benefits to our forebears, but

Becker thinks that duties of reciprocity exist even when it is impossible to give back to those who have benefited us. We can most fittingly discharge our duty, he argues, by passing on these, or comparable benefits, to people in the next generation.

Becker grounds his account of intergenerational obligations on the duty of reciprocity—on the obligation to make an appropriate return for a benefit. Others prefer to speak of a duty of gratitude. Lincoln's appeal to the sacrifices of the dead can be understood in this way, and so can many accounts of the duties associated with being a member of a trans-historical association like a nation. One is deeply indebted to one's culture and nation, says Jeff McMahan:

> They have provided the language in which one thinks and speaks, the intellectual and artistic heritage that informs one's sensibility and one's understanding of both oneself and the world, many of the values that give purpose to one's life and structure one's relations with others, numerous elements of the material and social infrastructures that make decent life possible, and so on, almost indefinitely. In short, the nation itself as a transhistorical entity is one's benefactor, and there are duties that one owes to it in consequence (1997: 130).

These duties, he says, include sustaining and strengthening the nation, preserving its treasures, heritage and institutions and passing them on to subsequent generations. McMahan speaks of a duty of gratitude to the nation rather than to past generations, but since a nation is an intergenerational association, his account seems to appeal to a similar idea of how obligations arise from being a recipient of benefits.

An obvious objection is that generations produce costs as well as benefits for their successors: they may have left them with an environmental mess or committed injustices that continue to cause harm to people in the present. How do these costs affect our relationship with past generations or to the nation as an intergenerational society? More importantly, what do they imply about our duties to our successors? If we perceive that we have inherited more costs than benefits, this might diminish, if not extinguish, our obligation of reciprocity or gratitude to pass on benefits to our successors. But even if our inheritance is overwhelmingly beneficial, it is not obvious that people have to feel grateful or duty-bound for benefits that they received as a matter of course or benefits that were produced without the intent of providing a benefit. Becker's argument depends on the intention of our predecessors to benefit us, but this means that an appeal to reciprocity leaves us without obligations if we do not believe in the existence or sincerity of such intentions.

Even in those cases where we do acknowledge a duty of reciprocity or gratitude, it is not obvious that we should discharge it by providing a benefit to future generations. In his discussion of Becker, Edward A.

Page wonders why we should be duty-bound to pass on goods that were not explicitly meant for *our* successors (2006: 122). Why not use them up ourselves or give them to impoverished people in other countries? If the injustices of past generations are the cause of disadvantages to present people, then an obvious thing to do with the benefits that we have inherited is to use them to overcome these disadvantages.

Becker meets such objections by appealing to the motivations behind the intention to benefit future generations:

> Imagine what social life would be like if we had no assurance from reciprocity that our good works would be honored by future generations, no assurance that after our deaths our families and friends would tie up the loose ends of our reciprocal relationships with them; no assurance that people would feel some obligation—*because* of the good work we have done—to carry on in the same fashion (234).

This defence depends not so much on requirements of reciprocity, but on the nature of our future-directed concerns. These concerns, and their role in generating intergenerational obligations, will be more closely examined later.

Duties of gratitude seem even less amenable to being tied to a particular response than duties of reciprocity. To the extent that we think that we have duties of gratitude to past generations or to the nation, we might respond by commemorating the deeds of past people or simply by being thankful. But the very existence of any kind of duty of gratitude depends in the first place on people regarding the acts of their predecessors as beneficial, or at least well intended. A significant number of citizens—especially those who are disadvantaged or oppressed—may not have this belief. Or they may think that they have duties of gratitude only to their parents or mentors and not to the nation or to past generations of their polity.[1]

By themselves relationships of benefactors to benefitters seem an inadequate ground for duties of intergenerational justice, but McMahan's defence of national partiality provides a context that makes an appeal to reciprocity or gratitude much more compelling. If people identify with their nation or polity as an intergenerational association, they will not only be predisposed to regard the inheritance they receive from their predecessors as beneficial, they will want to maintain these benefits and they will think that their national successors ought to be able to enjoy them.

Belonging to an intergenerational association like a nation can itself be a source of value, as David Miller emphasises:

> In the case of nations, people who deny the significance of their national identity . . . are missing out on the opportunity to place their individual lives in the context of a collective project that has been handed down from generation to generation, involving among other things the shaping of the physical environment in which they live, and whose future

they could help to determine, by political participation and in other ways (2007: 39).[2]

Those who value participation in this collective project will not only be predisposed to value the things that they receive from past generations, they will also regard these goods as an inheritance that their predecessors—as participants in the collective project—have provided for them. They will accept, as a matter of course, the duty to pass on these goods, along with their own contributions to the project, to future members. Their identification with their nation predisposes them to accept intergenerational obligations, including, Miller believes, obligations in respect to the debts of their forebears. Injustices of the past are not, in his view, a reason for rejecting intergenerational duties; for those who identify with their nation they are a source of obligation.

IDENTIFICATION AND INTERGENERATIONAL DUTIES

Identification with an intergenerational community like a nation leads naturally to the endorsement of intergenerational obligations. Neither of the non-identity problems stands in the way of their acceptance. Since intergenerational obligations arise from a relationship between present people and whoever in the future will be members of their community, the way in which future generations come into existence is irrelevant to the existence of these duties. Since group members want their association to endure, they accept an obligation to do their share to ensure its continuation and they act under the assumption that it will have future members to whom obligations are owed.

Nevertheless, difficulties plague any theory that founds intergenerational obligations on identification with an intergenerational association—especially the project of justifying and defining the duties of citizens of an intergenerational polity. One of these difficulties is that people have diverse identifications. Some identify with their nation rather than their polity—and this, as Miller points out, may not amount to the same thing (2007: 124). A polity can contain more than one nation, and if these groups come into conflict about the value of their political association (as the Americans did during the Civil War period), then the very existence of their political obligations, including intergenerational obligations, comes into question.

Citizens of modern polities are likely to belong to many different communities of identification: familial, ethnic, social and religious, as well as national or political. And some may have no particular attachment to any intergenerational group. Since their allegiances are various, the route from identification to obligations is not going to be straightforward. Moreover, not all citizens regard their polity or nation as the lodestar of their identity. Some citizens are patriots or nationalists who strongly identify with their nation or political society and what they believe to be its ideals; but for others, their family, church or ethnic community is the centre of their social world. Even among patriots or nationalists there are likely to be differences of opinion about the values and heritage of their society, and thus about what ought to be maintained for future generations. Taking into account these considerations, it is going to be very difficult to determine what, if anything, citizens owe to future or past generations of their polity.

Individuals commonly identify with some intergenerational group, but not everyone does, and not everyone identifies in the same way or to the same extent. A theory of intergenerational justice for a polity must be able to explain how the ways in which members identify, and the groups that they identify with, lead them to accept duties as citizens. It must explain why they should identify with an intergenerational community in the first place. Miller says that people find value in such an identification, but the value they find needs more explanation. It might seem plausible that they would find greater value in identification with their contemporaries—those they interact with, depend on or work with—than in identification with people of past and future generations or with an intergenerational group. Finally, it must tell us more about how intergenerational obligations arise from an identification with an intergenerational community and what they are.

Avner de-Shalit addresses some of these issues in his communitarian account of obligations to future generations (1995).[3] Like other communitarians he thinks that the very existence of a community—and the obligations associated with it—depends on the perception of members that they are united by a common conception of the good. Unlike some communitarians, he thinks that commitments to a good, and to a community, are chosen. Individuals adhere to ideas of the good because they have reason to believe that a life conducted according to them is of value. Community identity in its best form, he says, is something that a person accepts or affirms as the result of moral reflection and debate (25). There is no difficulty, as far as de-Shalit is concerned, in explaining why people identify as they do. But he provides no support for those who think that people *ought* to identify in a certain way—for example, with the nation or polity to which they happen to belong.

Unlike many communitarians de-Shalit does not require that all members of a community come to share exactly the same idea of the good. In his view, a community constitutive of identity is one in which members aim, through free and open debate, to define a common good (25). They are bound together by their common pursuit, and though they must be sufficiently of the same mind to regard their pursuit as common, they do not have to reach an agreement. The obligations of members of such a community are thus perpetually up for discussion; they are, presumably, among the things that they debate.

Future citizens are not direct participants in this debate, but de-Shalit thinks that their inclusion follows from the fact that people have interests that extend beyond their lifetimes. We want the things that we regard as good to flourish, but will inevitably be frustrated in our pursuit of this objective by our mortality. The only way we can immortalize ourselves is through activities that make our ideas available to future generations, who will be able to use them to continue the conversation about the good (1995: 34–40). By putting forward ideas that they will or could develop, present community members, according to de-Shalit, are participating with future generations in an interaction—a kind of partnership.

This idea about how citizens of the same and different generations, despite differences in their points of view, can be bound together by their participation in a common conversation has an obvious application to relationships within a political society. Ernest Partridge suggests that the debates that have been conducted over the generations concerning the interpretation of the US Constitution, a document enacted 'for ourselves and our posterity', provide a good example of the intergenerational interaction that de-Shalit has in mind (2001: 381). Those who participate in this debate do not necessarily have the same views about justice or other political values, but they nevertheless see themselves as belonging to, and valuing, their ability to participate.

De-Shalit takes it for granted that identifying with a community of the sort he describes gives rise to obligations to future, as well as present, people (and perhaps to past people, but he does not consider them). He does not tell us exactly how obligations arise from this identification, but his discussion suggests that the argument might take the following form:

> A community consists of those who identify with its good, or with its project of defining the good, which they pursue through their interactions. These members have an interest in perpetuating this project by passing on their ideas to those whom they hope will succeed them. Therefore, they have reason to accept an obligation to maintain the conditions that will make it possible for the project, and thus their community, to perpetuate itself.

A notable feature of this derivation is that the duty in question is conditional on valuing a good or the project of defining a good. If we want the project to survive, we ought to ensure that future people have the opportunity to pursue it. The concern in question is impersonal. Future members of our community are a means of maintaining something we value. We have, it seems, no responsibility *to* them. So understood, de-Shalit's conception of obligation does not give us an account that explains why members of future generations have entitlements that we ought to fulfil.[4]

We can overcome this difficulty if we suppose that the communal identification in question is not merely with the good that we are pursuing, but also with the people—present and future—who are or will be participants in the project of defining this good. These people do not merely include members of the succeeding generation. If our heirs value their inheritance and think that it ought to be perpetuated, they will think of *their* heirs as participants in perpetuating this good, and so on through the generations. No one in our generation or succeeding generations of our community can reasonably reject a principle that requires them to maintain the conditions which enable the intergenerational interaction to be perpetuated. If we were to act in a way that would make our heirs incapable of continuing the partnership, then we would be wronging them and those whom they regard as their heirs. This contractual interpretation of de-Shalit's position makes present members of a community answerable to their communal successors, whoever they turn out to be, and answerable to those who have reason to regard themselves as the rightful inheritors of the communal good.

This return to the idea of an intergenerational partnership makes more urgent a problem that de-Shalit shares with others who derive obligations from an identification with a community. Our obligations to future people exist if, and only if, we have reason to believe that they will maintain the pursuit of the good or at least want to do so. It is easy to be sceptical about moral commonality between generations. Ball (1985) doubts that future generations will share our moral ideas, including ideas about justice. But even if some commonality continues to exist, the belief that it does may fail and with it a motivation to accept obligations. Even generations near to each other in time can perceive each other to be irreconcilably different in moral outlook. In modern societies younger people are apt to think that they have very different ideals from their elders—to the extent that they sometimes resist the idea that they belong to the same moral community. Older people are sometimes appalled by the values of the young and think that discourse with them is fruitless. Even in political communities, differences of opinion can lead to ruptures between generations. Despite the continued existence of their Constitution, many Americans probably regard themselves as having different values, ideals and concerns from Americans of earlier generations. A view about obligation that depends on a *perception* of commonality seems very vulnerable to such attitudes—even when differences are exaggerated.

Moreover, the moral commonality that people regard themselves as having with others, including people of the future, is going to vary from person to person and from time to time. Individuals may think that their moral community is with people of their religion, their culture or political group, and not their political society. In fact, it is all too easy to doubt that members of a diverse and complex community like a polity will share a common good, even the general moral outlook that de-Shalit requires. All in all, the perception of people that they share a common moral standpoint seems a fragile basis for a view about intergenerational justice in a political society. The problems that beset a theory of intergenerational obligations based on identification are not solved by his approach.

However, there is a second way of interpreting the contractual position that I have attributed to de-Shalit. He holds that it is in the interest of members of each generation to be able to pass on their ideas and projects to those whom they think might value and further develop them. So why not suppose that the contract encompasses the members of all generations of a political society as individuals who have or will have an interest in cooperating to maintain institutions and practices that enable members to pass on things that they value to their successors? Intergenerational justice, according to this idea, means that each generation should do its fair share in maintaining these institutions and practices. This formulation, by making the maintenance of institutions rather than a conversation about the good the focus of cooperative relationships, seems to provide a better basis for a political conception of intergenerational justice. Moreover, it allows that individuals can have widely different conceptions of the good and different communities of interaction, and it maintains a connection between generations that is not so likely to be weakened by intellectual fashion or changes of circumstance. We can presume that the need for institutions that enable people to pass on what they value will remain, and thus that the motivation for accepting duties of maintenance will also persist.

This interpretation constitutes a return to a liberal conception of political relationships. Citizens are united by their support for institutions that embody, more or less well, their ideas about justice—not by an idea of the good or even a pursuit of the good (although their conversations about the ideals of justice on which their institutions and practices are based, or their attempts to achieve an overlapping consensus, might be regarded as constituting the pursuit of their good, as Partridge suggests). On the other hand, the interpretation retains a communitarian element. Individuals are motivated to accept intergenerational duties by something intrinsic to their nature as selves: their desire to transcend their own mortality. As in Rawls's account in *A Theory of Justice* they are psychologically motivated to accept intergenerational duties and to maintain intergenerational relationships, but this motivation is supposed to be (more or less) universal; it is not confined to representatives of family lines or even to individuals who have ties of sentiment to people of the next generation. By being a motivation that all individuals can be expected to have, it has the potential to overcome the most serious objections that Rawls's earlier theory encounters.

Indeed, an account of intergenerational obligations and entitlements which appeals to a basic human interest would overcome many of the difficulties that have been discussed in this chapter. But the interest in question—the desire to pass on valued things, above all ideas, to successors—is likely to be judged inadequate to the task of grounding a theory of intergenerational justice. Is it plausible to suppose that everyone has this interest? And even if so, is it strong enough to motivate people to accept intergenerational duties? Many people are likely to suspect that the answer to one or both of these questions is 'no'. Moreover, it is not obvious that the duties that these interests might motivate us to accept include all of the duties that a theory of intergenerational justice ought to prescribe.

Nevertheless, beginning in Chapter 4, I will defend a theory of intergenerational justice based on the approach that I have just outlined. I will argue that we have interests which are lifetime-transcending—interests that include, but are not exhausted by, the interest identified by de-Shalit. These interests, I will aim to establish, are central to our attempts to give our lives meaning. They not only cause us to have desires about the future, as de-Shalit believes. Some of our lifetime-transcending interests are a legitimate basis for making *moral demands* of our successors. In the following chapters I will show how the existence of these legitimate demands grounds duties in respect to past people, and will go on to show how an appeal to lifetime-transcending interests and demands also motivates the acceptance of duties to future generations.

4 Lifetime-Transcending Interests

Liberals—indeed most philosophers—in their accounts of the self and its interests tend to concentrate on the lifetime interests of individuals: the goals, needs and motivations that relate either to their present wants and circumstances, or to their ideas about what they want to achieve for themselves or enjoy during the course of their lives. Once an individual is dead, his or her account is closed. She has enjoyed or suffered her quantum of happiness or misery; her objectives have either been fulfilled or they have not; her life plan has been realised or it has not. Lifetime interests, it seems, give individuals no bonds with people of the past and future, no reason to think that anyone can have duties to the dead and no concerns for the future beyond one's lifetime. Rawls's supposition in *A Theory of Justice* that heads of families care about the fate of their descendants is often regarded as introducing a special interest into discourse about justice. The suggestion is that those who do not have this concern would have no reason to care about what happens after they are dead and thus no reason to accept duties to future citizens.

De-Shalit rightly questions a view of the self that concentrates on lifetime interests by pointing out that it is common, indeed natural, for individuals to care about the future beyond their lifetimes. The prospect of mortality concentrates the attention of individuals on the prospects for the survival of their ideas and ideals. They are predisposed to accept a duty to maintain the conditions that will enable successors to continue an interaction aimed at defining the good. It might be objected that such concerns are limited to some individuals or to particular times of life. Young people may not be inclined to worry about what will happen after their death; they are more likely to concentrate on satisfying their wants and realising their lifetime goals. Many people avoid thinking about their mortality and concentrate on day-to-day issues. But if we examine more closely the interests that individuals possess, including their lifetime interests, we will discover—intimations of mortality aside—that they either have lifetime-transcending concerns or that their lifetime concerns presuppose interests that transcend their lifetimes.

Parents care about the future well-being of their children and grandchildren. Members of ethnic, political and religious groups generally care about the fate of their community or ideals. People often labour to produce things for posterity and want their successors to continue their projects, or at least to be able to appreciate what they have done. Academics write books that they hope will make a difference to the future of their discipline. Artists paint pictures that they hope future people will appreciate. People sometimes have views about how their survivors should regard them after their death, how their bodies should be disposed of and how their possessions should be distributed. They may want their posthumous reputation to be respected or their children to enjoy an inheritance. Not everyone cares about all of these things. Some people may not care about any. But this survey suggests that the existence of hopes, fears and desires concerning the future beyond one's lifetime are extremely common, and some of the laws and institutions of society are designed to deal with the requests and demands that arise from lifetime-transcending concerns.

These concerns are obvious examples of what I call 'lifetime-transcending interests': interests concerning states of affairs that will, or could, occur in the future beyond one's lifetime. The existence of these interests has sometimes been used to ground duties in respect to the future. Rawls and de-Shalit are examples of philosophers who have appealed to them for that purpose. But there is also a possibility that they can ground duties in respect to past people. If, for example, a person makes a request while alive about how her body would be disposed of, most people would probably agree that this gives her survivors a duty to respect her wishes (unless there is a good reason not to do so). The main thesis of this book is that lifetime-transcending interests are the foundation for a theory of justice that encompasses duties to both past and future generations. In this chapter I will explain what lifetime-transcending interests are and why they have the potential to play this role.

INTERESTS

Let us begin with the notion of an interest. To have an interest, as I will use the term, is to have a reason for pursuing an activity, favouring an outcome or being attracted to a person or thing. A person can be interested, for example, in pursuing a hobby, becoming acquainted with the girl next door, the progress of his football team, the achievement an ideal or the well-being of friends or lovers. Interests have a point. An interest in another person, more precisely understood, may be an interest in becoming her friend or lover, or perhaps simply in her ability to achieve a certain goal. Interests belong to agents (which can include other entities besides persons), but not all interests are self-interests. People can have an interest in the fate of others, the achievement of world peace, moral goodness and many other things that transcend the self and self-centred needs and wants. Interests give agents a forward-looking orientation. Their interests are the focus and reason for their desires, fears, hopes, pursuits and propensities. A person who has an interest in the future well-being of his children desires that they will be able to live good lives, and because of this interest may be motivated to give them good advice or leave something for them in his will. But the subject of an interest can be events or people of the past. A person can have an interest in learning about past events or in remembering past people.

Interests are motivating. A person can have a detached, merely intellectual interest in the outcome of events—an attitude that merely amounts to a focus of attention—but in general a person's interests are her concerns. Interests are inextricably associated with propensities, desires, wishes, intentions, hopes and fears. An interest is at the centre of a related set of propensities, desires, hopes and fears; it is the theme that explains their relationship. People desire to achieve the objects of their interests; they wish for the success of projects in which they take an interest, or they fear for their failure. If a person has an interest in the well-being of his children or community, then he wants them to flourish and he is likely to want others to do things that increase their chance of flourishing. He may actually demand that they do so. Whether and when such demands are justified is a subject for moral philosophy. Whether and how a political society should accommodate them is a topic for political philosophy.

Interests breed interests. An interest in one thing often leads to an interest in another. A person can just have an interest—in fishing, for example—but in many cases interests call for further explanation, and in providing it, agents generally refer to other, more basic interests or to the values which inform or lie behind their interests. Values are themselves interests when they become reasons for actions, propensities, desires, hopes and fears. A person who has a value or ideal has an interest in pursuing it or an interest in its perpetuation or realisation, and thus an interest in the activities or states of affairs that might lead to such objectives being fulfilled. We should not assume that agents have a core interest that explains all of their other interests—and thus all of their desires, activities and propensities—but it is reasonable to suppose that some of an agent's interests will be of much greater importance than others to her life and her conception of herself, and that her most significant interests will be central to her identity and her view about the meaning of her life.

A person's interests, it is generally assumed, are what she takes an interest in. But if we think of interests as reasons, then it is also plausible to suppose that a person can have interests that she is not aware of having. This may be because she is not conscious of the interests behind her actions. She does not properly know herself. But it may also be because she does not know that something is in her interest. She does not properly appreciate the implications of her conscious interests. The idea that a person may not appreciate her own interests is contentious. We associate this claim with those who have paternalistic or authoritarian views about the interests that others ought to possess. But in some cases, it can be a reasonable judgement without paternalistic connotations. Living in a secure society is necessary for the pursuit of many aims, but some individuals may never have thought about the social prerequisites of their activities, or they may falsely believe that social conditions are not important. But nevertheless their other interests make it clear that they also have an interest in a secure society. So I will include among the interests that can be attributed to a person those that are *entailed* by his or her acknowledged interests, along with reasonable beliefs about the world. Rational, well-informed people would acknowledge that they have such interests.

LIFETIME-TRANSCENDING INTERESTS

A lifetime-transcending interest is an interest in outcomes, activities or processes that will, or could, take place in the future beyond the boundaries of one's lifetime. A person's lifetime-transcending interests give him wishes, desires, hopes and fears that do not depend on whether he can, or will, live to experience the outcome that he desires or fears. Some of a person's lifetime-transcending interests are about outcomes that will necessarily happen after his death; for example, his interest in how his body will be disposed of, or his interest in his bequests being honoured. But others are about outcomes that may be decided before his death. A person who has an interest in her children living a good life may live long enough to know whether her hopes for them are fulfilled. She may outlive her children. But the interest and the desires associated with her concern for the future of her children do not depend on her being able to experience her children's well-being. She has an interest in them living well, and not (merely) an interest in being gratified by their well-being. Lifetime-transcending interests can include interests in outcomes that we expect to be able to experience. Having sent his book to the publisher, John has an interest in it being published. He fully expects to be around to experience this outcome, but he has an interest in it being published whether he is or not.

Lifetime-transcending interests are many and various. They can be self-interests—having an interest in being revered by future people, for example—but they can also be altruistic, such as having an interest in the future well-being of one's family or members of a community. They also can be particular—such as an interest in the future well-being of a particular person or family—and they can be general, like an interest in averting global warming or in the achievement of a more just society. They can be interests in the survival of things valued for their own sake, or they can be interests in the persistence of institutions or conditions valued as a means to an end.

Lifetime-transcending interests are motivating. Those who care about the future of their community are predisposed to contribute to projects that will ensure its survival. They will avoid activities that could endanger it. Those who have an interest in perpetuating a tradition are likely to advocate it or to contribute to activities that encourage respect for the past. An artist who has an interest in how her works will be valued in future generations will make an effort to ensure that they survive. Those who have in interest in donating their bodily organs will be motivated to sign up to an organ donation program. Those who care about the future of their children may make a will in their favour. If so, they will want their survivors to honour the terms of the will. Indeed, they will regard this as something that their survivors ought to do. They may encourage their children to do things that will enable them to flourish in the future. They will be predisposed to believe that members of their society ought to act to ensure that their children, as well as the children of other people, will have secure and prosperous lives. Lifetime-transcending interests give rise to lifetime-transcending desires, and sometimes to lifetime-transcending demands. Whether these demands can ever be legitimate is something that we will need to investigate.

No theorist is likely to deny the existence of lifetime-transcending interests. On the other hand, few philosophers have paid them much attention. As a category of interest they have been largely overlooked. In my view, lifetime-transcending interests are not only very common but are extremely important to individuals, their identities and their views about their obligations and entitlements. They ought to be the concern of any political theory, in particular, any theory of justice that appeals for its justification to the needs and interests of the individuals of a society. However, this claim is going to meet with resistance. Some sceptics are likely to think that lifetime-transcending interests are far from universal, that they are merely the special interests of some people, and thus no basis for principles that are supposed to be endorsed by all citizens. But even critics who are persuaded that lifetime-transcending interests are common might consider them peripheral—not nearly so important as some of the lifetime interests of individuals—and thus not something that moral or political philosophy needs to concern itself with. Liberal political philosophers believe that individuals should be free to pursue their interests (under certain limitations), and lifetime-transcending interests might be regarded merely as interests that some, or many, individuals pursue, but not as interests that need to be given special consideration in defining principles of justice or constructing political institutions.

My contention is that they do have an important role to play, not only in a theory of intergenerational justice, but also in a re-evaluation of the importance of intergenerational obligations and entitlements in the affairs of a political society. The first step is to demonstrate that all individuals are likely to have lifetime-transcending interests and that they play an important role in their lives. If this is so, then a just political society ought to ensure that its citizens have an opportunity to acquire and pursue them.

Moreover, their existence is likely to justify the existence of political institutions that enable, or even require, lifetime-transcending desires of certain kinds to be fulfilled.

SIGNIFICANCE OF LIFETIME-TRANSCENDING INTERESTS

Not all philosophers have ignored lifetime-transcending interests. Miller, as we have seen, thinks that people value being part of an intergenerational community such as a nation. Lukas Meyer believes that most people have projects that 'are situated in practices that are historically formed and that themselves are defined against the background of past practices and the possibility of other practices being realised', and that some of these people engage in future-oriented projects, including those that will not bear fruit for many years, and think it important how their efforts are regarded and continued by their successors (1997: 141–3). He thinks that the fact that individuals want to dedicate themselves to such activities is a significant feature of human existence, and that any just society ought to provide opportunities for such undertakings.

Hannah Arendt argues that human life is futile unless people are able to engage in activities that produce something that endures (as opposed to things that are consumed to maintain life or satisfy desires). The highest activities, in her view, are those through which individuals immortalise themselves—an end that is made possible by the existence of an intergenerational polis in which people commemorate and build on the deeds of the past (1958: 135ff).

Arendt's views are the result of a reflection on human existence. Ernest Partridge presents a psychological case for the significance of what he calls self-transcendence: 'Well functioning human beings identify with, and seek to further, the well-being, preservation and endurance of communities, locations, causes, artefacts, institutions, ideals, and so on, that are outside themselves and that they hope will flourish beyond their lifetimes'. The endurance of these valued objects is for the agent 'a part of his inventory of personal *interests or goods*' (1981b: 204). Using my terminology, self-transcendence as defined by Partridge involves having lifetime-transcending interests. If a person values a community, not merely as something that contributes to her well-being, but as something with an independent value, she will have an interest in its continued existence. She will want it to flourish in the future beyond her lifetime. People who value a cultural endeavour like art typically have an interest in perpetuating artistic institutions or activities. People who value ideals or causes like justice, peace or socialism have an interest in the achievement of a society or a world which is just, peaceful or socialist, and an interest in engaging in activities that seem to contribute to its achievement.

Partridge makes three claims about self-transcendence: that it is common for individuals to have self-transcendent values; that having them is a prerequisite for living a meaningful life; and that self-transcendence predisposes individuals to care about the future and to accept duties to future generations. The latter claim, like de-Shalit's communitarianism, raises questions about how lifetime-transcending concerns generate obligations. But it is the second claim that Partridge is most concerned to defend. If there is reason to think that self-transcendence is necessary for living a meaningful life, then individuals have reason to acquire these values, to make them a central part of their lives and to accept whatever obligations to the future that they entail. They have reason to want their society to provide members with opportunities to acquire and live according to self-transcending values, and reason to give their collective consent to institutions that enable them to do so.

Partridge marshals arguments from common sense and a variety of moral and psychological perspectives to persuade us that self-transcendence is essential for a meaningful life. If the self is intrinsically social, as Mead and others argue, alienation from social concerns is a form of personality disorder; if we have a predisposition to attribute independent value to things that we value, then we are constitutionally predisposed to transcendence. Moreover, we know that we are mortal and subject to the contingencies of fate and a commitment to enduring causes, ideals and institutions is an important way of extending our influence beyond our lifetimes (as de-Shalit also argues). Not to be self-transcendent is to be trapped in a limited and unsatisfactory existence of the narcissist or the egoist. Healthy, well-functioning people, Partridge concludes, have a need to transcend themselves and 'to identify themselves as a part of larger, ongoing, and enduring processes, projects, institutions, and ideals'. Without the existence of posterity as an idea 'our lives would be confined, empty, bleak, pointless, and morally impoverished' (1981b: 218–9).

That self-transcendence is central to a meaningful existence is also explicit or implicit in accounts of the meaningful life or the human condition offered by many philosophers. 'To seek a meaningful life,' says Robert Nozick, 'is to seek to transcend the limits of one's individual life' (1989: 166–7). He suggests that there are two ways that this might be done: by connecting with external things or by incorporating these things inside ourselves—by enlarging our self-conception. The self that is transcended in the latter case is the self that confines itself to a narrow concern with its own person. Susan Wolf takes the first path outlined by Nozick by claiming that a meaningful life is one in which a person actively engages in projects of worth—a pursuit that requires commitment to something enduring (1997: 211). Loren Lomasky similarly claims that a commitment to long-term projects that persist over time and project into the future is an important component of a person's identity

(1987: 32). Charles Taylor takes the second path outlined by Nozick. Essential to a human agent, he says, is the capacity to be a strong evaluator—to evaluate the worth of one's projects or one's life—and this requires that she subscribes to a higher order of good such as justice, God, aesthetic beauty or knowledge, that makes her part of something larger than her own life (1989: 62ff). Communitarians, as we have seen, think that individuals do and should identify themselves with a community that persists through the generations and to regard its good as their good. Deep ecologists want us to expand the self by identifying with other living things (Naess 1973).

Self-transcendence has many supporters. Nevertheless, Partridge's thesis is not so self-evident as to be indubitable. Is self-transcendence really necessary for a meaningful life? Is it even a good thing? The first question can be asked because it seems that some people live satisfying lives, lives that are meaningful to them, without having any transcendent values. It even seems possible to imagine a society in which all or most people lack these values. Indeed, Arendt believes that most members of a modern consumerist society aim only to satisfy their desires and are no longer genuinely concerned with immortality (1958: 55). The second question arises because there are philosophies, hedonism for example, which seem to exclude self-transcendence.

Partridge himself doubts that everyone has self-transcendent values and he fears that the possibility of people living a satisfying life without these values could undermine his claim that self-transcendence is essential to a meaningful life. A playboy who lives for the pleasure of the moment, the miser who is obsessed with amassing and counting his gold coins, the businessman who is simply interested in accumulating a fortune or a collection of artwork which he values only because they give him the satisfaction of ownership—these people do not seem to have, or feel the need for, self-transcendent values. Egoists of these and other kinds pose a general problem for Partridge's thesis. A person who values people and things outside of himself only insofar as they contribute to his happiness or the achievement of his goals does not fit Partridge's conception of being self-transcending. Egoists undoubtedly exist, and some may be happy with their lives, so if valuing something for its own sake is necessary for having interests that predispose individuals to care about the future beyond their lifetime, then there are people who have no reason to care.

In our social world, people who have self-transcending values may be far more prevalent than those who do not (though Arendt's claim shows that this is by no means incontestable). But this does not mean that this is so in every society, or that it must be so in future generations. Golding, as we have seen, fears that future humans of a later generation might be preoccupied with immediate pleasures and not interested in things that could make them self-transcending. Nor are most of the people in *Brave New World* (1955), Aldous Huxley's fictional account of a society where people are constructed and conditioned to live life for the moment, taking drugs and having sex whenever something unpleasant threatens their perpetual state of bliss. A different, but real-world description of people who seem to have no use for transcendent values is presented by the anthropologist Colin Turnbull (1972), who studied a tribe in Uganda, the Ik, which, according to his account, consists of egoistic individuals who are preoccupied with getting the necessities of life; who place no value on mutual aid, honesty or fair dealing; who throw their children out to fend for themselves as soon as they are old enough to function independently and who leave old people to die.

One way of dealing with doubts about the prevalence or importance of transcendence is to raise questions about these examples of non-transcendence. Partridge wonders whether the playboy, the businessman or the miser is really able to do without self-transcendence, and if so, whether their lives are really satisfying (216). Some of Turnbull's critics claim that the Ik are not as he described them, but rather are victims of famine, drought, displacement and warfare—conditions that can drive people to extremes and take from them their hopes for the future. Or perhaps Turnbull's description misses something that is important to the Ik. In fact, it is hard to see how a society consisting of competitive, selfish people who do not care about each other or the future of their children could last for very long. In presenting their fictions about the future, Huxley and Golding assume that we will agree that people who live only for the sensations of the moment have degraded lives.

Another way of dealing with doubts is to question the way in which some philosophers conceive of transcendence. Owen Flanagan criticises Taylor for making too high the bar that separates truly human agents from those who live a meaningless life. Tolstoy's stories of peasant life, he thinks, provide examples of people who are living good and morally satisfactory lives, but who are not reflective or self-interpreting in the way that Taylor requires (1996: 149ff). Both Partridge and Taylor tend to think of self-transcendence as a commitment to long-term causes or ideals, but if it simply means valuing something outside of oneself, then Tolstoy's peasants clearly have self-transcendent values. They value their children, their communities, their religious tradition and other things that give them concerns about the future beyond their lifetime. A similar criticism can be directed at Arendt's contention that modern citizens have ceased to be concerned with the future. Her ideal is the Athenian polis in which citizens competed with each other to be immortalised by their deeds and left the labour of reproducing life to servants and women. But a concern for the future beyond one's lifetime can be expressed in more mundane activities: in the investments parents put into ensuring that their children will flourish, in the projects people pursue, the traditions that they want to perpetuate and ideals that they support. To have lifetime-transcending concerns it is not necessary that people be devoted to immortalising themselves in the public arena.

There is a further reason to think that Partridge and Arendt have raised too high the bar that separates those who have reason to care about the future beyond their lifetimes from those who do not. Consider the miser who cares about no one but devotes himself to hoarding gold—not because he wants to do anything with it, but perhaps because he simply enjoys possessing it. Let us say that he does not care what happens to it after his death; perhaps he intends to hide it away so that no one else can possess it. But it is notable that he gloats over a precious metal and not, like a magpie, over brightly coloured pieces of string. A reasonable explanation is that he values gold because people in the society to which he belongs have long regarded it as having great and enduring value, indeed a value by which the value of other things is measured. So if gold lost its status as a mark of value, or if the miser believed that its value was bound to decrease and finally disappear, he would find it difficult to regard his hoarding as meaningful. If this explanation is right, then the miser, whether he acknowledges it or not, has a lifetime-transcending interest in the persistence of a mark of value and a way of valuing. The businessman who is preoccupied with amassing a fortune and has no concern about what happens to it after his death may nevertheless care about his posthumous reputation. He would not want people spreading lies about how he made his money or denying that he earned his reputation as a wealthy man. He may care about the existence and persistence of social values and traditions that make running a successful business an admirable activity in his society. The artist who just enjoys painting and does not care if anyone values her works after her death is nevertheless likely to care about the existence and persistence of a tradition of making and valuing artistic objects. The self-centred millionaire who buys valuable paintings and locks them up in his vault may not care about artistic values or about what happens to his possessions after his death, but he would not get satisfaction out of owning great works of art if he did not believe that people in the present and future would continue to value them. If he thought that people would cease to appreciate art, that the value of his pictures was merely ephemeral, then his pleasure in owning the pictures would probably be much diminished. His egoistic pleasure, in other words, rides piggyback on a tradition of valuing works of art, and he has an interest in the persistence of this tradition as an objective way of valuing just as the miser has an interest in the persistence of gold as a standard of value. They may not acknowledge these interests, but that does not mean that they do not have them.

For Partridge, self-transcendence means having ideals, altruistic objectives or moral values. An egoist cannot be self-transcending. But egoists can have lifetime-transcending interests. In fact, they are likely to do so. Once we recognise that such interests are not confined to those who care about others and that the objectives that people pursue can depend on unacknowledged lifetime-transcending interests then it becomes much more difficult to deny their ubiquity and importance, and much easier to accept the idea that all or most people have reason to care about states of affairs beyond their lifetimes.

LIFE WITHOUT CARING FOR THE FUTURE

Lifetime-transcending interests are prevalent. In fact, they are difficult to live without. But that doesn't mean that everyone thinks they are desirable. Some people have views about the good or meaningful life that seem to eschew them entirely or to make them less important and motivating. Hedonists believe that the good life consists simply of having pleasant experiences; stoics believe that equanimity depends on detaching oneself from transitory things. Mystics believe that true fulfilment comes from having a relationship to God or by removing oneself as much as possible from the concerns of the temporal world. Hedonism denies Partridge's thesis about the meaningful life; stoicism and mysticism reject the idea that self-transcendence means caring about the future.

Hedonists face familiar objections. If a good life is a life that contains the highest ratio of pleasure over pain, then a person who lives a bestial life of pleasure is likely to count as having a better life than those who strive for great things but often suffer disappointments. If pleasurable sensations are the only things that count, then a person whose happiness depends on being deceived by others is living a good life. Most people find these, and other, consequences of hedonism difficult to accept. Fred Feldman, a contemporary defender of hedonism, abandons the classical version, which is concerned only with episodes of pleasure, and defends a version that includes the enjoyment people obtain from things like art or friendship (2004: Chapter 4). He gives these experiences a higher rating than sensual pleasure in the hedonist calculus. But his calculus suggests that a hedonist values friends or works of art only for the enjoyment that they give her. Why should she care about these things as independent objects that deserve respect? Most of us are likely to answer that valuing friends or art only for the enjoyment they give us would be self-defeating. For one thing, it would make it likely that hedonists will not have many friends to enjoy. Moreover, people who regard art or their friends as a means to enjoyment are not likely to get as much value from their relationships with these things or people as they would if they appreciated them for their own sake and regarded them as worthy of being valued. If this is so, then a hedonist ought to cultivate some lifetime-transcending interests.

Stoics and mystics do not abandon transcendence. Rather they seek to detach themselves from the desires and cares associated with temporal existence. Stoics concentrate on achieving a life of virtue and inner peace that will not be disturbed by the vicissitudes of fortune. They do not give up friendship or the enjoyment of beautiful things, but aim to cultivate a perspective toward the things they value that enables them to face their loss with equanimity.[1] Mystics want to lose themselves in the love of God or to achieve a perspective that transcends time and place, but not to abandon a concern for others. By loving God, the mystic, so far as she can, strives to love others in the way that God loves them. Buddhist meditation cultivates a compassion for all creatures. Mystics typically value their traditions and practices and want them to survive for the sake of future generations. They may compile teachings for this purpose.

This brief discussion is meant to suggest that hedonism, stoicism and mysticism are not so hostile toward lifetime-transcending interests as it first appears. The more important point to make about these philosophies, especially stoicism and mysticism, is that most people have neither the inclination nor the ability to put them into practice or are not in the position to do so. They are philosophies for people who have leisure time and are reasonably free of responsibilities. The outlook and discipline they require is hard to reconcile with being a parent or with citizenship in more than a nominal sense, and the more that they are reconciled with the responsibilities required by these roles, the more obvious it is that their practitioners will continue to have concerns about the future of their children, the survival and well-being of their community or the fate of ideals associated with it.

A political society is by its nature an association with a worldly mission. It is supposed to provide a collective means for avoiding or alleviating some of the misfortunes that can afflict human existence, as well as providing opportunities to individuals that they would not otherwise possess. A just society is supposed to guarantee to all of its citizens certain rights and protections; in particular, it is supposed to establish and maintain social relationships that enable them to determine and pursue their own interests, and it gives citizens a collective responsibility for maintaining these relationships. A political society should perhaps leave room for stoics and mystics and for others whose philosophical or religious commitments require them to eschew the political. (Whether there is room for hedonists depends on their willingness to conform to requirements of justice.) But citizenship is primarily designed for those who regard the purposes of politics as their concern and a theory of justice must assume from the start that it is (primarily) about relationships between people who share this concern. I have argued that lifetime-transcending interests are among the interests that individuals have reason to pursue, and a just political society must take this into account. How it should do so remains to be seen.

LIFETIME-TRANSCENDING INTERESTS AND OBLIGATIONS

Common sense, moral psychology and most philosophers support the thesis that people generally have lifetime-transcending interests of one kind or another and that they play an important role in their lives. Partridge's thesis, at least as I have interpreted and expanded it, seems correct. The question remains how it is to be translated into an account of intergenerational duties, in particular, intergenerational duties of citizens in a political society.

For Partridge self-transcending values always involve a moral concern for other people, including those who will exist after we have departed.

He assumes that a concern for ideals, artefacts, places or communities involves a desire that people of the future be in the position to realise, enjoy or maintain them. Our willingness to accept obligations to people of future generations arises from our concern to ensure that they will be in the position to enjoy their inheritance and to live meaningful lives as self-transcending agents, and he thinks that this concern extends far into the future beyond the lifetime of our immediate descendents. There are difficulties that Partridge doesn't consider. Some people's self-transcending values may not entail much of a concern for future people. Some people's self-transcendence extends no further than a concern for their family and friends and does not seem to motivate duties to people of the far future. Nevertheless, his account makes the relation between self-transcendence and obligation relatively straightforward. Lifetime-transcending interests, on the other hand, are not necessarily moral or altruistic interests and furthermore, they are extremely varied. The relation between these interests and intergenerational obligations stands in need of explanation.

There are two strategies for explaining how we get obligations from lifetime-transcending interests. The first makes use of the idea of a contract. Let us imagine that members of a society are behind the veil of ignorance with the object of determining principles of intergenerational justice. They do not know what interests they have or what generation they belong to. Nevertheless they know that they have an interest in developing and pursuing lifetime-transcending (as well as lifetime) interests. They know that they have, or will have, desires arising from these interests that they want their successors to fulfil. The previous discussion explains why these are reasonable assumptions. It follows that they have a lifetime-transcending interest in ensuring that their successors will be in the position to fulfil their interests. So they will be predisposed to accept a duty of justice that requires each generation to provide their successors with the institutions and conditions that will enable them to develop and pursue lifetime-transcending (as well as lifetime) interests. This contractual agreement, it should be noted, makes use of reasoning similar to that which I outlined in Chapter 3.

The original position is like the one described by Rawls in *Political Liberalism*, with one important difference. The contractors do not merely have an interest in maintaining conditions that enable them to pursue their lifetime interests; they have a lifetime-transcending interest in their lifetime-transcending desires being fulfilled. They will therefore want to perpetuate social relationships which give their successors the opportunity to fulfil these desires. And they will regard as their successors those who will be in the position to do this. This means that they will not want to act in a way that brings the social relationship between the generations to an end. They will want successors. The second non-identity problem, which Rawls fails to surmount, is overcome by an interest that everyone can be assumed to have in perpetuating their social relationships. And this interest does not depend on everyone caring for their descendants—a concern that we cannot suppose that all people have.

A number of objections can be made to this elaboration of the contract story. Though members of a society have an interest in their lifetime-transcending desires being fulfilled, they do not so obviously have an interest in their successors developing and pursuing their own lifetime or lifetime-transcending interests. So why shouldn't the contractors decide to give the young as little freedom as possible to develop their own interests and concentrate on indoctrinating them to believe that it is imperative to fulfil the interests of their predecessors?

The veil of ignorance makes this objection easy to answer. The contractors do not know what generation they belong to, so they will not accept a principle to which they do not want to be subjected. In particular, they will not accept a principle that allows citizens to indoctrinate their successors or otherwise restricts their freedom to form their own interests. And their interest in having their lifetime-transcending desires fulfilled means that they will not want to act in a way that brings it about that they are the last generation, and thus they have to suppose that they might be subject to any principle that they affirm.

However, a more serious problem for this conception of an intergenerational contract is similar to the main difficulty faced by de-Shalit. The very existence of an intergenerational relationship, and the duties associated with it, depends on a belief that it exists. Suppose that the contractors doubt that the succeeding generation will ever satisfy any of their lifetime-transcending desires or even consider the possibility of satisfying them. Such scepticism, it seems, would make it impossible for them to regard this coming generation as their successors, and would thus subvert any account of intergenerational justice that depends on the continued existence of an intergenerational relationship.

There is a further problem concerning successors. Everyone can be assumed to have lifetime-transcending interests. But this universality is achieved by cobbling together a collection of interests so various that there is a danger that they can provide no basis for any conclusions about intergenerational justice. The fact that the interests are so varied is not itself a problem: the veil of ignorance reduces this variety to the general knowledge that all individuals have an interest in developing and pursuing lifetime-transcending interests of some kind. What is problematic is that individuals, depending on the nature of their interests, have different ideas about who will count as their successors. Those who want to perpetuate an artistic tradition will think of their successors as being those people, wherever they are, who can be expected to carry it on. Those who want their religious or ethnic community to survive and flourish will regard as their successors members of this community, and so on. It is far from obvious how these particular relationships between the generations translate into a theory about obligations of justice between the generations in a polity. What seems to be needed is a demonstration that the perpetuation of an intergenerational polity that maintains certain political practices or institutions is essential to the perpetuation or protection of the intergenerational relationships that people value, whatever these relationships are. The need for such a demonstration is not unique to the approach I am taking. A theory of intergenerational justice that rests on the concern of representatives of family lines has to explain how an interest in the perpetuation of family relationships and the well-being of family members translates into an interest in establishing and maintaining just political institutions through the generations. Rawls in *A Theory of Justice* does not sufficiently discuss this matter.

It should also be noted that the contractual approach is not a suitable strategy for explaining how we can have duties in respect to the dead or their deeds. Those now dead had lifetime-transcending desires, and we may be disposed to fulfil them. But the contract gives us no reason for believing that we ought to do so. And the next generation is not required to fulfil our desires. This is what makes it possible for us to be sceptical about their being our successors.

These difficulties are addressed by the second strategy, which aims to show that certain lifetime-transcending desires, or commitments entered into because of these desires, impose moral requirements on successors. This idea has some plausibility. We think, for example, that people ought to keep promises made to those now dead (unless there is a good reason not to do so). We think that a person's wishes about how her body and possessions should be disposed of should generally be respected. We are inclined to think that members of religious or ethnic communities are entitled to provide a cultural inheritance to their descendants and thus to demand that future members of their society respect the right of these descendants to receive and maintain it. Such obligations and entitlements, if indeed they exist, would bind together the generations of a society in a moral relationship of rights and responsibilities. This moral relationship would ensure that the first problem—the doubt that succeeding generations will be related to us in a way that makes them count as our successors—does not arise. If succeeding generations are obliged to fulfil obligations in respect to their predecessors, then their status as successors cannot legitimately be doubted or denied. Moreover, a moral relationship between generations would give present people duties in respect to their predecessors. If we can bind our successors to fulfil some of our lifetime-transcending demands, then we ought to accept an obligation to fulfil legitimate demands of our predecessors.

The problem concerning intergenerational political obligations will be solved if we can establish that just political institutions and practices are essential to underwrite the fulfilment of intergenerational obligations and the securing of intergenerational entitlements. If this is so, then members of a polity will have a reason for maintaining through the generations political institutions and practices that secure their ability to fulfil their intergenerational responsibilities and obtain their intergenerational entitlements. And by cooperating to maintain these practices they will obtain intergenerational responsibilities and entitlements as citizens.

In the next two chapters I will make use of both of these complementary strategies. Using the second strategy, I will argue that individuals are sometimes entitled to make lifetime-transcending demands of their successors, and that in doing so they are tacitly endorsing an intergenerational requirement that gives them duties in respect to their predecessors. I will explain why these duties exist and what they are, and I will argue that the principles that they entail require us to accept a collective responsibility for maintaining intergenerational institutions that underwrite their application. Employing the first strategy, I will then go on to consider what members of a generation, as imagined participants in a social contract, ought to regard as their fair share of this responsibility.

5 Lifetime-Transcending Interests and Duties to Past People

Most of us believe that we have duties to past generations. Some of these duties result from personal or familial connections: for example, keeping a promise made to a dying friend or burying a relative according to her wishes. Some arise from membership in a community: for example, the duty of citizens to honour those who sacrificed themselves to defend their country or to make recompense for the injustices of past governments or citizens. Some require respect for a socially recognised entitlement: for example, the right of individuals to make bequests and the right of heirs to receive them. Some are predicated on the wishes or interests of the dead: protection of posthumous reputations, for example. Others have to do with their deeds: for example, making recompense for their wrongs. Some seem to be duties of piety or gratitude; others are more likely to be classified as duties of justice.

Some people have doubts about the existence of some of these duties. Egalitarians, for example, question the legitimacy of rights of bequest and inheritance. Pacifists may refuse to accept a duty to honour those who died in war. But any discussion of duties to the dead has to contend with a more fundamental form of scepticism. The dead, after all, are dead; our deeds cannot make their lives better or worse. The impression that we have duties to them seems to fly in the face of a common sense understanding of why we owe consideration to others. And the idea that we have an obligation to make recompense for the deeds of past people seems to be contrary to an equally common-sensical view of collective responsibility. If it is wrong to punish us for the injustices of others, then how can it be all right to make us responsible for making recompense for their deeds?

A theory that aims to encompass responsibilities in respect to the past must be able to deal with these sceptical objections, and it must also be able to provide criteria for determining what duties exist. A theory of intergenerational justice that aims to include duties in respect to past generations must explain how duties to the dead or in respect to the past are related to the duties of justice that citizens are supposed to owe to each other and to people of the future. These are the tasks of Chapters 6 and 7. In this chapter, I will defend the idea that we have duties to the dead by showing that some demands based on lifetime-transcending interests are morally justified. This defence, as I will show, provides a way of linking our duties in respect to the past with our duties to the future.

WRONGING THE DEAD

Most philosophers who have considered the question of whether we have duties to the dead believe that the answer depends on whether the dead can be harmed or benefited by our activities. On this issue, natural feelings and rational reflection seem to lead in different directions. Many people find it natural to believe that the dead can be 'the victims of injustice, slander, betrayal, and so on,' as George Pitcher says (1984: 183). If Bill promises his dying father to bury him in the family plot but instead sells his corpse to a medical school, then it seems right to say that Bill has badly betrayed, and thus harmed, his father. If Mrs White cared about the continued survival of the business that she built up during her lifetime, then its failure after her death harms her. But if we believe that death puts an end to the existence of a person or that the dead are translated into a realm that has no causal relation to ours, then it is difficult to understand how a dead person can be harmed. Our ability to harm things that *were* of interest to the dead does not seem to generate any duties to them. And it seems absurd to suppose that the interests had by the dead during their lives hang around like hungry ghosts demanding satisfaction.

Joel Feinberg (1974) and Thomas Nagel (1979) make a case for saying that we can harm, and therefore wrong, the dead by pointing out that a person can be harmed even when his life chances, mental states and relationships are in no way affected. Feinberg asks us to imagine that, in some remote area of the country, a person's reputation has been maliciously impugned. There is no chance that he or any of the people he knows will ever hear of this slander and none of his opportunities or relations with others will be adversely affected. Nevertheless, according to Feinberg, his interests have been set back. A person has an interest in having 'a good reputation *simpliciter* and not just an interest in avoiding hurt feelings, embarrassment, and economic injury' (1974: 4). But if a person's interests can be harmed when this does not affect his conscious experiences or have a detrimental effect on his opportunities, then, according to Feinberg, it makes sense to suppose that the interests of the dead can also be harmed.

The analogy is not convincing, for it might be the case that our willingness to believe that the maligned person has been harmed depends on the *possibility* that he might be affected—a possibility that no longer exists for the dead. In *Harm to Others* Feinberg makes a more plausible case for duties to the dead by adopting a position also advanced by Pitcher (1984: Chapter 2). They agree that interests cannot belong to 'postmortem persons' who are nothing but decaying corpses or heaps of ashes. But if the dead are thought of as 'antemortem persons'—as the people they were during some stage of their life—then it makes sense, according to Feinberg and Pitcher, that they have interests and can be harmed. By failing to fulfil the promise to his father, Bill harms him as an antemortem person—as someone who wanted to be buried in the family plot and counted on his son to carry out his wishes. If we reject the idea of backward causation, then nothing we do now can cause a dead person to suffer at any stage of his life. But what we do can make it true that a person was in a harmed condition before he died in the same way that the destruction of the world during the period in office of the next US president would make it true even now that George W. Bush was the second last president of the United States (to update an example used by Pitcher).

How should we understand this account of harming the dead? If we suppose that by setting back the interests of the dead an agent makes a real change to the world—makes something the case about their past lives that was not the case before—then we are invoking backward causation, which Feinberg and Pitcher agree is implausible. If we suppose that the harm exists because it was true of the dead person when she was alive that her interests would be set back after her death (as Pitcher's discussion suggests), then the account seems to have unacceptably fatalistic implications (Lamont 1988: 204–05). In any case, how can a posthumous event harm a dead person? 'It is simply not the case that posthumous events are harmful to Smith. Rather, it is the fact that they will come about which is harmful to him. Once they do come about, Smith himself is beyond harm' (J. Callahan 1987: 345).

On the other hand, we can interpret Feinberg and Pitcher's position as an appeal to the common sense idea that events that occur after a person's death can affect how we understand and describe his life and activities (Grey 1999: 361). If I mistakenly erase the disk containing a philosophical work that a dying friend left in my care, then his colleagues will regard the effort he put into writing this work as 'tragically wasted' and his desire to communicate his philosophical ideas as 'thwarted' by my careless act. In other words, what happens after a person dies can change the story we tell about their lives as well as our assessment of their life and work. But this non-metaphysical interpretation of Feinberg and Pitcher does not support the conclusion that the dead can be benefited or harmed. It is difficult to understand how doing something that changes the story that we tell about a life constitutes a harm or wrong done to the dead.

There are further difficulties. Most discussions of harm to the dead take place in the context of an argument about whether death is a harm. This means that theorists pay little attention to questions about the nature and seriousness of the wrongs that are committed by causing this harm, or when we should judge that a wrong is actually committed. Even if we agree that it is possible to harm the dead, it is not obvious that doing so is very wrong. Aristotle allows that the dead can be harmed but thinks that the effect of our actions on them must be 'weak and negligible', a description that suggests that harming their interests is not nearly as serious as it would have been to harm these interests when they were living or to harm comparable interests of living people (1980: 23). Pitcher points out that antemortem persons have interests that deeply matter to them. But since they are no longer in the position to care about them, the question remains whether harming these interests can count for very much. It seems possible for people to accept his view about antemortem harms and yet have very different opinions about how much these harms matter. Moreover, the theory about antemortem harms does not tell us how we determine our duties to the dead. Not all the ways in which we can harm the dead count as wrongs. For example, we do not generally think that it is wrong to tell the truth about a person in a posthumous biography, even though making this truth public might be judged to harm an antemortem person who didn't want the truth to be known. We need criteria to tell us when harming the dead is wrong, and an appeal to the great harm that our actions can cause to antemortem persons is not sufficient.[1]

The thesis that the dead can be harmed is therefore not only difficult to understand, but it also fails to give us a proper basis for a theory about duties to the dead. These considerations give us good reason to look for another approach. In what follows I will be agnostic about harms to the dead. Nothing I will say rules out the possibility that they occur, but nothing will depend on it.[2]

LIFETIME-TRANSCENDING INTERESTS AND COMMITMENTS TO THE DEAD

The interests of the dead that we can promote or set back are, by necessity, lifetime-transcending interests. If Mrs White thought of her business only as a means of providing her with a living, then we would have no reason to think that her interests are harmed when her business collapses after her death. The harm occurs because she wanted her business to survive as 'a monument to her industry and skill', as Pitcher says (1984: 183). It makes sense to suppose that we harm the interests of a dead person by telling malicious lies about her because most people care about how they are remembered after their death. But when a person is concerned only that an unpleasant truth not be revealed during his lifetime, then we cannot harm his interests by telling it after his death. Pitcher's account of how we can affect the interests of antemortem people depends on their having had desires and interests that can be thwarted (or satisfied) after they are dead. If it is ever wrong to thwart desires had by someone now dead, or if it is ever a duty to satisfy them, then this must be because of the nature of these interests and the reasons why the person, when living, could have demanded that her survivors fulfil them. This suggests that the way to determine whether we have duties to the dead, and how important they are, is to consider whether and when a person can make legitimate lifetime-transcending moral demands of her successors. But if they can make such demands, then we do not need to appeal to harms done to the dead in order to explain why their survivors have duties.

To show how this can be so, let us begin with an idea of obligation that almost everyone would endorse. Your friend Algernon, who is about to undergo a serious operation, asks you to promise that you will deliver his manuscript to the publisher if he is unable to do so. You promise. Algernon dies during the operation. Since it is reasonable to suppose that he had a lifetime-transcending desire to have his manuscript published, it is also reasonable to believe that he had a lifetime-transcending interest in you keeping his promise in the event of his death. But now he is dead. He will not suffer disappointment if you fail to keep your word, or relief and pleasure if you do. And perhaps no one else knows or cares about the promise. If Feinberg and Pitcher are right, then you would harm his antemortem interests by failing to keep it. But suppose that you are sceptical about antemortem harm, or suppose that you think that the interests of the dead are subordinate to the interests of the living and regard delivering the manuscript as too much trouble. 'A promise is a promise', many people would say, implying that the mere making of it gives you an obligation to keep it. But an insistence on following a rule needs to be backed up by a reason for believing that it applies to the case in question. We think it is important to keep a promise because those to whom it was made, or their friends and dependents, are depending on the promiser to honour it and it would be a breach of trust to fail, or we think promise-keeping is important out of respect toward the promisee. But neither reason seems to apply to this case. Algernon is dead and he is no longer dependent on you for anything (nor are his associates, if no one knows of the promise); and if you are sceptical about antemortem harms, then you will wonder how any act can count as disrespect to someone who is dead. It seems that death must put an end to any relationship of trust that existed between yourself and the person concerned, including the relationship that brought the promise into being. If the manuscript contains important contributions to scholarship, then you are doing a disservice to the academic community. But this is a different issue.

If you make a promise, someone might reply, then you are subscribing to a moral practice that requires you to keep it unless exceptional circumstances apply (for example, if it was made under duress or if fulfilling it becomes much more onerous than you or others expected). You should fulfil it even if the person to whom it was made would not be harmed by your refusal, even if no one depends on your performance. Let us assume that this is the understanding implicit in promise making. But why couldn't things be different? Suppose that we live in a society where it is accepted that promises and similar commitments become null and void once the promiser or the promisee is dead. No one has an obligation to keep a promise made to the dead. No one ever has an obligation to fulfil a promise made by a person who is now deceased. If promises of the deceased were to become null and void at their deaths, Feinberg says, 'there could be no confidence in promises regarding posthumous arrangements; no one would bother with wills or life insurance policies' (1974: 58). Feinberg suggests that a world without the possibility of posthumous arrangements would be undesirable. But why should this be so?

In a world where it is accepted that promises and contracts become null and void once the promiser or the promisee is dead, no one can commit others to pay a debt or fulfil an agreement after her death. In this world it is going to be much harder to do business or to make secure arrangements. People's ability to trust that commitments will be fulfilled and to make long-term plans on that assumption is considerably diminished. They are not able to entrust anyone to fulfil bequests to their children. They are not able to guarantee that a debt will be paid no matter what happens to them. They are not even able to guarantee that they can keep agreements during their lifetime when doing so depends on others keeping their promises. If I can pay my debts only if another pays his debt to me, and that person dies, then I cannot fulfil my commitments. In the imagined world, people cannot place so much trust in promises, and even if this does not undermine the practice of promise making altogether, it subverts some of its important purposes.

A convention that makes promises void when one of the parties dies would be bad for business and inconvenient for individuals. It would undermine trust and damage social relationships. But it is especially important to recognise that it would directly harm individuals by undermining their ability to ensure that their lifetime-transcending interests will be fulfilled. It is important to Algernon that his book be published. Mrs White wants her business to be taken over by someone who will appreciate it and run it well. Bill regards it as important that he be buried beside his wife in the family plot. A person who has had a long-term intimate relationship may want to ensure that her partner will be able to carry on their common project or obtain a beloved possession. A person who has laboured to assemble a collection of pictures by the same artist may regard it as important that the collection remain intact. In a society where agreements do not survive death and no one is required to keep a commitment to someone now dead there is little that people can do to ensure that the interests that are important to their lives will be fulfilled by their survivors. Their peace of mind, their sense of achievement, even their ability to invest their activities with meaning would be seriously compromised in a world where the means of obtaining this assurance is not available. Hence there is a good reason to accept a practice of posthumous promise-keeping: that is, a principle or convention that requires us to honour promises made by and to the dead and the entitlements and obligations that this convention requires.

Partridge conceives of such duties to the dead—or, as he prefers to put it, duties *in respect to* the dead—as derivable from an intergenerational social contract. The living have an interest in having their wills, contracts and promises respected after their deaths and in having agreements made by those now dead fulfilled. Thus they have reason to participate in an arrangement

Lifetime-Transcending Interests and Duties to Past People 61

that requires them to fulfil the contracts and honour the bequests of the dead, and to keep promises that were made to them. 'That is to say, it is in the interest of the living (out of concern for their own to-be-posthumous "interests") that they maintain the stable and just institutions that secured the wishes expressed by the deceased during their lifetimes' (1981a: 261). He is presuming that the living will always have this interest and thus that the practice will continue through the generations.

However, Scanlon's contractual approach to moral obligations seems more in keeping with the reasoning in the previous discussion. No one can reasonably reject a principle that requires the living to keep promises made to those now dead because of the harms that failing to have such a practice of promise-keeping would cause to the living. The reasoning used to establish the conclusion is moral rather than prudential. It involves appreciating why people like Algernon are entitled to demand that the promises made to them be kept, even (or especially) in the event of their death. Moreover, making a promise to someone makes us answerable to him, and although the dead cannot call us to account, it seems intelligible and proper to regard ourselves as answerable *to* them. We might, for example, be required to account for our behaviour to someone who represents them.[3]

Support for the practice of posthumous promise-keeping comes from a consideration of what we owe to each other and not from a prudential agreement between self-interested contractors. This makes it possible to respond to the following objection. Suppose you recognise that Algernon's peace of mind depends on you promising to deliver his manuscript. So you promise and he gets his peace of mind. The promise has served its purpose. Now that he is dead and doesn't care whether the promise is kept, you see no reason to keep it. When someone objects that by failing to keep the promise you are imprudently undermining a convention that you might later depend on, you reply that you are never going to ask anyone to do something for you after you are dead, and consequently you have no interest in maintaining a practice of posthumous promise-keeping. One response is to point out that it may be difficult for you to avoid becoming involved in a contract or agreement that involves posthumous undertakings. But the crucial point is that the reason for supporting a practice of posthumous promise-keeping is moral; it appeals to the consideration that we should have for the interests of others. This means that what is important is not whether you will ever want to make a posthumously valid promise, but the reasons you have for acknowledging that if you *were* to ask someone to promise to do something for you after your death, and they did promise, then you *would be* entitled to demand that the promise be fulfilled.

DETERMINING DUTIES TO THE DEAD

The moral reasons for supporting obligations to keep promises made to people now dead do not depend on the belief that the dead can be harmed by a failure to keep those promises. This is an advantage, given that there is reason for being sceptical about whether the dead can be harmed. It is a further advantage that my account explains why such obligations are important, why the living can be required to make sacrifices in order to fulfil them. Harms to the dead may be negligible, as Aristotle says, but the interests of the living that are served by the practice of posthumous promise-keeping are not insignificant. Furthermore, the account provides a way of determining what are our duties to the dead.

In *A Theory of Justice*, as we have seen, Rawls says that agents in the original position should determine what duties they owe to their descendents by considering what they think they would be entitled to claim from their forebears (1999a: 256). By inverting this criterion, and taking into account the situation and interests of our predecessors, we can use it as a reference point for determining our duties to the dead. We ought to do for our predecessors what we think we are entitled to demand from our survivors. If I think that my survivors ought to fulfil certain demands (were I to make them), then I have to accept a duty to fulfil relevantly similar demands that were made, or could have been made, by those whom I survive. If my predecessors were entitled to make a demand of me, then I would, if my situation were relevantly similar, be entitled to make a similar demand of my successors.

Consider, for example, the view that survivors should respect the requests made by those now dead concerning the disposal of their bodies. Most of us think that we are entitled to demand respect for such requests and we do not hesitate to accept a duty to respect similar demands of those now dead. We are critical of survivors who, without good reason, go against the wishes of the deceased. Our reasons for believing that we are entitled to make this demand sometimes have to do with the importance of a lifetime-transcending desire. Bill always wanted to be buried beside his wife in the family plot. Aunt Mabel strongly believes that she should be given a proper Christian burial and her peace of mind depends on a belief that her desire will be fulfilled. Jim is a supporter of organ donation and wants his own organs to be used to save lives. Perhaps our belief that we have an entitlement to make demands is also influenced by our relation to our bodies and our belief that we ought to be able to make a decision about the fate of something that is so intimately connected to who we are.

But not all people care about how their bodies are treated. Suppose that I, Aunt Mabel's only surviving relative, am one of these people. I am not inclined to make any demands of my successors about the disposal of my body. Can I then conclude that I do not have a duty to bury her as she wished? The criterion properly applied does not support this conclusion. It requires that I consider what I would be entitled to demand of my survivors if I were in her position with her beliefs about the importance of a Christian burial.

Embedded in our reflections about the demands that we might make of our successors and the demands that our predecessors might make of us will be moral considerations that might tell against accepting an obligation, and thus persuade us that a demand is illegitimate. Some demands that people might be predisposed to make of their survivors can be ruled out for moral reasons. A person cannot legitimately demand of his children that they take revenge on the children of his enemies. He cannot do this even if he would have been prepared to accept an obligation to take revenge on the children of his parents' enemies. Individuals ought not to fulfil a demand that they have reason to believe is immoral.

Sometimes moral considerations require that we do what a dead person ought to have demanded rather than what they did demand. Suppose that Andy, my business partner, made an informal promise to a contractor to do him a special favour. Andy is now dead and I have to consider whether I have a duty to keep the promise. As a matter of fact, I know that Andy had no intention of fulfilling this particular promise. However, promises ought to be fulfilled unless there is a good reason not to do so. So I reason that if I had made a promise of the kind that Andy made, I would judge that my successors ought to fulfil it. The practice of posthumous promise-keeping is justified by the importance of lifetime-transcending interests to individuals, but this does not mean that, in following its requirement, we are always fulfilling a dead person's interests. By keeping Andy's promise I might be frustrating one of his schemes.

Some demands that individuals might be predisposed to make can be ruled out because fulfilling them would unduly restrict the freedom of survivors. In a liberal society we do not believe that parents are entitled to demand that their grown children live their lives in a particular way or that they continue to support a religion or subscribe to a particular cause or ideal. We do not believe that children are obliged to accept commitments made by their parents. Suppose, for example, that philanthropic parents have contributed a percentage of their income to a particular charity all their lives. They promise (without consulting their children) that after their deaths the family tradition will continue—that their children will continue to contribute a part of their income to the charity. The children may or may not do what their parents want. But most of us believe that they have a right to refuse. Individuals, we believe, have a right to determine how they will live their lives and what commitments they will make.

For the same reason most people in a liberal society are likely to reject the idea that they have an obligation to continue or complete the projects of the dead or to maintain the institutions that they created. Indeed, it might be argued that duties to the dead do not, and cannot, amount to much in a society where individual freedom is accorded such a high value. This seems to be confirmed by a comparison of contemporary views about such duties with requirements that are accepted in more traditional societies, or have been accepted at earlier times in modern societies. In some societies family elders can make commitments that their descendants are obliged to keep. In earlier times, many people believed that deathbed promises were sacred, however reluctantly made and unreasonable their terms. It was commonly believed that children had an obligation to pay the debts, both monetary and moral, acquired by their parents, and that children could have a duty to follow their parent's profession. Most people in contemporary liberal societies do not accept these ideas about duty. And in conflicts between the desires of the living and the desires of those who are now dead, the law in most liberal societies is likely to favour the interests of the living. In many countries, slander of the dead is not against the law; in many countries, relatives can override the wish of a dead person to donate her bodily organs, however much she wanted to donate and however clearly she expressed her wish. In part, this tendency of the law to favour the living can be explained by pragmatism: the living are the ones who can make a fuss. But it might also reflect the reluctance of a liberal society to interfere with the freedom of the living in favour of the interests had by those now dead.

In short, history seems to demonstrate a decreasing willingness of people in liberal societies to accept duties to the dead, and the duties that remain don't seem to amount to much. So if the glue that holds members of an intergenerational society together in relationships of obligation and entitlement is supposed to be practices that give the living an entitlement to make demands of their successors and an obligation to fulfil demands of their predecessors, then it seems that this bonding agent is rather patchy and wearing increasingly thin.

The danger that a society will dispense altogether with duties to the dead is not very real. As we have seen, a world without the possibility of posthumously valid promises is undesirable—not merely because of social inconvenience but because of the importance to individuals of their lifetime-transcending interests. Moreover, it could be argued that people in contemporary liberal societies care less than they should about duties to the dead, or fail to recognise duties that they ought to acknowledge. The failure of philosophers to attend to lifetime-transcending interests and their role in the lives of individuals—the emphasis on lifetime interests that is so prevalent in liberal philosophy—may reflect, as Arendt believes, the ethos of a consumer capitalist society where short-term interests and immediate wants tend to take precedence over long-term concerns, including lifetime-transcending interests. A society that encourages people to concentrate on satisfying lifetime desires is likely to exaggerate the importance of having the freedom to satisfy these desires and to be impatient with suggestions that people can be burdened by duties in respect to the past. The people of such of a society may fail to properly appreciate the nature and importance of their lifetime-transcending interests or they may be prevented from making legitimate lifetime-transcending demands by a misplaced fear of illegitimately interfering with the freedom of their successors.

In the following sections I will argue for the existence of two categories of duties to the dead that are not universally acknowledged in contemporary liberal societies but which can be justified by reference to lifetime-transcending interests. In both cases, the existence of these duties can be made plausible by considerations similar to those that are used to defend duties that are already accepted in a liberal society. The first category of duty has to do with respect for the projects of the dead; the second with inheritance.

PROJECTS, ACHIEVEMENTS AND REPUTATIONS

The duty to the dead that Feinberg and Nagel are especially concerned to defend is the duty to protect posthumous reputations from malicious lies and slander. They regard it as obvious that most people want this protection, and that their reputation is of concern to them even when they are not in the position to experience the consequences of slander. If we inquire into why people are likely to have this lifetime-transcending interest, there seem to be two obvious answers. First, that they are concerned about the harm that lies and slander could cause to the projects they pursue, the ideals they believe in and the people they care about; and second, that they want their efforts, accomplishments and objectives to be properly appreciated after their death by those whose opinion they respect and by the groups and institutions to which they have tried to make a contribution. A concern about posthumous reputation can thus be understood as a lifetime-transcending interest that exists because people have lifetime-transcending interests of other kinds, and it gives rise to duties because of the importance of these interests to people.

The centrality of some of these interests to a person's identity and the meaning of her life makes the prospect of lies or slander especially appalling. Slander can harm a person's family and community, or cause her contributions, projects or ideals to become objects of ridicule or false insinuations. It can frustrate her desire to have her projects and endeavours appreciated and fairly judged. If people have reason to think that their posthumous reputations would be vulnerable to those who have no compunction against telling malicious lies for their own gratification or profit, they could not with confidence pursue lifetime-transcending projects and causes, or believe that what they did would make a contribution or have a chance of being appreciated. They could not be sure that their attempts to provide benefits for their children and community would not be undermined by the suffering that slander would cause. Lacking confidence in the future of their endeavours, they would be less inclined to pursue lifetime-transcending objectives, and an important source of meaning would be less available to them. So failing to protect posthumous reputations would be bad for individuals. It would also be bad for a society. People are not so likely to labour for the good of their successors if they think that these successors will denigrate their contributions and intentions or harm those whom they care about.

These considerations give individuals a good reason to demand that their survivors protect their posthumous reputation and to insist that this protection is their entitlement. It also gives them a reason for demanding that their successors restore their reputation if it has been wrongly maligned and if they are unable to rehabilitate themselves by their own efforts.[4] Thus we have grounds for endorsing a moral practice that requires survivors to protect the reputations of the dead from malicious lies and slander and for restoring the reputations of the dead who have been wrongly maligned. That a moral principle requiring such a practice cannot reasonably be rejected follows from basic moral considerations. Those who respect others must also respect their important interests, particularly those that are central to their ability to live good lives. The question that remains is whether reasons similar to those that require us to protect posthumous reputations give us duties in respect to the lifetime-transcending interests of individuals that are not so often appreciated.

The demand that posthumous reputations be protected is predicated, in part, on the importance to people of their lifetime-transcending interests in their projects and endeavours. Let us agree that individuals cannot reasonably demand that their successors continue their projects or approve of their endeavours. In a liberal society people are free to make up their own minds about what projects are worth pursuing and what endeavours deserve approval. But it does not follow that we have no duties in respect to the projects and endeavours of the dead.

As well as running her business, Mrs White was a strong supporter of her local community. She put a lot of time, effort and some of the proceeds from her business into a program for young people that was supported by both community leaders and many of the community's members. She provided facilities for the use of the young and established a home that cared for abandoned and abused children. Her aim was to provide a lasting contribution to the well-being of future generations. But shortly after her death, the community voted in new leaders who decided to abandon the program for young people. The services that Mrs White built up were discontinued, the facilities sold off, and now no one remembers Mrs White or what she contributed.

Community leaders, we have agreed, did not have a duty to carry on the project of Mrs White. But it is hard not to get the impression that they did something wrong in respect to her interests (as well as the interests of the young people). Mrs White may not have made any demands of her successors, but given her dedication to the future of the community and the contribution she made, she surely was entitled to have her contribution remembered and properly appreciated by her successors. Let us consider what this means.

To remember the contribution of someone is to put it on record and perhaps to commemorate it and to teach young people about it. How long and in what way a community or family should remember a contribution depends on its nature and on their means of commemoration. Mrs White could reasonably demand that her more immediate successors remember her contribution, but probably not that it should be remembered in 100 years' time. On the other hand, many people think that those who died to defend their country should be remembered as long as the country exists. How a group remembers a contribution depends on its nature and customs: it might sponsor an official history or keep a museum or simply depend on members passing on information to later generations. But in any case, the duty to remember implies that intergenerational communities have a duty to maintain and use means of commemoration.

What it means to appreciate a person's contribution can have weaker or stronger interpretations. A very weak interpretation is simply that it should be remembered. A somewhat stronger interpretation is that the person's reasons for making the contribution, as far as they seem relevant, should be considered when members of a community are making a decision about how they should treat her project. The strongest interpretation is that we should make an effort to understand the point of view of the person who made the contribution, to understand why she thought it important to make the contribution and how she wanted it understood. According to this interpretation we are required to regard her views as if she were a participant in our discussion about how the project to which she contributed should be treated or assessed. De-Shalit believes that members of a community are participants in an intergenerational communication. The duty of appreciating the contributions of past members requires that this communication take place. Successors cannot simply ignore what their predecessors thought and did.

My claim is that the third interpretation best answers to the importance of a person's lifetime-transcending interests concerning her contributions to future generations of her community or family. The duty that it gives members does not require that they maintain projects that they now regard as pernicious or inappropriate. It does not prevent them from changing their priorities. The views of past people should not count as if they had votes and could, through their numbers, decide the matter in their favour. Present people are the ones who are entitled to make a decision according to what they regard as the strength of the better reasons. But fulfilling the duty to appreciate the point of view of past contributors to the community makes it less likely that projects will be abandoned without serious consideration of why they were initiated or maintained. Such appreciation is all that we can reasonably demand of our successors, but we can at least insist that they give us that.

There are, however, cases where it seems that people can demand more of their successors. Suppose that our community forebears put time, effort and money into establishing a system of public parks as a gift to posterity. But we no longer care about parks and the kind of recreation that they afford, and we propose to destroy the parks and replace them with shopping malls, restaurants and gymnasiums. What seems wrong in this case is not merely that we are failing to appreciate why our forebears thought it important to establish the parks, but the fact that they established them for posterity and not merely for us. We are destroying a legacy which was meant to be the inheritance of all future members of our community.

The mere fact that our forebears wanted to preserve something for posterity cannot require us to preserve things that we regard as pernicious or that require large sacrifices to maintain. But if the sacrifices are not great and the thing in question is particularly valuable in providing a connection to past generations or an insight into their values, then it would be wrong to destroy it. We ought to keep some, if not all, of the parks as a monument to the efforts and values of past generations and as a legacy for our successors. Past generations are entitled to demand that we make that much of an effort on behalf of their interests.

Members of families and communities have good reason to endorse practices that entitle them to make demands of their successors in respect to their contributions or legacy and, in turn, give them obligations in respect to the legacy they have received from their predecessors. These practices bind members of these groups together in intergenerational relationships of entitlement and obligation. Their existence has implications for a political society as a whole. One of them is that they require a respect for the rights of bequest and inheritance.

INHERITANCE AND JUSTICE

> Confiscatory inheritance taxes run roughshod over the deceased's interest in the ends his property will serve . . . It is an especially cruel injury because it deprives the dead of one of their last opportunities for securing the goods that they value. The dead can no longer offer loved ones their advice, their encouragement, sympathy in times of hardship, and joy when things go well; all they can do is pass on worldly goods to intended beneficiaries. To be robbed of that opportunity is to have one's ability to exercise agency sharply curtailed. (Lomasky 1987: 270).

Loren Lomaksy's plea on behalf of the dead appeals to the injuries that they receive from taxes that have the effect of confiscating their bequests. But his point can be put without an appeal to injuries done to the dead. Many people care about how their possessions are disposed of after their deaths. Mrs White, the businesswoman of Pitcher's example, may have wanted her business to go to her son or daughter. She may have built it up with the idea that it would be an inheritance for her descendants. A person's ability to regard her activities as meaningful may depend to a considerable extent on her ability to dispose of her possessions according to her wishes. An artist may want to give his remaining paintings to a friend who helped him in an earlier part of his career. A small farmer who inherited his farm from his father may think it important to carry on a tradition and keep it in the family. A parent may want to give her child her valued collection of jewellery that she taught him how to appreciate. An art collector may want her collection, which she laboured all her life to build up, to go intact to a museum rather than being split up by her next of kin.

These are the kinds of cases that Lomasky probably has in mind. But it is important to note that inheritance can be communal and that it can involve other things besides material goods. An individual can endeavour to leave something of value to her community or the members of a group might collectively provide a legacy for their successors—as in some of the examples in the previous section. The legacy can be cultural rather than material, as when members of a religious or ethnic group pass on their cultural heritage to their children. I have argued that those who receive an inheritance, cultural or material, have an obligation of memory and appreciation—though not an obligation to endorse it. But the intergenerational practice that requires memory and appreciation is predicated on the entitlement of individuals and collectives to provide an inheritance—and this entitlement, as Lomasky indicates, has sometimes been questioned.

Bequest and inheritance have been questioned for a number of reasons, but above all for the unfair advantages that it gives to heirs.[5] Bruce Ackerman, for example, thinks that inheritance offends against the neutrality which a liberal society is supposed to exercise in respect to the interests of all of its members, in future as well as present generations, by giving unjust advantages to those who are favoured by their predecessors. It is permissible, in his opinion, only if those who are not so fortunate agree to allow it. Wealth and other goods must be transferred to succeeding generations in one way or another but Ackerman thinks that the only transfers that are unambiguously just are transactions that occur in the pursuit by individuals of their goals—for example, through commercial exchanges (1980: 201–12).

Let us agree with Ackerman and the other political philosophers who insist that people do not have an *unchallengeable right* to distribute their property in whatever way they please. There remain two ways of questioning his complaints about inheritance.[6] The first is to argue that it is wrong for a society to prevent people from giving gifts as expressions of generosity, affection or concern to those whom they love or care about. It would be a mean, interfering society that did not allow expressions of love and affection between parents and children, friends and relations. Indeed, Ackerman does not want to prohibit gift-giving between people who are pursuing the good of friendship, and it would be difficult for him to prohibit similar gift-giving between the generations.

The second way of objecting to Ackerman's position is to stress the importance of lifetime-transcending interests to individuals. A person may care about the future well-being of her family or community, or, as in Mrs White's case, about her child being able to carry on her business. The point of intergenerational bequests and other gifts is, in many cases, to make it more likely that others will be in the position to carry on or realize something that the giver regards as good. A society that did not allow these exchanges would interfere with the ability of individuals to pursue lifetime-transcending interests that are of central importance to their lives and their idea of the good. In some cases it would prevent them from acting according to their ideas of duty or virtue. This second criticism locates the wrongness of Ackerman's account not in a failure to allow for special relationships but, more broadly, in a mistaken conception of the individual selves that make up a liberal society.

Neither of these defences of bequest and inheritance requires that individuals should be allowed to give whatever they please to their heirs. A defence of a practice of bequest and inheritance that appeals to lifetime-transcending interests is different from the libertarian defence of bequest as a corollary of a fundamental right to property. It does not reject the concerns of those who fear that inheritance can subvert egalitarian values, liberal neutrality or equality of opportunity. Indeed, a concern for the ability of individuals to pursue their interests, including lifetime-transcending interests, could be used to defend a more egalitarian distribution of resources. If some individuals can pursue lifetime-transcending interests and provide a legacy for their successors and others cannot, then the former have access to an important source of meaning that is unavailable to the latter. What this suggests is that some accommodation must be made between rights of bequest and inheritance and the pursuit of equality. This accommodation should take the form of moral principles that cannot reasonably be rejected by those who are heirs and those who are not (as Ackerman suggests). What exactly they would be is beyond the scope of this study, but some parameters can be put in place.

D.W. Haslett proposes that intergenerational gift-giving should be limited to goods of little value. Goods of greater value, like businesses, should be sold after the death of the owner, allowing children the first opportunity to purchase them at market prices (1986: 138). This proposal seems to give too little weight to the lifetime-transcending interests that motivate the support of a practice of bequest and inheritance. Many of the projects that people pursue get part of their meaning from the possibility that designated others will have the opportunity to continue them. It may be extremely important to Mrs White to be able to hand over to her children a business she has nurtured for them as much as for herself. The farmer may think it extremely important to carry on a family tradition and pass on his farm to his son. A collector may particularly want to bequeath his paintings to his children, who he has taught to appreciate them. The owner of a literary magazine may want to hand it on to someone whom she believes will maintain its standards and values. The practice of inheritance is, after all, not merely about passing on wealth from one generation to another. It is also about passing on goods that have meaning to the donor to those whom she believes can appreciate and maintain their value. The practice establishes a relationship between the generations that enables people to pass on their projects, causes, values and things that they have invested with meaning. To virtually abolish this practice would be seriously detrimental to the lives of many individuals, as well as to their ability to maintain a relationship between the generations.

However, Haslett is right to stress the injustice and inefficiency that occurs when a practice of inheritance allows wealth and property to be concentrated in a few hands. So if an extremely wealthy person wants to pass on all of his wealth to his children, it would not be wrong to tax their gains heavily. If all the agricultural land comes to be owned by family dynasties and there is no opportunity for others to become farmers, then there is reason to break up the monopoly. If the children of the art collector sell their inheritance, then it seems reasonable that they should attract a tax comparable to what they would pay on extra income. An appeal to lifetime-transcending interests should not give individuals an entitlement to pass on whatever they want to their heirs, however strongly they desire to do so.

COMMUNAL INHERITANCE

An inheritance can be communal and it can take the form of a cultural heritage. Members of a church, a political party or an ethnic group aim to pass on their valued heritage to younger generations. Since the identity of these members and the meaning that they find in their lives is likely to be invested in the lifetime-transcending nature of their group's ideals and traditions, they are likely to regard their ability to pass on this heritage as being of supreme importance.

It is reasonable to presume that members of groups have an entitlement to provide their heritage to those whom they deem to be their successors. This means that if governments or other agencies act to prevent people from maintaining and passing on their heritage, we can presume that they are committing an injustice. A wrong of this kind was once committed by Australian and Canadian governments against indigenous people by removing their children, sometimes forcibly, from families and communities in order to induct them into mainstream society and prevent them from inheriting the language and customs of their culture (HREOC 1997). Those who now criticise this practice are often concerned about the abuses committed against the children in schools and foster homes. But the wrong done transcends abusive practices and would have existed even if the children had been treated well. The policy violated an intergenerational entitlement and, as such, was not only a wrong committed against the parents and elders of the communities who wanted to pass on their culture to the young, but also an injustice to the children who had an entitlement to receive this inheritance.[7] In a liberal society individuals have a right to reject their religious or cultural inheritance, but they also have a right to obtain it.

However, recognising an entitlement of groups to pass on their heritage, like the recognition of a right of bequest, creates problems for a liberal society. Members of some groups treat their members, especially women, in ways that liberals are bound to find unacceptable, or they aim to indoctrinate children in a way that imprisons them in their group. Some traditions or cultures are so pernicious that it seems reasonable to judge that they should not be continued. We have to allow that it is not always wrong to rescue children from a communal culture or to ban a religious or political organization. As in the case of bequest and inheritance it is necessary to find an accommodation between a respect for the intergenerational entitlements of members and liberal concerns about individual freedom and equality. But it is important to note that in both cases, the reason for seeking an accommodation is found in liberalism itself; in a respect for the interests of individuals, which includes their lifetime-transcending interests as well as their interest in freely choosing and pursuing a life course.

LIFETIME-TRANSCENDING INTERESTS AND POLITICAL SOCIETY

Let us imagine, in the manner of Rawls, that members of a political society are in the original position behind the veil of ignorance. They know that they are members of the same generation but they know nothing about its situation or about its historical relationship to other generations. However, they do know that they are likely to have lifetime-transcending interests that are important to their lives and to their identities as individuals; they know that they make, or are entitled to make, lifetime-transcending demands of their successors; they know that they have or could have responsibilities in respect to predecessors. Given this knowledge they are likely to choose a principle (or principles) of intergenerational justice that underwrites their ability to pursue objectives associated with lifetime-transcending interests, to form and maintain families, communities and other associations in which these objectives can be fulfilled and to make and satisfy legitimate lifetime-transcending demands. They will be predisposed to accept a conception of justice that requires each generation to do its fair share to maintain institutions and practices that satisfy these requirements. They will not be tempted to favour themselves in a way that would make their generation the last generation in their political society. The conception of justice that satisfies these conditions determines what it means for a society to be an intergenerational polity. This conception, as I will argue in Chapter 6, gives them duties to, and in respect to, their political predecessors as well as to members of succeeding generations.

6   Taking Responsibility for the Past

A just society ought to protect the intergenerational concerns of its members. It must offer them opportunities to develop and pursue lifetime-transcending interests, to continue projects of predecessors and to pass on their ideas, projects, heritage and other goods to their successors. It must protect their ability to make, fulfil and have fulfilled legitimate lifetime-transcending demands. How it should do this is a question that a theory of justice must answer. The answer that many philosophers favour is that citizens can ensure that their intergenerational interests are protected simply by perpetuating through the generations institutions that maintain just relations between contemporaries. The assumption is that institutions that give individuals the freedom and opportunity to formulate and pursue their ideas of the good will enable them to develop and pursue lifetime-transcending interests as a matter of course.

Chapter 5 presented some reasons for doubting this view. Lifetime-transcending interests give us a reason for maintaining a right of bequest and inheritance for individuals and groups (within reasonable parameters). They also give us a reason to recognise the right of members to maintain their intergenerational communities (given protections for the rights of individuals). There may, of course, be non-diachronic reasons for endorsing bequest and inheritance or group rights, but intergenerational concerns, at least, put limits on what kind of theory of justice is acceptable. A theory of distributive justice that does not allow for bequest and inheritance will not adequately serve the lifetime-transcending interests of citizens. A theory that does not properly acknowledge the lifetime-transcending interests and duties of members of families and communities is clearly inadequate. The requirements of a theory of justice must be formulated with these interests in mind and it must assume that future members will have the same interests.

A more serious challenge to synchronic theories of justice is posed by the claim that citizens of a polity have responsibilities in respect to the commitments and deeds of their political predecessors. A polity is often conceived of as an agent which persists through the generations and which can be held responsible for its past deeds. It is supposed to keep its agreements and promises, including those that were made by past officials—unless there are good moral reasons for not doing so. That a polity has this obligation is assumed by international conventions and accepted by most citizens. A polity as an intergenerational agent is also supposed to take responsibility for injustices of the past: for breaking agreements, committing aggression or for violating the rights of citizens or foreigners. It can be required to pay reparations for the harmful deeds of past generations and/or to acknowledge and apologise for its injustices. Most citizens and leaders accept this responsibility.

However, from a synchronic point of view, these requirements are problematic. A 'promise of state' is supposed to give existing citizens an entitlement to bind their successors. It is supposed to give young and unborn generations an obligation to fulfil its terms and existing generations an obligation to fulfil the commitments made by their predecessors. Taking responsibility for the injustices of the past means that citizens, through their representatives, are required to apologise and/or make reparation for the deeds of their forebears. Jefferson and Paine, as we have seen, question whether citizens of a democracy should be required to accept obligations that are imposed on them by their predecessors. Although favourable to the view that white American citizens owe reparation to descendants of slaves, Boxill expresses a common doubt about conceptions of historical responsibility that rest on the collective responsibility of citizens. At one time, he says, the US government had a duty to pay reparation to slaves:

> None of this supports the claim that the present US Government owes present day African Americans the reparation an earlier US Government owed their ancestors but never paid. Since present day US citizens were not complicit in the crime of slavery that claim can only be based on the morally repugnant idea that individuals can be burdened with the duties that other people incurred (2003: 71).

The belief that members of a group should be held responsible only for their actions, failures to act or the actions of those whom they choose to represent them, is a corollary of the synchronic view of justice. It follows from a consideration of how contemporaries ought to act toward each other and when they should take responsibility for harms to others that they are implicated in causing. A view of justice that gives individuals responsibility for agreements made in the past and for apologising and making reparation for the deeds of past generations must challenge in a fundamental way synchronic ideas of justice and responsibility. In this chapter I will consider how this challenge can best be made.[1] In Chapter 7, I will consider whether citizens have additional duties in respect to the projects and deeds of their political predecessors.

IDENTITY AND INHERITED DEBT

If people identify with their polity or with its past members, then they may be predisposed to accept responsibility for the deeds of past officials and citizens. Indeed, those who take pride in the good deeds of their predecessors seem at least psychologically inconsistent if they fail to feel shame for their unjust deeds. Raimond Gaita (1999: 87) thinks that having a national identity involves being ashamed of the injustices done by our nation and being prepared to make recompense to the victims or their descendants. Farid Abdel-Nour (2003: 694) says that we acquire historical responsibilities by identifying with our forebears. If they did good things, then we will be predisposed to commemorate their deeds and to carry on their work. If those we identify with committed injustices, we will want to put things right by making recompense. MacIntyre, as we have seen, thinks that a communal identity brings with it, as a matter of course, obligations in respect to the past.

However, we have also seen that identity with a polity or nation is an uncertain basis for intergenerational obligations. It excludes from responsibility those who don't have this identity—unless some moral reason can be found for insisting that they ought to have it. And it is by no means obvious that identification with a community or past people must result in the acceptance of historical, or other, intergenerational obligations. We might think it sufficient simply to feel shame for our polity's past injustices. We might refuse to identify with those people who did wrongs, or our identity may lead us to deny that they did wrong according to their understanding. We might believe that the polity that committed the wrongs is no longer the same polity that commands our allegiance. Or we may simply lack MacIntyre's tribal certainties concerning responsibility. Most people in contemporary Western societies do not accept responsibility for the moral debts of their parents. Why should they think that they have a responsibility for historical injustices of their polity?

A more promising defence of historical obligation appeals to entitlements that I defended in Chapter 5. Individuals and communities have a right to provide an inheritance for their heirs and the heirs are entitled to receive it. A just society protects these entitlements. If they are violated, then heirs may have a right to restitution from those who committed the injustice or their heirs. They may also have a claim against the polity itself for failing to protect their entitlements. Since the entitlement is intergenerational, so is the obligation. If individuals or communities can legitimately demand that their political successors protect the entitlements of their heirs, then present citizens have no moral grounds for denying responsibility. The fact that they did not commit the injustice is not relevant, nor is the chain of events that brought the heirs of the victims into existence. Let us consider some ways of elaborating this approach to historical obligations.

INHERITANCE AND RECTIFICATION

Robert Nozick makes historical rectification into a key element of his conception of justice (1974: 151–3). In his theory, justice requires respect for the historical fact that goods have come to be owned by particular people. So if sometime in the course of history a rightful possessor is wrongly dispossessed, then justice now requires that the possession, or something equivalent in value, be returned to the victim or his heirs. Nozick's account of rectification has an obvious application to the claims of indigenous people for land that was unjustly taken from their forebears. But some of those who argue for reparation for slavery also make a case based on property rights. They claim that by being enslaved, the ancestors of present African Americans were illegitimately denied the fruits of their labour, and thus their descendants have a right to the equivalent of the wages that their ancestors ought to have earned, with appropriate interest payments calculated (Mumford 1996: 428).

Boxill's argument for reparation for slavery does not focus merely on loss of property. Slave owners and everyone who consented to slavery (Boxill assumes that they included most Americans living at that time) harmed those who were slaves and owed them reparation because of this harm, he says. This unpaid debt has been inherited by the white population of the United States (including immigrants who took advantage of assets to which slaves had rightful titles). 'Since present day African Americans are the slaves' heirs, and have inherited their rights to reparation, it follows that they have inherited titles to a part of the assets held by the entire white population' (2003: 77).[2]

Let us ignore the practical problems concerning who owes what to whom and focus on a basic objection to these appeals to right of inheritance. Both Nozick and Boxill depend on an account of ownership rights that gives heirs a claim that persists through the generations. The hardship of those who owe rectification for a historical loss may be a reason for denying the claim—but the wealth of those to whom it is owed is not a reason and nor are other, less dire, changes in the circumstances of those who owe the debt. To many advocates of social justice this consequence of a historical account of ownership rights is insupportable. Jeremy Waldron, for example, argues that rights to restitution tend to be superseded by time and change (1992: 18–9). A person centres her life and plans on her ability to make use of the things she owns and this, Waldron says, is generally a good reason for acknowledging and protecting her rights of ownership and for rectifying violations. But if rectification is not made and the years pass, then, by necessity, she and her heirs will have to find another way of living their lives. Meanwhile, ownership of the property passes into the hands of others and becomes central to their lives. The claim of the original possessor fades away. Indeed, Waldron suggests that historical claims succumb fairly rapidly to changes of interest and conditions.

Waldron's belief that historical claims are superseded by the interests and needs of present people depends on the assumption that the interests that count are lifetime interests. A focus on lifetime-transcending interests and the role they play in enabling people to live meaningful lives, give us a basis for resisting the supersession thesis—at least in some cases. It seems reasonable to insist that a family retains its right to an heirloom long after it was stolen and that members of a tribe can legitimately demand the return of cultural artefacts that were unjustly taken from their ancestors. Even Waldron admits that the attachment of indigenous communities to land of cultural and religious significance gives them a resilient claim (1992: 19). These claims depend on the interest of members of families and groups in maintaining an intergenerational heritage and the reasonable demands that they can make for the return of property central to these interests. But an appeal to lifetime-transcending interests is not likely to support all historical claims. In particular, we might be sceptical about the survival into present generations of claims for unpaid wages or reparation that was once owed to slaves. Why not suppose that duties of justice to the descendants of slaves consist only of reparation for harms done to *them* and/or compensation for the disadvantages that they now suffer?

CLAIMS OF THE DEAD

If we assume that the dead can be harmed or benefited by our actions, then, according to Michael Ridge, we can justify reparations for slavery as a duty owed to dead slaves. Of course, we cannot directly compensate them, but we can benefit them by promoting objectives that we have reason to believe that they cared about. 'Most slaves probably cared very much about the welfare of their descendants, so the United States could provide reparations to the slaves by promoting the welfare of their descendants' (2003: 44).

The assumption that the dead can be benefited or harmed is problematic but sceptics can fall back on the reasoning of Chapter 5. People now alive can make legitimate lifetime-transcending demands that their successors will have the obligation to fulfil. The living owe to the dead whatever the dead could have legitimately demanded of their successors when they were alive. A slave as an individual could have reasonably demanded that the wrongs done to her should be remembered by her survivors and appropriately acknowledged by those members of her society who committed injustices against her or who were complicit in these injustices; she could have demanded that they not commit similar injustices to her children and grandchildren. It is not so obvious that she could have demanded that benefits be given to her distant descendants; that her suffering should be remembered not merely by her more immediate successors but also by people of more distant generations, or that people distant in time who had nothing to do with the injustice should take responsibility for apologising or making reparation for the injustice of slavery. The question of why existing citizens should take responsibility for the wrongs of their political predecessors remains unanswered.[3]

David Miller explains the existence of this collective responsibility by insisting that members of a nation who regard themselves as the rightful heirs of benefits created by past generations—and who believe that they are entitled to use and control these benefits—also inherit a responsibility for putting right injustices that stem from acts of dispossession and exploitation committed by past generations (2007: 154ff). But the idea that a national inheritance includes moral debts incurred by the deeds of past generations raises some of the same questions as appeals to reciprocity and gratitude. Why should citizens think that duties attach to the benefits that they happen to have received from past generations? In particular, why should they think that these benefits give them a duty to remedy historical injustices? They might believe instead that their inheritance should be used to fulfil requirements of distributive justice—to relieve the poverty of the least well off. Why should they think that they ought to apologise for wrongs that they did not do? Miller's position depends on citizens valuing their nation as an intergenerational society and thus being predisposed to believe that membership gives them duties in respect to its past as well as duties to present and future members. If members do indeed regard their nation as intrinsically valuable and identify with the endeavour of maintaining it through the generations, or with past people who have contributed to this project, then they *may* be prepared to accept intergenerational responsibilities. But once again we are forced to rely on an uncertain basis for obligation. Let us take a different approach to the issue of collective responsibility for the historical past by returning to the question of why polities should be required to act as responsible intergenerational agents.

POLITIES AS INTERGENERATIONAL AGENTS

My thesis is that the obligations of the polity as a responsible intergenerational agent, and thus the responsibilities of citizens for the deeds of their political predecessors, is predicated on their reasons for valuing a political association capable of exercising this agency. They do not have to identify with it or believe that it is intrinsically valuable, but they do have to believe that it protects, or can be made to protect, their ability to pursue lifetime-transcending interests and to make and fulfil legitimate lifetime-transcending demands, and that it respects the ability of other individuals, inside and outside of the polity, to do the same. I have argued that the polity ought to respect and protect the ability of individuals to make and fulfil—and have fulfilled—lifetime-transcending contracts; that it ought to respect and protect rights of bequest and inheritance, and that it should respect and protect communities within which individuals develop their lifetime-transcending, as well as lifetime, interests and, in which, as members, they acquire intergenerational entitlements and obligations. Let us then consider how these requirements determine the form a polity ought to take and its responsibilities as an agent.

If a polity is to protect the intergenerational interests of its citizens, then it must promote and maintain intergenerational institutions and/or ensure that groups and individuals can do so. It must exercise an intergenerational agency sufficient to ensure that this protection can be perpetuated. In a world of polities the need to exercise this kind of agency is particularly obvious. International conventions which require states to keep their long-term agreements answer to the desire of citizens to promote their lifetime-transcending, as well as immediate, interests by securing a framework within which they can perpetuate their intergenerational communities, pass on an inheritance to their survivors and pursue their projects with a reasonable expectation that their successors will have an opportunity to continue them. To protect these interests and to ensure that their responsibilities to their successors can be fulfilled and that their successors can fulfil their responsibilities to them, citizens have reason to endorse a principle that entitles each generation to make long-term agreements with other polities or intergenerational agents when appropriate. (We can assume that the Rawlsian contractors described in Chapter 5 would agree with this proposition.) By accepting the principle, they also accept the obligations that it entails, including obligations in respect to the past.

This pragmatic justification for requirements imposed on the agency of a polity is not the only basis for its responsibilities. In Chapter 5 I argued that intergenerational communities deserve respect as associations in which individuals develop and pursue their lifetime-transcending interests, pass on projects to their successors and make and fulfil legitimate lifetime-transcending demands. Polities ought to treat these communities respectfully, recognising and perhaps even promoting their interests—unless there is good reason not to do so. Their members can reasonably demand that this respect be offered and maintained. A polity has similar reasons for respecting other polities—at least those that protect the interests, including intergenerational interests, of its citizens. The duty of respect does not mean that we have to respect a polity that is aggressive to outsiders or unjust to its citizens, or to respect oppressive institutions or traditions. But the very fact that a polity does protect the intergenerational interests of its members is a reason for respect, though this mark in its favour may be outweighed by other moral considerations.

Polities ought to keep their commitments, and citizens have reasons, moral and pragmatic, for accepting obligations that enable their political society to be a responsible intergenerational agent. The duty of commitment-keeping has a corollary. If polities fail to keep their commitments without good reason, then they ought to acknowledge the wrong and make recompense to those whose entitlement was violated. Since the commitment-making obligation is intergenerational, so is the duty of reparation. If our predecessors violated a commitment and failed to make amends, then the obligation falls on us. The fact that we had no part in committing the offence is irrelevant.

The making and keeping of intergenerational commitments is based on mutual respect and on concerns that come into existence as the result of interactions between polities or with other intergenerational communities. A polity that interacts with other intergenerational polities or communities ought to treat them with respect. It ought to recognise, appreciate and respect the interests of its members or citizens. Citizens ought to cooperate through the generations to maintain these respectful relationships. They ought to make appropriate commitments and agreements when their interests intersect; they ought to repair respectful relationship when these have been damaged and they ought to make reparation for unjust violations or failures of respect. The maintenance of respectful relationships requires intergenerational cooperation, and repairing these relationships or making up for violations are obligations that citizens can acquire as the result of the acts of their predecessors—just as keeping an agreement or making reparation for the failure to do so is an obligation that a generation might inherit from its predecessors.

The requirement of respect for other intergenerational communities means that a polity can owe reparation to a community not merely for breaking an agreement but for a failure to appropriately recognise and respectfully interact with it. When Europeans who settled in Australia refused to make treaties with Aboriginal communities they not only harmed existing people, they also failed to respect the entitlement of Aborigines to protect their intergenerational interests and fulfil their intergenerational responsibilities to their predecessors and successors. These acts of injustice, which were never fully acknowledged by succeeding generations of white Australians, require an appropriate response from present Australian citizens to members of Aboriginal communities.

REPARATION FOR SLAVERY

If a polity commits acts that undermine the intergenerational interests of other polities or communities, then it owes appropriate reparation to these communities, and if reparation has not been made, present citizens may acquire the responsibility. This account of how citizens acquire historical obligations and why they are owed to members of an intergenerational association suggests a different approach to the issue of reparation for slavery. The problem, as we have seen, is that rights of inheritance appealed to by Nozick and Boxill are not likely to persist through time and change. Though individuals can make demands that survive their deaths, the legitimate demands that could have been made by slaves do not seem to explain why present white citizens of the United States should regard themselves as obligated to make apologies for slavery or provide reparation in the form of an apology and/or benefits to descendants of slaves. However, it is not so implausible to suppose that citizens can owe reparation to members of family lines for the harms done to families as intergenerational associations.

The family is an intergenerational group central to the ability of individuals to develop and pursue lifetime-transcending interests. Individuals develop many of these interests as the result of living in families; they pass on projects and property to family members, and their interests are often directed toward the future well-being of their descendants and other family members. A polity ought to respect families as intergenerational groups, and a good reason for supporting families and pursuing policies conducive to their flourishing is the important role they play in the intergenerational affairs of a society and as the focus of the lifetime-transcending interests of many individuals.

Some of the injustices committed by polities and other agents are not merely crimes against individuals; they are also wrongs done to intergenerational family lines. Genocide is an obvious example. Its wrongness consists not merely in the fact that those who practice it murder or oppress large numbers of individuals, but also because their intent is to wipe out a people by wiping out their families or their culture—by trying to bring it about that there are no successors. Slavery as it was practiced in the southern United States was a crime against family lines as well as against individuals. It was designed to perpetuate itself by enslaving families (unlike the slavery involved in the use of convict labour in the early history of the American and Australian colonies). Descendants of slaves, even those fathered by slave owners, were also doomed to be slaves, and the system of persecution and discrimination that succeeded slavery had a similar objective: to keep the descendants of slaves in a position of perpetual subordination. Injuries to family lines, in other words, are intergenerational wrongs, and they may require that reparation be given to present members of families just as wrongs to a tribe or polity may require reparation to present members.

DUTIES OF REPARATION

Citizens are morally bound by the commitments of their political predecessors and they acquire responsibility for reparation for historic injustices. These responsibilities exist in the framework of requirements of intergenerational justice. Obligations in respect to the past are derived from an obligation to respect the lifetime-transcending interests of individuals, members of families and communities and their ability to make and fulfil lifetime-transcending demands. This does not mean that making reparation for historical injustice is really about healing individuals or improving relationships between existing people. To construe it in this way is to ignore that we as citizens have duties to those now dead; that they, as individuals or members of communities, made or could have made demands that we ought to fulfil. It ignores that our obligations to communities and families have to do with protecting entitlements that result from the interests and actions of past generations. However, locating historical obligations in context of a theory that also gives us duties to present and future people is bound to affect the way we understand these obligations and how we ought to fulfil them.

It influences, first of all, our ideas about what we owe in reparation. If maintaining through the generations just and respectful relationships between individuals and communities is the focus of our concern, then reparative justice must be compatible with this objective. Requiring that unjustly taken property be returned to victims or their descendants and that victims be returned to the situation that existed before the injustice are not only impossible demands in many cases, but they also do not give sufficient attention to intergenerational concerns. Waldron is right to insist that the validity of historical claims is affected by changes of circumstances and the needs and interests of present and future people, and that these claims can be superseded by the changes brought by time (though I have argued that some claims persist longer than he supposes). Reparation for historical injustices should aim to repair the harm done to relations of respect between individuals, families or communities in a way such that each can, from its point of view, regard the settlement as just basis for cooperation through the generations.

One consequence of viewing reparative justice in this way is that it makes a satisfactory result depend on parties negotiating in good faith, taking into account each other's point of view, present needs and intergenerational concerns. It gives history its due but it does not require that we return people to a situation that might have no relevance to their present interests as members of families or communities. It does not ignore the interests of the successors of those who did the wrong. Reaching a satisfactory result would require negotiation in good faith and a willingness to appreciate each other's concerns as individuals and as members of communities who have responsibilities to past and future generations.

Let us now consider how this conception of the objective of reparation applies to demands for reparation for slavery. If freed slaves and their descendants had been able to take their place in American society as equal citizens, if they had been given an equal opportunity to obtain the things that their society had to offer, then the wrong done to their family lines would have been repaired and present descendants would have no reason or justification to demand reparation for slavery, and white Americans would have no duties of reparation other than the obligation to remember the wrongs of the past. But this did not happen. African-American families continued to suffer from the effects of slavery and from injustices that were intrinsically related to the social divisions that slavery caused. So it is reasonable to insist that reparation is owed to these families for a history of injustice to family lines that includes slavery. What is owed depends on present needs and the desires that family members have for themselves and their descendants. Reparation may require the provision of special benefits to black families or programs of positive discrimination. But even if it requires citizens to do no more than to ensure that the members of African-American families have their fair share according to the requirements of distributive justice, the historical obligation of reparation gives the fulfilment of this requirement an urgency and priority that it otherwise might not have. A failure to appropriately address historical wrongs compounds the injustice and fails to give African-American families assurance for their future.

An account of historical obligations that locates them in the context of a theory about just and respectful intergenerational relationships also explains why an apology or other official acknowledgments of wrongs play an important role (Thompson 2008). An apology is a mark of respect in the sense that it acknowledges responsibility for a wrong and addresses this acknowledgement to the wronged individual or community. It expresses the intention of avoiding similar wrongs in the future, and thus answers to the requirement of perpetuating relationships of respect. An apology can be a watershed event in the lives of communities by making it possible for them to come to terms with the past so that respectful relationships can exist in the future. An apology may also make individuals feel better, but this healing effect is secondary to the role of apology in the intergenerational relationships of communities.

PERSISTENCE OF RESPONSIBILITY

Some people fear that once we accept responsibility for events in history, there is no limit to what we can be held responsible for, but this is not so. Historical responsibility viewed in the framework of a theory of just intergenerational relationships persists as long, and only as long, as history is relevant to the interests and situation of present and future citizens. Italy does not owe reparations for the injustices of ancient Rome; no one is owed reparation for the dispossessions that followed the Norman invasion of England. These wrongs are not relevant to issues of justice that exist among present members of polities. They have been superseded by changes brought by time.

On the other hand, historical claims and commitments can survive radical political and social changes. This consideration enables us to deal with a problem that is implicit in Boxill's objection to making present US citizens collectively responsible for slavery. If we doubt that the United States before the Civil War is identical to the United States as it exists today, should we also be sceptical about its responsibility for making reparations for slavery? This question can be answered by recognising that the agency and responsibilities of polities do not depend on a criterion of self-identity. They are predicated on the lifetime-transcending interests of citizens and on continuities of interest within the generations of individuals who are part of the polity or are affected by its actions.

This is recognised in international law. No one doubts that New Zealand, a country that did not exist when the British government signed the Treaty of Waitangi with Maori chieftains, inherited responsibility for the Treaty and now has responsibilities in respect to it. Intergenerational responsibilities can persist through political change, including changes that bring about the birth of new polities and which give old polities a different character. This is not surprising once we take into account the fact that individuals continually make lifetime-transcending demands that their successors ought fulfil; they continue through the generations to have an interest in their successors being able to carry on their projects; communities continue to pass on their heritage from one generation to another and want their successors to be able to inherit it. However great the political changes, these continuities mean that responsibilities endure and must be passed on from one political body to its successor. Even revolutions do not supersede all commitments or the obligation to maintain respectful relationships with communities and families whose intergenerational interests persist through change. Questions remain about what, if any, political changes can render invalid agreements between polities or communities or relieve present citizens of responsibilities in respect to the past. We might hesitate to make present citizens take responsibility for the crimes committed by a former dictatorship, and yet there are cases where it seems right to do so. It seems justified, for example, to expect German citizens to make reparation for the crimes of the Nazis, not only because of the political and social continuities between the Nazi polity and the German polities that succeeded it, but also because present Germans must accept the responsibility of establishing and maintaining just relationships between citizens and communities through the generations, and this requires facing up to and making appropriate recompense for the wrongs of the past.

INTERGENERATIONAL JUSTICE AND RESPONSIBILITY FOR THE PAST

The issues raised by reparative justice require a more detailed examination. But the discussion in this chapter explains why citizens can have obligations of reparation for historic injustice and, by locating this responsibility within the framework of a wider conception of intergenerational justice, it also shows how some of the difficulties associated with reparation can be overcome. We have duties in respect to commitments and unjust deeds of our political predecessors. Do we also have an obligation to remember their sacrifices or to maintain the heritage and institutions that we have inherited from them and to pass them on to our successors (as Burke supposes)? Answering this question requires a consideration of what members of a polity should cooperate to maintain through the generations. This is the subject of Chapter 7.

7 Just Inheritance in an Intergenerational Polity

There are two approaches to the question of what members of each generation of a polity ought to provide for their successors. One of them abstracts from the conditions and history of a particular polity and provides a universal, idealised account of intergenerational duties of justice. This approach is taken by Rawls and is embodied in the 'just savings principle'. Each generation, he says, has a duty to accumulate capital until the society reaches a level of civilization and culture that enables just institutions to be established and maintained through the generations (1999: 257). The other approach is particular and historical. It focuses on a polity as an entity with a particular nature and history and gives citizens duties in relation to the deeds of the past and the traditions, values and projects that are the products of its history. This is the approach commonly taken by communitarians, nationalists, patriots and traditional conservatives.

Those who take the universalising approach recognise that establishing and maintaining a just polity is a historical process that requires the labour of citizens of many generations and that the form their institutions take is the consequence of their history. They may allow that polities can acquire obligations from the commitments they make, their relationship with other communities and the injustices of the historical past, as discussed in Chapter 6. Those who take a historical approach generally acknowledge that citizens should be able to take a critical stance toward the traditions and institutions of their polity, and in liberal democratic polities (and indeed in polities that are not so liberal and democratic) universal ideas about justice and right are a basis for criticising and reforming existing institutions and practices. The two approaches distinguish themselves in their attitude toward history, tradition and the deeds of past members. The universalising approach emphasises the duty of citizens to cooperate in establishing and maintaining institutions and resources. Although it might allow that what the polity did in the past can create historical obligations for present members, its principal concern is to maintain goods that are likely to serve the interests of present and future people. It denies that we have any obligation to carry on the traditions and projects of our forebears. It is Jeffersonian in spirit. The historical approach, on the other hand, regards the history of a polity as a primary source of obligation. Lincoln, as we have seen, appealed to the deeds of the dead, including the acts of the founding fathers of the Republic, as a reason for accepting the responsibility of maintaining a democratic polity. Like others who take the historical approach he believed that citizens have an obligation to carry on the political project of their forebears—not merely because it is a project beneficial to future generations, but because their predecessors laboured and made sacrifices to provide them with this inheritance.

Those who take the universalising approach and those who believe that obligations derive from a particular history are also likely to express a difference of opinion about the value of the polity itself as an intergenerational inheritance. The universalising approach gives us a duty to maintain just institutions and other goods that will serve the interests of those who count as our successors. It does not give us an obligation to maintain a particular polity or a particular political culture—except when doing so provides the most sure or convenient way of maintaining just institutions. If just institutions could be maintained through incorporation into a larger polity or if they could be preserved through secession or radical political change, then the universalising approach gives us no reason to prohibit these developments. But those who take the historical approach are predisposed to believe, as did Lincoln, that the polity itself, with its particular institutions and traditions, is an intergenerational project that citizens have an obligation to maintain. To allow it to expire, be dismembered or lose its identity would be a betrayal of the efforts and sacrifices of past generations—even if there was no loss as far as the ability of present and future people to live under just institutions and enjoy benefits and opportunities. Those who take the historical approach are also likely to accept an obligation to maintain as an inheritance for future generations goods particularly associated with their polity and its past: for example, a particular political culture, an environmental or cultural heritage, monuments to the deeds of forebears or traditions and goods that citizens of the past especially valued and wanted to perpetuate. Those who take a universalising approach see no reason to accept these ideas about duty.

In this chapter I aim to bring together the universalising and historical approaches in determining what citizens of a polity ought to provide as an inheritance for their successors. I will argue that a consideration of the lifetime-transcending interests of citizens and the legitimate demands that members of each generation can make of their political successors influence a view about just inheritance in two ways. First of all, these considerations have a bearing on the general question of what citizens should provide for their successors. Some views about what should be transferred between generations answer better than others to the lifetime-transcending interests of citizens of a polity. Secondly, some of the ideas about obligation that come from the historical approach find a justification in a consideration of what citizens of a particular polity can reasonably demand of their successors.

JUST INSTITUTIONS

A just polity underwrites the ability of its members to freely define and pursue, individually and collectively, their lifetime and lifetime-transcending interests, to fulfil their obligations to each other, including their predecessors and successors, and to obtain their entitlements. It acts as a responsible agent in respect to other communities and polities, inside and outside of its borders. Following in the footsteps of Rawls, let us begin with the proposition that a polity is intergenerationally just if and only if each generation does its fair share to establish and maintain the conditions, resources, goods, institutions and practices that will enable its successors to enjoy just relationships and act justly toward others. These include institutions and practices that give citizens responsibilities in respect to past generations. To make this proposition into a theory of intergenerational justice we have to specify what counts as a fair share and be more specific about what resources, goods, institutions and practices should be established and maintained through the generations. But let us first consider whether it is an adequate starting point for theorising about intergenerational justice.

Intergenerational justice, according to the proposition, has to do with what a generation, consisting of those who are now in the position to make or influence political policies, should collectively provide for its young and not-yet-born successors as their political inheritance and what it should regard as its responsibilities to, and in respect to, past generations. In Rawls's framework, a synchronic theory of justice tells us how goods, including freedom, should be distributed among individuals. A theory of intergenerational justice tells us how the generations should share in the labour of establishing and maintaining the institutions that distribute goods, leaving it up to each generation to distribute them according to its understanding of what justice requires. The last two chapters suggest that this division of labour needs to be questioned. How a political society distributes goods to individuals not only affects their life chances; it also has an impact on their families and communities and thus on succeeding generations. A society that systematically discriminates against individuals of a certain kind is also committing an injustice against their family lines. A society that fails to protect the entitlements of individuals to leave legitimate bequests is not only committing an offence to them, but also a wrong against their heirs. Some institutions of a society—for example, those that protect the inheritance rights of individuals and those that ensure that a polity can act as a responsible agent through the generations—are essentially intergenerational. The idea of intergenerational justice that we have inherited from Rawls deals only with one aspect of intergenerational justice. But this aspect is of great importance and is the centre of attention to those concerned about sustainability and the political and social inheritance that we are providing for our successors. So let us consider how this conception should be elucidated. What resources, goods, institutions and practices should we maintain for our political successors?

Rawls, as we have seen, says that each generation should accumulate capital so that just institutions—institutions that protect individual freedom and fairly distribute primary goods—can be established and maintained.[1] Just institutions, he believes, can only be established and maintained in a society where there are sufficient resources to enable all citizens to live a decent life. But he also insists that capital accumulation has a limit:

> Eventually once just institutions are firmly established and all the basic liberties effectively established the net accumulation required falls to zero. At this point a society meets its duty of justice by maintaining just institutions and preserving their material base (1999a: 255).

We are not obliged to make our successors wealthier or even to ensure that they will be as wealthy as we are. We do them justice if we ensure that they have sufficient capital to maintain just institutions. Whether this view is acceptable—and more generally, what each generation should regard as its fair share of the labour of maintaining just institutions—is a matter that I will consider later (in Chapter 9). But let us now focus on two kinds of criticisms of Rawls's idea of what each generation should provide as an inheritance for its successors: those claiming that Rawls includes too many items on his list of what we have a duty to maintain and those who think that he includes too few.

JUSTICE AS AN INTERGENERATIONAL PROJECT

Those who take to heart Ball's contention that future generations are likely to have ideas of justice that are different from ours might wonder why we should be so concerned to pass on to our successors *our* institutions. Why not concentrate on transferring capital—which they will need whatever ideas about justice they come to hold? Or why not go along with Jefferson and accept only a duty of justice to transfer the procedures that will enable each generation to make its own social contract and establish its own institutions of justice?

In commenting on Jefferson's proposal of a periodic social contract, James Madison made the point that having institutions that are not up for periodical review means that the citizens of a polity can concentrate on other political tasks without the distraction of continually being forced to debate the terms of their association (cited Holmes 1988: 216). Having this distraction would be morally undesirable, as well as inconvenient, if it means that people do not concentrate on ensuring that their institutions are properly run. Good institutions are not likely to come into existence with the stroke of a pen on a constitutional document. They need to be shaped and reformed; their unintended consequences have to be appreciated and dealt with. If each generation thinks of itself as constructing institutions only for its own use, they would probably be makeshift and badly resourced. Citizens would generally regard it as more rational to put up with their imperfections rather than to sacrifice a lot of time and energy to reform something that is only temporary. Creating just and workable institutions demands intergenerational cooperation.

Reflection on what motivates citizens to engage in this effort reveals a more fundamental difficulty with a minimal conception of just inheritance. Justice is a lifetime-transcending ideal. The very nature of justice as a moral concept (as I argued in Chapter 2) requires people to believe that their reasonable, well-debated beliefs about justice ought to be accepted by everyone, including their successors. When they construct institutions of justice they are bound to think that they are building something for their successors as well as themselves. On the other hand, they do not suppose that their ideas are beyond rational criticism. They recognise that some aspects of this inheritance may turn out to be justifiably criticised and rightly rejected. A commitment to justice means a commitment to an endless process of debating and criticising ideas about justice and reforming or rebuilding the institutions that are supposed to embody them. Any attempt to establish justice in a polity involves participation in attempts to reach an overlapping consensus with those who have different conceptions. So citizens who are committed to establishing a just polity are predisposed to conceive of themselves as participating in an intergenerational project of making, unmaking and reforming institutions of justice. They inherit this project from their predecessors and given that this project has succeeded in establishing institutions that are reasonably just, they have an obligation to pass them on to their successors. Future generations can make their own judgments about their value, but the possibility that they might have completely different ideas of justice does not undermine the existence of the obligation.

PREREQUISITES OF JUSTICE

We have an obligation to transfer the fruits of our labours to create a just polity to our successors along with the capital needed to ensure that the project can be maintained. But is this all that we are obliged to do? Environmentalists, in particular, are likely to criticise Rawls's account of intergenerational justice for leaving sustainability and environmental values out of consideration. Paden (1997) believes that Rawls's theory can be rescued from such criticisms by noting that the prerequisites of justice—the conditions that must be obtained before a just society becomes possible—extend beyond the provision of capital, even in Rawls's extended sense of what this means. To maintain liberal institutions, Paden claims, we must ensure that our society can defend itself and, for the sake of its future security, that it contributes to achieving a more just world environment. We must make sure that the level of resources does not fall below what circumstances of justice permit, and we must preserve structures that underwrite the development of moral personality (34).

David Miller adds that 'those features of the environment that are really essential to a sustainable human existence—like breathable air—have first claim on resources in the same way as, say national defence' (1999: 159). Indeed, if our purpose is to maintain just institutions and not mere human existence, then environmental values of many kinds will have a claim upon our resources. Just institutions are unlikely to survive and flourish if our successors are impoverished by the destruction of ecosystems on which their economic prosperity depends; if their health is affected by the lack of access to clean water and clean air; if they are irradiated or debilitated by harmful substances or if vital resources are depleted. What environmental economists refer to as 'natural capital' must also be maintained for the sake of future generations.

By making explicit the prerequisites of a just society we obtain a more plausible, though more demanding, conception of intergenerational justice. However, doubts remain about whether by satisfying these requirements we would be doing all that we need to do in order to be just to future members of our society. Fulfilling these requirements will not necessarily prevent our successors from suffering from environmental degradation or from a deterioration of social amenities. Their general health and life expectancy may be worse than ours—but not so bad that they cannot maintain institutions of justice or make and pursue rational plans for their lives. They may live in an environment that lacks many of things that we value and enjoy. They may inherit a world that is ugly, that has lost many of its natural environments and species, its historic buildings and monuments to the past. To avoid these outcomes, most people are predisposed to think that their duties to future generations must go beyond the duty to maintain just institutions and their prerequisites.

Many philosophers agree. Brian Barry thinks that we have a duty to ensure that future generations can live good lives according their conception of what a good life is: 'This should surely include their being able to live good lives according to our conception but should leave other options open to them' (1999: 104). Peter Laslett thinks that 'each generational entity must deliver the world to its successors in the condition in which it was received' (1992: 29). R.M. Green sets down as a basic principle 'that the lives of future people ought ideally to be 'better' than our own and certainly no worse' (1981: 91). Marcel Wissenburg requires that 'no goods shall be destroyed unless unavoidable or unless they are replaced by perfectly identical goods . . . '(1998: 123). 'No rock, animal, or plant should be destroyed, no species made extinct' (126). All of these positions require that we pass on to future generations things that we find valuable or beneficial, or at least that we provide an equally valuable substitute.

Some of these ideas about our obligations are disputable. Do we really have a duty to replace everything we destroy by something of the same kind or by an equally valuable equivalent? Do we really have a duty to ensure that our successors are just as well off as we are? Rawls doesn't think so, and neither do Wilfred Beckerman and Joanna Pasek (2001: 69). These ideas also suffer from vagueness. Every generation makes changes in the world. What criteria do we use to determine whether we have delivered to our successors a world that is in the same condition as it was when we received it? What counts as an equal opportunity or an equivalent benefit? If we pollute the air so that it is no longer pleasant or safe to engage in outdoor recreation, have we fulfilled our duty if we provide our successors with a wider range of indoor activities? If we deprive them of good health and shorten their life expectancy, can they be compensated by increased wealth? These questions need answers, but first let us consider whether we commit any injustice at all by worsening the conditions under which future members of our society will live—providing that they can still maintain just institutions and practices.

Suppose that in two countries, A and B, citizens have different attitudes toward the value of good health. In country A, improving the health of the population has long been a priority, and people take pride in the progress made in public health and the provision of medical resources. People in country B, though equally wealthy, have always had other priorities. They greatly value individual freedom, risk taking and individual self-sufficiency, and as a result the government has never spent much money on health care and has never attempted to limit people's choices for the sake of their health. As a result, the people in country A are generally healthier than people in country B—life expectancy is higher and they are less likely to suffer from chronic diseases. But it seems mistaken to think that the people in country B are suffering from an injustice—even though they could have been as healthy as people in country A if their government had pursued different policies. If this is right, then why should we think that it would be unjust if the people of country A, by failing to prevent environmental deterioration or by allowing its health infrastructure to deteriorate, bring it about that people in following generations are somewhat less healthy?

The answer is not simply that future generations have no say. People born into country B also have no say—at least not until they become old enough to vote. What seems to make an important difference to the way in which we judge these two cases is a matter of history. In country A, citizens have traditionally placed a high value on health and have embarked on an intergenerational project of improving health; the evidence is in their policies and in the attitudes of citizens. Since the people of this society regard high standards of health as a social value—a value that all citizens, so far as possible, should enjoy—they have put themselves under an obligation to ensure, so far as they can, that their successors will also enjoy that good. This means not only that younger generations are likely to share the same values, but also that they have an entitlement to the conditions that will enable them to enjoy the same standards of health as their predecessors and can complain of injustice if, because of the actions of these predecessors, they fail to inherit these conditions.

Citizens of different societies are likely to have different ideas about what is socially valuable and thus will have different intergenerational projects. The intergenerational obligations that citizens possess thus depend in such cases on the values of their particular society. These values determine what equal opportunities or equal benefits mean when they are used to make judgements about intergenerational relationships. People of society A have an obligation to ensure that their successors will have an equal opportunity to enjoy a high standard of health. People of society B do not have that particular obligation. Citizens may of course change their values. They may also find that their values conflict. A society that values both health and wealth may find that pursuit of the latter undermines health standards by causing environmental problems. Such conflicts require the making of choices—not just about how values should be pursued, but about which values should take priority.

We are likely to have views about what values a society ought to pursue, but as long as its values do not conflict with universal requirements of justice—requirements that we have reason to believe that citizens of every polity, or at least every liberal democratic polity, should accept (allowing for reasonable differences of opinion that exist in debates about justice)—then it is up to citizens to determine what they value and regard as the rightful inheritance of their successors. The resulting requirement of intergenerational justice can be summed up as follows:

> Each generation of citizens has a duty to ensure, so far as possible, that its successors will have an opportunity to enjoy and pass on to their successors institutions and practices that embody requirements of justice that all polities (of its kind) should accept and resources and conditions necessary for the maintenance of these institutions; and in addition it has the duty to ensure that successors will be able to enjoy and pass on to their successors the goods that it values as products of an existing or prospective intergenerational project—so long as these goods or the way they are pursued do not conflict with general requirements of justice or with each other.

VALUES IN A DIVERSE SOCIETY

The previous discussion assumes that citizens of a polity are pretty much in agreement about their priorities, and thus about what goods ought to be transferred to succeeding generations. But this is often not the case. Some citizens value and want to preserve old-growth forests or other environmental goods; some value an artistic heritage and its products; others want to preserve buildings or monuments with a heritage value; yet others value the particular sporting tradition that is associated with their country or region. But people who value nature may not value sport, those who value sport may not care about artistic endeavours and some people may not value any of these things. These different ways of valuing give rise to a problem that has been much discussed by liberal philosophers. A liberal polity, it is commonly believed, should be neutral concerning ideas of the good. By questioning the favouritism inherent in practices of bequest and inheritance, Ackerman (as discussed in Chapter 4) presents a strong version of this thesis. Neutrality means that laws or policies ought not to favour particular individuals by endorsing or supporting their particular ideas of the good—unless doing so is agreeable to everyone in the society. According to Rawls:

> There is no more justification for using the state apparatus to compel some citizens to pay for unwanted benefits that others desire than there is to force them to reimburse others for their private expenses (1999a: 250).

He sets up the original position so that the contractors cannot be influenced in their choice of principles of justice by their ideas of the good, and this limitation is transferred as a matter of course to considerations of intergenerational justice.

However, the prohibition flies in the face of common practice. In many countries governments provide resources to protect heritage: they declare national parks, maintain museums of art and natural history, finance opera companies and provide money for sport. Ronald Dworkin, who in other contexts supports neutrality, defends these policies. Without public support of art, a rich convention will be unavailable to our successors (1986a: 231). Without conservation of the environment, he says, 'a way of life that has been desired and found satisfying in the past' will not be available to future generations (1986b: 202). Dworkin's reasoning echoes the views of many citizens who are motivated to demand that environments, buildings, museums or traditions be preserved 'for the sake of posterity'.

But is this widespread conviction about what we ought to maintain defensible? David Miller thinks not. People have different views about the value of ways of life, he says, and in cases where decisions have to be made about how public resources should be used, the fact that a life close to nature was valued by some people is a flimsy basis for environmental conservation (1999: 159). However, Miller's understanding of Rawlsian neutrality can be challenged in two ways. First of all, it can be challenged by pointing out that the value that people often find in nature, art and other such things is lifetime-transcending and thus cannot be separated from their views about what their successors should inherit. Second, it can be challenged by making a case for saying that the values of our predecessors are sometimes a good reason for preservation.

VALUES AS LIFETIME-TRANSCENDING INTERESTS

People commonly value natural environments or artistic achievements not merely because they find them beneficial in their own lives, but also because they believe that these things have a lifetime-transcending value. This way of valuing makes a difference to the case for the preservation of the things that they value. First of all, their values are not based simply on what they happen to like. People think that posterity ought to be able to appreciate certain things because those things are worthy of being valued, and they can often make a good case for their belief. That art is worthy of appreciation can be defended, for example, by reference to the way that it enhances our ways of seeing, broadens our appreciation of beauty, connects us with a heritage and so forth.

The second point to note is that people do not have to appreciate things in nature or artistic creations in order to agree that members of future generations ought to have an opportunity to value them. Parents often think that their children should be exposed to things valued by the people of their culture even when they don't care about these things themselves. And since a case can be made for the value of art or the environment, it is not implausible to suppose that citizens will agree to policies that ensure that their successors will have this opportunity. Agreement is particularly likely if the people of this society have a tradition of obtaining value from these things and thus are exposed to the positive evaluations of past and present people.

Suppose, however, that members of a society diverge on values to such an extent that they cannot reach an agreement about what things should be maintained for successors. Each contending group believes that its values should be maintained, but refuses to accept that the things valued by the other groups are sufficiently worthy. Andrew Dobson says that a liberal society can maintain its neutrality and yet act to preserve values by ensuring that the conditions that enable people to enjoy the various things they value are maintained for future generations (2003: 164–5). In his view, future generations should have an opportunity to value as many of the things that people now value as possible, as well as to acquire their own ideas of the good. How much is possible to maintain is, however, a critical issue. A society is not likely to have the means of preserving everything that its citizens regard as good. Moreover, attempts to preserve some things that people value would require a considerable amount of political intervention—more than is likely to be tolerable in a liberal society. Valued ways of life disappear because of economic and technological changes that result from the free choices of others. To preserve every valued way of life in the face of these changes would be beyond the legitimate powers of government. Choices clearly have to be made and the problem of maintaining neutrality arises once again.

It might be suggested that people with lifetime-transcending values could and should fulfil their preservationist aims by using their own resources to achieve their objective. Environmentalists might collect money to buy the ecosystems that they want to preserve. Those who love art could fund their own galleries, and so on. A polity could then confine itself to providing a social and legal framework that enables groups to pass on things that they value to those who they assume will appreciate them, and to ensure that their heirs are able to acquire their rightful inheritance. But this proposal has its disadvantages. Private initiatives are often a precarious means of fulfilling the aim of people who want to maintain the things they value for future generations. Their immediate heirs may be unable or unwilling to maintain their inheritance—thus undermining the objective of making valuable things available to more remote successors. Decisions of others in their society may get in the way of preservation: land may be acquired for a freeway; a gallery may succumb to economic pressures. So it is not surprising that those who want to maintain values for future generations seek the active support of governments. Polities are generally in a much better position than groups of private citizens to preserve what is valuable (to protect wilderness areas, for example) and to ensure that the young are educated so that they are able to appreciate things of value. They are in a better position to provide this opportunity to all young people, poor as well as rich.

Given that citizens generally believe that preserving valuable things for future generations ought to be a public concern supported by the government, they will be predisposed to agree to a decision procedure for determining what, in a particular circumstance, ought to get this support. We can supplement Dobson's attempt to show that liberal neutrality is compatible with preserving things that particular citizens value by demonstrating that there is or could be a fair procedure—a procedure that everyone has reason to endorse—for making such decisions.

A procedure that decides all issues by rule of the majority would not count as fair—the larger group would get its way every time. But it does not seem impossible to devise a system that is fair to minorities. Suppose that public debates about what deserves to be valued produce a short list of the types of good that a society should maintain for future generations, and that all members of this society agree with a policy of maintaining goods of at least one of these types. We can imagine an arrangement that asks supporters of each type of good to nominate particular candidates for preservation to a body that makes decisions according to a policy that requires equal support for these ideas of the good. What decision-making method should be used requires much more discussion, but it does not seem impossible that people motivated to adopt a procedure will be able to find one that they can all regard as fair. And if so, the objective that they all subscribe to—maintaining things that they value for future generations—can be achieved without violating the requirement of neutrality.[2]

In conclusion, citizens ought to accept a collective obligation to pass on to their successors those goods that they believe future members of their society should have an opportunity to appreciate. Differences of opinion about these goods do not constitute grounds for rejecting the obligation. Differences mean that citizens are obliged to enter into negotiations about what ought to be maintained and to reach a decision according to a procedure that they can agree is fair. Their obligation to accept the decision is motivated by their belief that their successors ought not to have to live in a world where the things that they now value will not exist.

THE VALUE OF AN INHERITANCE

I have taken the universalising approach in arguing that citizens ought to pass on to future generations those things that they have reason to value. The position I am defending nevertheless allows that citizens can make different collective decisions depending on the procedures they accept and on their culture and history. But there is another way in which history enters into the reasoning of citizens who want to preserve their values. Many of the things that people value have been handed down to them from their predecessors, and the sacrifices and accomplishments of these past people are often a reason why they value their inheritance and think it ought to be maintained.

This way of valuing raises two issues. The first is the familiar question of why the deeds of past people should give us obligations, and the second is whether such obligations—if they exist at all—have much of a role to play in determining what we should maintain for future generations. Lincoln thought that the value of a society conceived in liberty was reason enough to maintain it. Why should we also need to appeal to the sacrifices and deeds of the dead?

To explain how the deeds of predecessors can give citizens obligations we can make use of the reasoning in Chapters 5 and 6. Individuals do not have a duty to carry on the projects of their predecessors. The mere fact that past people valued something and made an effort to maintain it for their successors is not a sufficient reason for us to value it. We might judge our inheritance to be valueless or worse. But we do have a duty to remember and to make an effort to appreciate what our predecessors did for our sake. This means that if we want to reject our inheritance and abandon our predecessors' project, the onus of justification falls on us. We are answerable to our predecessors for rejecting what they laboured to provide for us to the extent of being required to explain our reasons for rejection in a way that takes into account their point of view. It means that if we reject an inheritance not because it is pernicious but because we now value something else, we might nevertheless have a duty to ensure that our successors have an opportunity to inherit it (depending on our means and the difficulties involved).[3]

These ideas about duty can be translated into a view about the intergenerational entitlements and obligations of citizens. The citizens of each generation are entitled to demand that their successors remember the sacrifices they made for the sake of posterity. They are entitled to demand that their successors make an effort to understand and appreciate the intergenerational goods that they inherit, and appreciate why their predecessors wanted to provide these things as an inheritance for future generations. They are entitled to demand that their successors should not turn their back on their inheritance without being prepared to justify themselves—that is, to take seriously the reasons why their predecessors made an effort to provide it. They are entitled to demand that their successors make their ideas about value—and in some cases, the things they valued—available to succeeding generations so that these more distant successors have an opportunity to understand them and maintain their link with past generations.

The idea that successors should remember and appreciate the efforts of their predecessors to provide them with things of value comes up against some familiar objections. Some critics might wonder why future generations should be obliged to appreciate our efforts when all we are doing is fulfilling our duty to provide them with (more or less) just institutions and other things of value. Remembrance and appreciation seems better reserved for those who have gone beyond the requirements of duty in providing benefits for their successors. But even if this is so, citizens will not lack duties to their predecessors. In the frictionless world of Rawls's ideal theory each generation bears no more or less than its fair share of costs and receives its fair share of benefits. No special effort of memory or commemoration seems called for, but in the real world, the task of maintaining institutions of justice has its difficulties and dangers in most generations. Institutions have to be reformed, injustices have to be corrected, reparations have to be made, threats to the perpetuation of just institutions have to be met. Some generations will have to make great sacrifices to defend their institutions. All generations will have to use their ingenuity and courage to apply principles of justice under difficult circumstances and to resist the forces that can erode just institutions. Remembering and appreciating how the people of past generations coped with their difficulties is not only important because their deeds can generate duties for their successors. Our predecessors are entitled to be remembered for their accomplishments.

Another common objection to the idea that we have a political obligation to remember and appreciate the contribution of past citizens is that there is likely to be a considerable amount of disagreement in a polity about who should be remembered and what should be appreciated. Citizens interpret national history in diverse ways according to their communal allegiances or their ethnic and racial identities. They have different ideas about the identity of national heroes and villains. A government that requires citizens to honour designated heroes or to commemorate particular deeds is surely violating the requirement of neutrality.

One response to this objection is to point out that citizens of a polity, however diverse their views, share the project of building, reforming and maintaining just democratic institutions and making decisions about the values that ought to be preserved. Because they have this project in common, they are likely to agree that certain contributions ought to be appreciated. But even when they disagree, this is not necessarily a bad thing or a fatal objection to the idea that citizens have duties of memory and appreciation. A pacifist may not care to celebrate those who have died in war, but will prefer to promote the contributions of past citizens who worked for peace. Members of minority groups who have been persecuted in the past are likely to have their own ideas about who in their national history should be celebrated as a hero or condemned as a villain. These differences of opinion not only contribute to a democratic debate about the past and future of the polity, they also ensure that the contributions of more people will be properly remembered and appreciated. The duty of memory and commemoration does not require an official act sanctioned by government. It can be carried out in different ways by groups of citizens who, in their acts of commemoration, contribute to the debate about the meaning of the history of their polity and the heritage that it has received from the past. And in cases where it seems appropriate for governments to officially remember and honour people of the past, they can do so in an inclusive way.

KEEPING FAITH WITH PAST GENERATIONS

We have a duty to keep faith with our predecessors, as explained previously. This has implications for a view about what ought to be passed on to future generations. We should enable them to learn about the deeds and points of view of ourselves and our predecessors. We should maintain records, memorials and other forms of commemoration. We should preserve the heritage of past generations and the things that they regarded as valuable—at least to the extent that this does not impose unacceptable burdens on us. We should maintain channels of communication between the generations. In some cases this may mean the perpetuation of a language and other aspects of culture that enable later generations to appreciate the point of view and contributions of earlier generations.

Our duty to keep faith with the past can also influence our decisions about what particular institutions and political formations we should maintain and pass on to our successors. We do not have a duty to carry on the projects of our predecessors. We can reject political traditions, institutions and practices that we believe are unjust, inefficient or inadequate given existing circumstances. But the deeds, values and aspirations of our predecessors ought to be given their due when we make decisions concerning institutions and practices, and in some cases the weight of these considerations may be decisive. Jefferson was wrong. The earth does not belong wholly to the living—or just to us and to future generations.

Keeping this in mind, let us return to Abraham Lincoln and his conviction that the South was wrong to abandon the project begun by the founding fathers by seceding from the Republic. Our judgment about this case is bound to be affected by the fact that the objective of the Confederacy was to perpetuate conditions in which slavery could flourish. So let us imagine a situation in which such an obvious objection to secession does not exist. Suppose that the people of a polity composed of two groups with different customs, religions and ways of life have, for many generations, struggled and made sacrifices in order to build their political institutions. People of both communities worked together on equal terms with the conviction that it was possible and desirable to construct a society in which both cultures could flourish and where citizens could work together to maintain a just society through the generations. The people of this society have faced war and difficult times together; they have defended their country against foreign invaders; they have participated in forming and reforming their political institutions; they have built for the future. Some have made great sacrifices. But now one of these groups wants to secede and form an independent polity. Its members believe that they can better pursue their way of life if they have a polity of their own. They are tired of the compromises they have to make to accommodate a group with a different culture.

Is the fact that their predecessors laboured to maintain the polity a moral consideration that tells against secession? Could it ever be a decisive consideration? Allen Buchanan, when he details the reasons against secession, focuses on concerns relating to rights of property and sovereignty, distributive justice and the prospects of present and future people (1991: Chapter 5). He does not even consider whether labours and sacrifices of the past generations might have a moral weight. Nevertheless, he makes it clear that the burden of proof falls on secessionists. If they have no good reasons for secession, then it would be wrong for them to seek a political divorce. Unlike some liberals, he does not think that secession is simply a choice that free people are entitled to make. My claim is that the considerations that weigh against secession, that require those who want to secede to make a good case, are not merely the economic and political problems that secession might cause, but the weight of the past: the sacrifices and contributions of past generations who were labouring for posterity.

If we agree that these past sacrifices and contributions have weight, then we would expect this weight to be decisive in cases where those who want to secede or make some other political change that breaks with the past have no strong moral case for their proposal: where they are reacting to difficulties that are likely to prove temporary, or when a mutually acceptable compromise seems possible. Liberals and conservatives are likely to differ about what circumstances justify a break with the past. But liberals, as well as conservatives, have reason to accept that the past can give us reasons for maintaining political institutions and relationships, and that sometimes these reasons can be decisive.

GENERATIONAL INSTITUTIONS

In this chapter I have presented answers, general and historical, to the question of what each generation of a political society ought to maintain for its successors. We have a duty to develop, maintain and pass on to succeeding generations just institutions along with other things that we have reason to believe are worthy of being valued through the generations; to maintain the conditions necessary for them to appreciate and enjoy these institutions and good things; and a duty to keep faith with our predecessors.

Do these answers suffice? There is an important matter that has, so far, not been discussed. The perpetuation of a political society, its institutions and the things that its citizens regard as worthy of being valued, depend on children being born, nurtured and educated. The institutions that perform these roles have an important place in an intergenerational political society. In Chapter 8, I will consider whether and how these and other institutions that provide benefits and burdens to different generational groups should be incorporated into a theory of intergenerational justice.

8 Generational Rights and Duties

Individuals are not first, or forever, autonomous agents with the duties and entitlements of citizens. They begin their lives as children whose well-being depends on others. They go through a long period of tutelage; they need education and support in order to become independent individuals and responsible citizens. Eventually they become workers and often parents. They pay taxes, some of which are used to educate and care for younger members of society and to pay the pensions of the old. They age, retire, and often end up being dependent on others. It is a central fact of a society that it consists of generational cohorts, each of which is at a different stage in the progression through life, and whose members acquire different needs, interests, obligations and entitlements as they move from childhood to old age.

However, this generational progression has not been central to the concerns of most political philosophers. In classical theories, care of children and the very old is assumed to belong to families, and the family is located outside of the political sphere. This assignment of generational responsibilities, and the associated separation of society into the public sphere of political and economic life and the private sphere of the family, have been rightly criticised by feminists and others. It meant, in classical theories, that women, defined by their familial role, were not regarded as citizens, and it had the anomalous consequence that activities essential to survival of a political society—the raising and educating of children—were not regarded as a matter of political concern. Lack of attention to generational relationships among co-existing people, or the assumption that they are politically irrelevant, is also responsible for familiar assumptions that I have highlighted by means of the distinction between synchronic and diachronic justice.

One of these assumptions is that justice between co-existing citizens has nothing to do with their membership in generational cohorts. Intergenerational justice, according to most theorists, is about the relationship between present citizens and their successors: that is, the young and not-yet-born individuals who will inherit the social world of those who are now in the position to make political decisions. It is this familiar idea of the subject matter of intergenerational justice that I left unchallenged in Chapter 7. The assumption that intergenerational relationships are a one-way street goes along with this picture. Present citizens give and future people take, or, alternatively, present citizens bring about conditions, bad or good, which later people have no choice but to accept. This idea has already been challenged in the last three chapters. We depend on our successors to fulfil our legitimate lifetime-transcending demands. The relationship between the generations is not a one-way street, but the belief that it is gets its plausibility from the common conception of intergenerational relationships. This conception also encourages the belief, challenged in this book, that intergenerational justice is a secondary concern.

Peter Laslett and James Fishkin, who criticise the way in which philosophers treat generations as discrete units that succeed each other, suggest that we think of the temporal dimension of a society as being rather like a procession of indefinite length. People are continually joining and leaving the procession (Laslett and Fishkin 1992). They march along, intermingling with others in their vicinity. Laslett and Fishkin point out that the division of these marchers into generations is at best artificial and at worst misleading, and they prefer the term 'processional justice' for what the people in the march through time owe to each other. However, the processional analogy does not capture the way in which people change as they move through life, acquiring different needs, interests, entitlements and obligations and different relationships with people both older and younger—changes that are related to the position that they share with those who entered the procession at a similar time.

Nevertheless, the processional analogy is useful because it provides another way of challenging the common conception of intergenerational relationships. It makes it clear that time is a dimension of a political society, and that temporal relationships permeate its entire existence. Co-existing people also participate in intergenerational relationships and can thus be conceived as subjects for a theory of intergenerational justice. Intergenerational justice so conceived would not merely be about the relationship between present people and their successors and predecessors; it would also be about relationships between existing generational cohorts. This conception, if it can be justified, will provide another demonstration of the centrality of intergenerational justice to a political society. It will give us another way of showing that some of the institutions of a society are essentially concerned with intergenerational affairs and that no account of justice among citizens is complete without including the responsibilities and entitlements that generational groups owe to each other.

An obvious reason for insisting that a theory of justice must pay attention to the ways in which benefits and burdens are distributed among co-present generational cohorts has to do with the facts about life described previously. In their procession through time, members of a generational cohort acquire different responsibilities and entitlements in respect to other cohorts. It seems reasonable to suppose that these duties and entitlements are subject matter for a theory of justice. In particular, a theory of intergenerational justice seems necessary in order to make sense of the debate that is taking place in many countries about the relative burdens of older and younger generational cohorts. As stated in Chapter 1, a primary issue in this debate is whether it is fair to require a relatively small cohort of younger people to support a relatively large cohort of older people. Although the issue is about relationships between contemporaries, it also seems to be a matter of intergenerational justice. In this chapter I will defend this perception. I will argue that generational cohorts have duties of justice to each other, and that these duties are best understood in the framework of a theory of intergenerational justice.

In a discussion of the relationships between co-existing generations, there are two senses of 'generation' that come into play: one social and one familial. A generational cohort is simply a group of individuals whose birth dates fall within specified dates and who move through life together. In a family those who count as members of the same generation are defined by their relation to their parents or, more generally, by their position in a family tree. Although generational cohorts can be defined in a way that matches, more or less, generational relationships in families (given that people have their children at about the same time in their lives), the two senses of generation often part company. If your parents came from families in which there were wide gaps between the birth of children, you and your first cousins may be members of different generational cohorts. For a theory of justice, the relevant conception of generation must be the social one. Indeed, I will argue that it is a mistake to model an account of justice between generational cohorts on familial conceptions of duty. Nevertheless, a discussion about justice between generations makes it necessary to attend to familial relationships and the role of the family in managing intergenerational affairs. The topic of the family forces us to come face to face with one of the most difficult problems of political philosophy: explaining how the duties and entitlements of family members are related to requirements of justice. This chapter will draw attention to some of the difficulties, which will also be discussed in Chapter 10.

JUSTICE AND GENERATIONAL COHORTS

Although there are reasons for thinking that relationships between generational cohorts raise issues of justice, this supposition might be resisted in a number of ways. One of them is to question the very notion of justice between cohorts. How a cohort is defined—what birth dates are selected—is an arbitrary matter, as the processional analogy makes clear. So a sceptic might wonder how it can make sense to speak of justice between generational cohorts when these groups can be defined in whatever way we please.

References to generational cohorts are really about individuals who are related by the similarity of their birth dates. In measuring how a generational cohort fares relative to others, we are interested in how its members fare. But justice in a society is best measured by comparing relevant groups and not by comparing individuals. How a particular individual fares is determined by many factors, some of which are irrelevant to justice. But if members of a group are generally worse off or more heavily burdened than members of another group, and there is no morally satisfactory reason why this is so, then an issue of justice is likely to be at stake. How we define the groups depends on the issue in question. If we are worried about the burdens imposed on some members of society by demographic change, then the relevant groups to compare are cohorts that result from a high birth rate and those that result from lower birth rates.

The response raises another objection to the idea that relationships between generational cohorts raise issues of justice—this time from those who object to the very idea of social justice. A libertarian would claim that how cohorts (and other social groups) fare relative to each other is not an issue of justice. Members of society are not entitled to demand that others help them support and educate their children or support them in old age. Rational members of a libertarian society would presumably have no more children than they could support and educate, and they would save to support themselves in old age. But if it turns out that many old people are poor, or that some generational cohorts are much better off than others, a libertarian would not regard this as unjust.

The trouble is that not all individuals are in the position to control their fertility; not all children are born to parents who can afford to give them a good start in life; not all people can save adequately for retirement. Individuals, however careful, cannot ensure that they will not have a child with special needs or that they will not incur expenses in old age that exhaust their savings. Libertarianism is a political philosophy designed for relationships among able-bodied, independent individuals. It is not an attractive position for a society that consists of people of all age cohorts. It does not answer well to the vicissitudes and contingencies of human lives. A society in which individuals, no matter how hard they try and however responsibly they act, have no reliable way to ensure that they will be able to live reasonably well in their old age or that their children will obtain what they need lacks the qualities of a decent society. If a libertarian society is to be a decent society, then care for children with special needs and for many dependent old people is going to depend either on its members accepting a duty of charity or on families that regard it as their responsibility to make great sacrifices in order to care for their members. Perhaps anyone who has a child can be regarded as having consented to take on a responsibility, however onerous this turns out to be. But the needs of the old create theoretical, as well as practical, difficulties for libertarians. To the extent that the responsibility for fulfilling their needs falls on private persons or members of families, then it seems that some people in a libertarian society (mostly women) are going to acquire duties that they did not volunteer for (Post 1990). In other words, the fundamental tenant of libertarianism—that obligations should be based on voluntary acts—cannot be followed in practice.

This criticism of libertarianism is likely to provoke the response that familial and personal duties are not duties of justice and thus, whether voluntary or not, are not a concern of a theory of justice. If this is right, and if the duties that we are predisposed to think of as generational duties are properly understood as belonging to families, then we have another way of objecting to the idea that relationships between generational cohorts raise issues of justice. This objection is not confined to libertarians. We could hold that justice requires citizens of society to re-distribute resources among themselves and yet insist that relationships between co-existing generations are a familial and not a political concern. This is the way that they were pictured by classical social contract theory, which conceived of justice as being about relationships between independent individuals, and relegated care of children and the aged to the private world of the family.

As a matter of fact, most modern societies do not leave these matters to the family. They provide or subsidise schools and make education for children compulsory; they monitor, to a greater or lesser extent, the way in which families nurture children. More affluent societies provide pensions for the elderly and institutions that provide them with care. Because public institutions have these responsibilities it is natural to raise questions about whether the burdens and benefits of fulfilling them are fairly distributed among members of a society: to question, for example, the fairness of a pension scheme which burdens some age cohorts more than others.

However, it is important to note that issues of justice are not confined to societies that provide public institutions to educate the young and care for the old. If citizens decide to leave these tasks to the family, then this is a political decision, and it is reasonable that those who are heavily burdened raise questions about its justice—as feminists have done. It is also reasonable to wonder whether this decision can deal adequately with the needs of individuals in an intergenerational political society. In many contract theories, as we have seen, these questions are avoided by an unexplained shift in the identity of the contractors. Individuals are first assumed to be representatives of family lines, and it is reasonable to think that they are responsible for looking after the interests of their dependents and would want to consider whether generational duties can be adequately carried out within families. But when they actually make the social contract they are transformed into independent individuals who are concerned only with preserving as much freedom for themselves as possible. One of the effects of this change of identity is that it avoids making generational duties into a matter of political discussion. But generational relationships do raise issues of justice and any adequate theory must address them.

JUSTICE AND AGE GROUPS

Objections to an idea of intergenerational justice that includes relationships between co-present generational cohorts have so far consisted of attempts to deny the existence of social justice or to reduce generational duties to family duties. But it is possible to agree that these duties are a matter of political concern and nevertheless insist that they do not belong to a theory of intergenerational justice. Synchronic theories of social justice prescribe distributions of resources to meet the needs of individuals, including those with special needs. So it might be argued that 'generational' duties are merely the responsibilities that a society as a whole has to those with special needs or disadvantages because of their age—responsibilities that include providing education for the young and pensions for the old. In a synchronic theory of justice philosophers generally take as given the needs and disadvantages of citizens and consider how resources should be distributed to provide for these needs or lessen the disadvantages. At some times during its history members of a society may have more needs to provide for. In periods of high unemployment more people will need unemployment benefits. If an earthquake destroys homes and social infrastructure, more people will need relief and support. Those who have to make additional sacrifices—perhaps in the form of higher taxes—to provide support for those made homeless or unemployed might count themselves as unlucky, but it seems wrong for them to complain of injustice.

Andrew Levine takes this view about care for the aged. He thinks that we ought to support institutions that provide pensions to the elderly simply because meeting the needs of the elderly is something that a society ought to do (1998: 308). If at a particular time there are many old people and a relatively small number of tax-paying citizens to provide for them, then these tax payers can regard themselves as unfortunate, but not as the victims of an injustice. To think that they are is, in his opinion, simply a mistake. This way of looking at the issue seems to be reinforced by those feminists who regard care as a central responsibility of a society—in the public as well as the private realm. If care is an imperative, then we ought to care for whoever needs care and not ask ourselves whether it is just that these demands are made of us.

What counts against this reduction of diachronic to synchronic justice is that some institutions of society—in particular those that are concerned with the care and education of children and support for the old—seem to require the diachronic point of view. Social emergencies, like economic setbacks or earthquakes, occur unpredictably from time to time, and it is appropriate to think that those who have to bear the costs of supporting those who are rendered needy by these events are simply unlucky (as are the needy themselves). But young and old people will always be around, and if a political society is to persist and ensure that its citizens will continue to have their needs met in each generation, then families, or whatever takes their place, will have to continue to nurture children and educational institutions will have to be maintained. Members of each generational cohort will eventually retire and will need a means of support—however this is provided. The public good of having a just pension scheme depends on there being institutions which can be relied on to persist through the generations and provide benefits for each cohort in its turn. But this means that it is difficult to avoid questions about how the entitlements and burdens are shared between generational cohorts, just as it is difficult to avoid, in other cases where care is required, questions about how the benefits and burdens are distributed among members of a society.

Governments, exercised about the problem of demographic change, tend to assume that maintenance of pension schemes and other benefits for the old raise issues of intergenerational justice. For example, a recent Australian Government report on how to deal with the problems posed by an ageing population warns that, 'the current generation of tax payers is likely to impose a higher tax burden on the next generation'; and argues that, for the sake of intergenerational equity, policies should be adjusted so that this will not happen (Commonwealth of Australia 2002: 1, 14). The idea of justice between generational cohorts that this report embodies needs more discussion. But the important point to note is that it is natural and reasonable to assume that the prospect of an ageing population raises issues of intergenerational justice.

Adopting this reasonable approach means making a distinction between justice between generational cohorts and justice between age groups. One of the reasons why it is tempting to collapse the first into the second is because one of the issues that governments are particularly concerned about when they discuss demographic imbalance is the growing cost of pharmaceuticals and medical technology. Governments that subsidise medical care of citizens face the prospect of an ever-increasing, and ultimately unsupportable, demand on their resources—and much of the demand will come from older people. However, the problems associated with financing and distributing health services are distinct from concerns about justice between generational cohorts. With or without an ageing population, societies will increasingly face problems about financing medical care. An ageing population simply exacerbates the problem. To prevent medical costs from taking resources away from other important public goods and services, decisions will have to be made about how expensive medical treatments should be distributed among those who could benefit from them, and it may happen that societies will decide to distribute them in a way that favours younger people. This would raise questions about justice between age groups—whether there is a justification for favouring the young—but a policy that distributes benefits or costs between age groups should be distinguished from a policy that distributes burdens and benefits between generational cohorts.[1]

Justice between generational cohorts has to do with the distribution of the benefits and burdens of the institutions that fulfil generational responsibilities. What justice requires depends on how we conceive of cooperation between generational cohorts.

INTERGENERATIONAL COOPERATION

Co-existing generational groups interact. They can provide benefits and impose burdens on each other. For this reason many theorists assume that their cooperation is a matter of reciprocity. Richard Posner, for example, treats retirement benefits as an appropriate return from younger to older generations for benefits received:

> Adults of working age pay taxes to support the public school system, in effect lending the young money with which to purchase human capital. The young repay the loan when they become adults of working age and the generation that paid for their public school education reaches retirement age . . . (1995: 254).

Daniel Callahan thinks that children acquire a debt, not merely because of the expenses of their education, but also from being nurtured, brought up and provided with the advantages of a society, and he thinks that the benefits received from older members of this society gives them a duty to make a return (1980: 77). These views about the nature of intergenerational reciprocity are somewhat different, but the basic idea of justice is the same: generational cohorts who receive significant benefits from older generational cohorts should compensate them in due course by providing them with comparable benefits.

This account, if acceptable, makes justice between existing generations different from justice between generations who are not in the position to provide a return for the benefits that they have received. Indeed, justice as reciprocity between co-existing generations can be regarded as another way of putting the relationship between these generations into a synchronic framework. Many accounts of synchronic justice insist that those who provide us with benefits are owed a return; the fact that reciprocity might have to take place many years after the benefit was provided does not seem significant.

The idea that justice is a matter of reciprocity between interacting generational cohorts is attractive not only because benefits and burdens can move in both directions between co-existing groups, but also because reciprocity is the basis for most accounts of filial duties. Most views of why children have duties to their ageing parents make reference to the services that parents performed for their children in an earlier stage of their lives. 'That we exist at all puts us in debt to those who conceived us,' says Callahan (1981: 77). Though Nancy Jecker does not think that we have a duty to parents simply because they brought us into the world and brought us up, she does think that we owe duties to parents when they performed acts beyond the requirements of duty and performed them in a praiseworthy manner, or when their efforts required great sacrifices or produced special benefits (1989: 75).[2] Mark Wicclair thinks that our duties to parents cannot be precisely specified, but should be proportional to the sacrifices they made for us (1990: 177). Though there is some disagreement among these philosophers, the basic idea is that our parents have done things for us at an earlier stage of our lives and therefore we ought now to do things for them. So it is natural to suppose, as Callahan does, that when generational duties become a social concern—when they are transformed into duties of younger to older generational cohorts—their justification must be similar. But this is a mistake. For one thing, the analogy between familial duties and the duties of generational cohorts breaks down upon closer examination. The duties of parents to children and children to ageing parents are predicated on a personal concern for the well-being of another. Parents act with the intention of benefiting their children; they respond to them with loving concern, and it is not surprising that children who have benefited from this personal attention should regard themselves as having duties of gratitude to their parents, perhaps even when their parents were no more than adequate. But the exchanges between younger and older cohorts of a society are impersonal. The tax payers whose contributions help to educate younger members of society do not generally intend to help younger generations; they are forced to make contributions and may do so unwillingly. There is no reason why members of younger cohorts should feel gratitude, nor does it seem that they have a duty to reciprocate just because they received benefits.

Since filial duties are duties of gratitude, it is not necessary to specify exactly what we owe to our parents in return for services rendered. But duties of generational cohorts are presumably duties of justice and some explanation is needed of what counts as a fair exchange. This is where we strike the most serious difficulty with accounts based on reciprocity. Generational cohorts can create costs and benefits for other cohorts in all sorts of ways, and the obvious question is which ones are relevant for an account of justice. The differing views of theorists suggest that this question is not going to be easy to answer. Should we simply insist that the overall costs and benefits that each generational cohort receives as the result of interactions ought to be equal, and that those that incur greater costs ought to be compensated by generations that incur greater benefits? But this idea is impossible to apply, since total costs and benefits to a younger cohort may not be determined until long after it becomes impossible to compensate an older cohort or receive compensation from it. Moreover, changing circumstances as well as generational interaction will inevitably affect the level of costs and benefits that falls to the share of each cohort, and it is going to be difficult, if not impossible, to distinguish between costs and benefits that can be regarded as a matter of luck and those for which compensation is owed.

It is also difficult to specify what counts as a fair return for a benefit. Has a younger generation succeeded in discharging its debts to its elders by providing them with pensions, or does it owe them additional benefits? At what point do the demands of elders become unfair? Levine thinks that the difficulty of providing a standard for making judgments about fair reciprocity between generations is a good reason for rejecting the very idea of justice between generational cohorts. A more reasonable conclusion is that we need to adopt a different view of intergenerational cooperation.

This conclusion is supported by other considerations. Some of them are advanced by Brian Barry (1979) and Allen Buchanan (1990) in their criticisms of justice as reciprocity. Does reciprocal justice, applied to generational cohorts, mean that a poor generation that cannot afford to spend much on education deserves only a niggardly provision in old age? We might reject this proposal by insisting that reciprocity should depend on the sacrifices that older generations made rather than the actual amount that they spent. But problems remain. If members of a large older cohort do not need to sacrifice much in order to educate a small younger cohort, does this mean that they deserve little in return? Should the fact that they had fewer children than their parents count against them—or is this something for which they should be rewarded (given the environmental threat posed by a growing population)? But now we return to the earlier problem of determining what benefits require a return.

Noting the difficulties associated with generational duties based on reciprocity, Laslett argues that we should regard the social entitlements of the old as resulting from a relationship of trust made possible by the welfare state (1992: 31-3). In their productive years citizens subsidise the retirement of the old and expect that they will be supported by the succeeding generation in turn. This arrangement, Laslett argues, is distinct from the 'tri-generational contract' between non-contemporary generations, which gives present people rights in respect to the preceding generations and gives them duties to their successors. In a tri-generational contract, responsibilities move from a generation to its successors; in the relationship between co-present generations, they move from younger to older cohorts.

Laslett's account comes closer to the justification that people often give for the belief that their society should, if necessary, support them in old age. By putting an emphasis on production as a justification for entitlements, he might be accused of denying them to those who, for one reason or another, were not productive, but this is probably not his intention. Citizens of a welfare state can collectively commit themselves to providing assistance for all those who have needs of certain kinds. However, a disadvantage of his account is that it separates the provision of benefits for the old from other social responsibilities that exist between generational cohorts—for example, the responsibility of educating children. More seriously, by making the provision of benefits to the old into the business of current generations, it ignores long-term considerations. Like views based on reciprocity, his account of a generational cohort's responsibilities is compatible with it neglecting institutions in a way that makes it likely that people of more distant generations will suffer—for example, failing to save or make changes to pension schemes to ensure that they are sustainable for many generations to come, and not just for those who are now in their productive years. In this respect, institutions that ensure support for the aged are like the institutions discussed in Chapter 7. Maintaining them should be regarded as the intergenerational responsibility of members of a political society.

INTERGENERATIONAL INSTITUTIONS AND GENERATIONAL DUTIES

My thesis is that the account of justice that best answers to the role that institutions and practices which support or perform generational duties ought to play in a political society takes the same form as the conception of intergenerational justice discussed in Chapter 7. Institutions that educate the young and support the old should be regarded as vital to the existence of a polity as an intergenerational society. They give members of each generational cohort entitlements and obligations as they move through the stages of their lives: from children to contributing adults to old-age pensioners. Maintaining these institutions is the collective responsibility of members of an intergenerational society, and justice between generational cohorts is achieved if each cohort gets its fair share of entitlements and responsibilities. It is no objection to this account that the responsibilities and entitlements flow in different directions: to younger members of society in the case of educating children, and to older members of society in the case of providing pensions. Intergenerational justice gives us duties both to our predecessors and successors. By embracing the duties between generational cohorts, a theory of intergenerational justice acknowledges that requirements of justice govern relationships of co-temporal generations.

Incorporating generational duties into a theory of intergenerational justice has the advantage of providing a means of relating family duties to justice between generational cohorts. Let us assume that family duties are not duties of justice; that parents care for their children out of love or because they think that they have a basic duty of care; and let us agree with Jecker, Wicclair and others that adult children generally have duties of gratitude to aged parents. This does not preclude members of families from regarding themselves as participating in familial relationships of intergenerational cooperation that require members of each generation to carry out traditional responsibilities to children and elders, and entitle them in turn to receive care from their children. But whatever motivates family members to care for younger and older members, they are contributing to the maintenance of the intergenerational relationships of their society. They are ensuring that some of the intergenerational responsibilities of a just society are fulfilled.

Families, then, should also be counted as institutions that are essentially intergenerational. It is their nature to fulfil intergenerational responsibilities, even when their members are motivated by other considerations. By doing so they play an important role in the intergenerational polity, and justice requires that citizens provide appropriate support to families—or that they establish institutions which fulfil the same responsibilities. What a political society should do to support families, and how it should ensure that generational duties of families are well performed, is a difficult theoretical as well as political issue. Since family relationships are based on love and intimacy, since the raising of healthy children depends on intimacy and since families have traditions and things of value that they want to maintain and pass on to descendants, it would be wrong for a government to interfere in family relationships by insisting that children be raised in a particular way or by heavy-handed monitoring of what parents do. A polity cannot manage families as it manages unemployment benefits or old-age pension funds. But a polity has a vital interest in how family responsibilities are discharged. Some kind of political involvement in family affairs seems unavoidable. To leave families alone—to put them beyond the scope of politics—is not only bad for some of their members, but it also imposes unjust burdens on individuals and on less well-off families. How citizens should deal with these problems and what kind of family policy they should adopt is largely beyond the scope of this study, but I will have more to say about the matter in the context of a discussion of population in Chapter 10. There I will suggest a way of mediating between the entitlements of individuals as family members and the interests of citizens of an intergenerational society.

INTERGENERATIONAL JUSTICE AND FAIR SHARES

Each generation has a duty to do its fair share to develop, maintain and pass on to younger generations just institutions and other things that it regards as good; each generation inherits a responsibility to fulfil long-term commitments and make up for past wrongs; and each generation has a duty to maintain institutions that provide appropriate care and education for the young and which support the old. These are the conclusions that have been reached in the last two chapters. But what counts as a fair share? The issues raised by demographic change require an answer to this question. Is it unjust that younger generational cohorts in many countries will have to sacrifice comparatively more than earlier cohorts in order to support the elderly? Is it wrong for members of a polity to incur a national debt that younger generations must pay? The answers to these questions are going to depend on a general account of equity between the generations, which I will provide in the next chapter.

9 Fair Shares

The just savings principle, Rawls says, 'can be regarded as an understanding between generations to carry their fair share of the burden of realizing and preserving a just society' (1999a: 257). Chapters 7 and 8 considered what each generation needs to maintain in order to preserve a just society and to be just to its future members. Each generation ought to maintain institutions of justice, the prerequisites of a just society and those intergenerational institutions and practices that enable polities to maintain respectful intergenerational relationships with other polities and communities. It ought to maintain institutions that fulfil the generational responsibilities of a society. It ought to pass on to its successors those goods that its members believe that their successors should have an opportunity to value. The question that we must now consider is how the generations should share the burdens and benefits of intergenerational cooperation. What counts as a fair share?

Rawls's answer depends on the stage that the intergenerational project has reached. Those generations that have not yet established just institutions have an equal duty to save relative to their wealth. This duty puts a restriction on the application of the difference principle—the requirement that wealth should be distributed in favour of the least well off members of a society. Once just institutions are achieved, saving is no longer required. Each generation does its duty by 'maintaining just institutions and preserving their material base' (257). This includes, as we have seen, preserving the environmental and social prerequisites of just institutions. So long as just institutions can be maintained, Rawls does not require that each generation pass on to its successors wealth equal to its own. Justice does not require equal benefits or burdens between generations.

There is a tension in Rawls's position so understood. On one hand, he insists that each generation should make an equal sacrifice to accumulate capital for the sake of establishing institutions of justice. But on the other hand, he seems to imply that it doesn't matter that some generations may sacrifice more than other generations to *maintain* institutions of justice. Jane English claims that if all generations were represented in Rawls's original position (as she thinks they ought to be), then the parties 'would not be indifferent as to how primary goods are distributed among generations' (1977: 103). Frédéric Gaspart and Alex Gosseries hold that Rawls's principle should be reformulated to require generations who have achieved just institutions to maintain a steady state as far as resources are concerned—a requirement that would not allow 'dissavings' (2007: 201).

In this chapter I support the common view that each generation or generational cohort should do what is in its power to ensure that other generations or generational cohorts will not have to bear greater burdens than itself in order to establish, maintain and/or receive the same degree of benefits from institutions of justice and other intergenerational goods. I will call it the 'fair shares principle'. This principle, though intuitively plausible, faces both conceptual and moral difficulties. It needs to be defended from those who believe that it is too demanding and from those who do not think that it is demanding enough. I will discuss how these objections should be met and how the principle should be interpreted.

JUST SAVINGS

Rawls's prescription about how the generations should share the labour of saving for the establishment of just institutions is in accordance with the fair shares principle. Each generation should make an equal contribution according to its means. Earlier poorer generations should contribute less, and later richer generations should contribute more until the objective is reached. Rawls tells us that the members of existing generations should measure their contribution by reference to what they think their predecessors ought to have contributed. Thus what counts as just savings is determined by a judgement about what each generation should be prepared to sacrifice for the sake of establishing just institutions. Questions arise about how much each generation should be prepared to sacrifice and whether Rawls's way of determining this is adequate. But first we need to consider why the generations of a political society should embark on the project of constructing just institutions when this means that poor generations will have to save and pass on resources that could instead be used to improve the position of the least well off among their contemporaries. Behind the veil of ignorance they might reason as Rawls supposes (so long as each generation apart from the first benefits from a policy of saving). In the real world, where a generation knows its true situation and has many competing claims on its resources, this issue cannot be ignored. Where does the motivation to adhere to the just savings principle come from?

Rawls believes that societies have a natural duty to realize and maintain institutions of justice (1999a: 293), but he does not explain why individuals would accept this collective duty when they are not able to enjoy the benefits and when saving would take away resources that could be used to improve the condition of the least well off. This problem of motivation is likely to be particularly acute in a poor society where more resources could make a significant difference to the worst off. Gaspart and Gosseries say that the principle of maximising the liberty which each member of a society can enjoy—a principle that takes priority in Rawls's theory—requires that each generation participate in an effort to realize institutions that protect basic liberties. But their reasoning depends on accepting as basic the requirement to save:

> If one is not ready to care for some people's needs less than for those of other future people in order to invest and enable all the following generations to meet the basic-needs threshold, we remain unable to justify the positive savings that Rawls requires from the first generation (2007: 200).

The problem remains: why should the people of a poor society accept an obligation to save?

The motivation for the sacrifices that must be made by poorer generations—and in particular by the least well off people in these generations—must be founded on their lifetime-transcending interests. For some people justice is an ideal, as Rawls supposes, and they are predisposed to accept a duty to participate in bringing into existence just institutions. But others are more likely to be motivated by a concern for their descendants, for the preservation of a communal good or the ability to engage in projects and to pass them on to their successors. It is reasonable to suppose that such interests will be better served by establishing just institutions or at least by moving in that direction. And if people of a society join together to build just institutions—whether they see these as intrinsically valuable or as means to other ends—then they are predisposed to see themselves as participating in an intergenerational project which gives them a duty to pass on the fruits of their efforts to their successors, and gives their successors a duty to properly appreciate what they have done. Given that the interests and ideas of justice of these successors are similar, they will accept a duty to continue the effort to create just institutions and to pass on this project to *their* successors.

Supposing that the members of an intergenerational polity have embarked on this project, how great a sacrifice does justice require of each generation? Motivated by their lifetime-transcending values and interests, members of a generation might prescribe a large rate of savings for themselves and their successors. On the other hand, it seems unjust to require people to make great sacrifices for an objective that they will never fully enjoy. Rawls's abstract, gradualist approach suggests that the just rate is a mean between extremes, but in reality the sacrifices that citizens accept as fair are likely to vary according to their situation and will be influenced by how strongly their interests and their present conditions motivate them to build just institutions and by the sacrifices made by past generations.

In Chapter 8 I argued that history plays a role in determining the intergenerational duties of citizens. In respect to the project of constructing just institutions, history may also play a role in a consideration of what counts as a fair burden. If past generations have made considerable sacrifices, then present generations will be predisposed to believe that they should be prepared to do no less. If present generations are now faced with the prospect of having to make a great sacrifice to maintain the project of constructing just institutions so that their successors will not have to begin the work all over again, they are likely to accept the burden—not only for the sake of their successors, but also because of the labour and sacrifices of their predecessors. History gives the project a moral momentum that can obligate present generations.

TREATING LIKES ALIKE

The work of forming and reforming just institutions and protecting the other goods that intergenerational justice requires is never completely done. Some resources of a society will always have to be used for these purposes. But if an affluent polity has managed to establish institutions that are reasonably just, does it matter whether present generations contribute more or less than their successors toward maintaining these institutions? Rawls seems to think that it does not. If he is right, then we would not do our successors an injustice if we impose on them burdens greater than those we have borne—so long as their ability to maintain just institutions and other good things is not threatened. This conception of our obligations is not uncommon. Beckerman and Pasek do not think that we a have a duty to ensure that the benefits our successors enjoy will be equal to our own, though they believe that future generations will in fact be more well off (2001: 69, 90). Achieving sustainability, according to the World Commission on Environment and Development (1987: 43), requires that we ensure 'development which meets the needs of the present generation without compromising the ability of future generations to meet their own needs', but not that we have to ensure that our successors will be as well off as we are. Levine, as we have seen, believes that it is not an injustice if young people in a reasonably wealthy society have to make greater sacrifices than did their predecessors to provide pensions and services to the old. However, according to the fair shares principle, imposing such burdens would be unjust. Factors beyond our control may result in greater burdens for the young and future generations, but it would be wrong for us to impose these burdens or to do nothing if we can foresee that they will exist.

Some people regard the fair shares principle as self-evident. Robert Goodin takes it to be a fundamental principle of justice that 'likes be treated alike'—that it is unjust to make some people pay more than others for receiving the very same thing (1999: 193). He applies this principle to the population imbalance caused in some societies by demographic change and concludes that, all things being equal, the large older generation of these societies should have been running its pension accounts at a considerable surplus in order to reimburse the next generation, and this smaller generation would be justified in running their pension accounts at a deficit, thus borrowing from their more privileged successors (197). However, the plausibility of his principle may depend, more than Goodin supposes, on the proximity in time of those who are treated alike or unalike.

Rawls points out that the difference principle—or any other distributive principle that requires mutual adjustments of benefits and burdens between individuals or groups—cannot be applied to relationships between generations. There is nothing we can do to improve the position of the less fortunate, earlier generations (1999a: 254). We cannot better the living standards of the dead or reimburse them for the sacrifices they made. We can only accept a duty to remember and appreciate their sacrifices.

However, reimbursement of the earlier generations is not a requirement of the equal shares principle that I am defending. It does not require that the burdens of past generations be made equal to those of later generations. It merely requires that we do what is in our power to avoid unfair burdens to other generations. Since nothing we can do will relieve the burdens of past generations, we have no obligation to do so. In any case, transfers between generations are not altogether impossible. As Goodin explains, older generations can transfer resources to younger generations or they can impose burdens on them by running up a deficit. In these familiar ways, the costs of maintaining institutions, and in some cases the benefits that derived from them, can be transferred from one generation to another. The difference principle cannot be applied to all of the generations of a political society, but an idea of fair shares more demanding than that of Rawls is obviously possible.

EQUALITY AND COOPERATION

Another reason for rejecting a principle that aims for equality between generations is emphasised by Beckerman and Pasek (2001: 49). Inequalities, they note, can have detrimental consequences among people who interact with each other and share the same political and social institutions. Wealthier people are in a better position to obtain the things that people in their society value. They are likely to have more political power and social prestige. Differences in wealth in a society where wealth is much valued can affect self-esteem. So there are good reasons why a theory of justice should be concerned about how wealth and power are distributed among co-temporal citizens. But between people of different societies or different generations there is less direct interaction. So long as people are not needy, live in a just society and have equitable relationships with their contemporaries, why should it matter whether they are, on average, less wealthy than preceding or succeeding generations, or have to make greater sacrifices to maintain just institutions?

The position of Beckerman and Pasek is predicated on a view about the value of equality. If we insist that inequality between generations is unjust despite it having no detrimental consequences for individuals, then, according to their argument, we are supposing that equality is intrinsically valuable. But the idea that equality is intrinsically valuable has unacceptable consequences. It would imply that we ought to reduce our share of wealth and other goods to make it equal to the share available to earlier poorer generations. If we are not prepared to sacrifice current welfare to reduce intergenerational inequality, 'then the claim that intergenerational equality has some intrinsic value begins to look a little like humbug' (56). But if we reject the view about equality that leads to this result, then, apparently, we should also reject the fair shares principle when it is applied to relationships between generations.

One obvious problem with this argument is that it relies on a flawed conception of the relationship between the generations. Once we recognise that generations co-exist and that intergenerational relationships exist among contemporaries, it is no longer possible to think of them as groups who live in separate temporal worlds. Generations overlap and the individuals within them interact with each other. But the argument can be challenged for more basic reasons. It ignores one of the reasons why people regard equality as valuable and think that inequality is unfair.

If people cooperate to achieve something of equal value to each of them, then it is reasonable to insist, unless there is a good reason for making an exception, that the burdens should be equally shared. To impose heavier burdens on some individuals without a justification is to treat them as less than equal. It is a violation of a basic moral assumption: that all individuals are equally worthy of respect. That departures from equality have to be justified is basic to Rawls's contractualism and to Ackerman's advocacy of neutrality. And it is undoubtedly the reason why Goodin's insistence that likes should be treated alike is so intuitively appealing. The generations cooperate to establish and maintain institutions and other goods which (we assume) each of them has an equal reason to value. And thus each of them should share the burdens equally unless there is an overriding moral reason why sacrifices should not be equal.

Does this defence of equality in cooperative relationships succumb to Beckerman and Pasek's levelling down objection? Are we committed to reducing our share in order to make it equal to the shares of earlier poorer generations? The defence of equality that I have offered presupposes a cooperative relationship between the generations of a political society. This framework provides us with an overriding moral objection to accepting a levelling down requirement. The aim of our cooperation is to establish and maintain institutions of justice and other intergenerational goods—not to pursue equality for its own sake. Equality of shares is a subordinate moral requirement predicated on the basic moral equality of individuals and the nature of their cooperative relationship. If a poor generation were required to level itself down to the condition of the even poorer generation that preceded it, the aim of cooperation would never be achieved. This is obviously a good reason for not accepting, in the name of equality, a commitment to levelling down. If the generations in question are affluent enough to maintain institutions of justice but our generation is wealthier this does not oblige us to reduce our level of affluence. We might decide that we prefer the simpler, frugal way of life of our predecessors or we might think that environmental crisis gives us a duty to reduce our standard of living to ensure that our successors will not have to bear heavy costs. But we have no reason to accept, in the name of equality, a duty to level down. By levelling down we do nothing to advance the intergenerational project that we share with other generations. If reducing our share contributes nothing to the ability of other generations to establish and maintain just institutions, if it does nothing to advance the project to which we are all committed, it cannot be a moral requirement.

TRANSFERS BETWEEN GENERATIONS

The fair shares principle has so far been defended against those who think that it is too demanding. But it also needs to be defended against those who think that it is not demanding enough. If we are required to treat likes alike, as Goodin believes, then we should not only avoid imposing unequal burdens on others; we are also entitled to act to ensure that unequal burdens are not imposed on us. Goodin emphasises this point in his discussion of justice between generational cohorts. If we face the prospect of having to pay more than previous generations to enjoy a pension in old age, then we are justified in pursuing policies that will require later, more privileged generations to subsidise us. If his reasoning is sound, then why shouldn't it apply universally to intergenerational relationships? If we have reason to believe that our successors will be more affluent than us, and thus less burdened in performing their duties of justice, then why shouldn't we make them subsidise us by taking out loans or running up a public deficit that they will have to pay? The position of Gaspart and Gosseries suggests that *not* pursuing such a policy would impose an unjust opportunity cost on the least well-off members of our generation (2007: 204). By allowing our successors to enjoy a surplus, we will have less to distribute to the least well off of our generation. By not doing as much for these contemporaries as we could, we are committing an injustice. In their view, justice requires, under conditions of reasonable affluence, that a generation should *not* save to make its successors better off. So if there is reason to think that succeeding generations will be wealthier than us, then justice presumably requires—all things being equal—that we take steps to redistribute resources in favour of our generation.

It should be noted that the fair shares principle that I have been defending does not merely require that a generation should ensure that its successors do not have greater burdens; it requires that it should ensure, so far as this is within its powers, that other generations—older as well as younger—are not overburdened. This means that it would be wrong if a younger generation puts most of its resources in its own pension funds and doles out a niggardly amount to its elders. However, the principle does not prevent a generation from doing more than its fair share. It does not expressly forbid a poorer generation from obtaining subsides from wealthier succeeding generations, but it also doesn't require it to do so. It doesn't forbid a reasonably wealthy generation to save to make its successors even more well off, but it doesn't require that they do so. The question is whether a principle of intergenerational justice ought to forbid or require any of these things.

BORROWING FROM THE FUTURE

Many people are predisposed to think it is unjust for the present generations of a political society to borrow from the future by wracking up public debts. Jefferson was of this opinion. In stating that 'one generation is to another as one independent nation to another', Jefferson was, above all, criticising the practice of imposing a debt on younger generations:

> Again suppose Louis XV, and his contemporary generation had said to the money lenders of Genoa, give us money that we may eat, drink, and be merry in our day, and on condition you will demand no interest till the end of 19 years. . . . Would the present generation be obliged to apply the produce of the earth and of their labour to replace their dissipations? Not at all (1984: 961–2).

But our disapproval is likely to have a lot to do with the facts that the debt benefits the very wealthy, the money is spent on frivolous consumption and that poorer people are going to be the ones who pay the costs. When these drawbacks do not exist—when those who pay are well off, those who benefit are not so wealthy, and when the debt is used for a good social purpose—Jefferson's complaint seems less compelling.

In describing how the US pay-as-you-go social security system works, the economist Paul Samuelson makes a future-directed distribution of costs into a virtue:

> Everyone who reaches retirement age is given benefit privileges that far exceed anything he has paid in . . . How is this possible? It stems from the fact that the national product is growing at compound interest and can be expected to do so for as far ahead as the eye cannot see. Always there are more youths than old folks in a growing population. More important, with real incomes growing at some three percent a year, the taxable base upon which benefits rest in any period is much greater

than the taxes paid historically by the generation now retired (cited World Bank 1994: 105).

Samuelson inadvertently reveals why this system has become problematic. But so long as his assumptions hold, the scheme clearly benefits all generations. Indeed, by ensuring that the elderly get a larger pension than most would be able to afford by their own efforts, it distributes wealth to a group that tends to be among the least well off. Why should we not agree with Gaspart and Gosseries that such redistributions among generations are not only allowable but should be required as a matter of justice?

An obvious reason for rejecting this idea is that we cannot be certain that younger generations—particularly those who are as-yet unborn—will be in a position to assume the burdens that we impose on them. Samuelson's first assumption—about population growth—is no longer true in many countries; and his second, more important, assumption about increasing wealth has become questionable, given the environmental problems that we face. But even if we had no reason to disbelieve Samuelson's projections, something unanticipated could happen to upset them. Our successors could be impoverished by an unforeseen disaster. Uncertainty about the future is a reason for being cautious about tapping into the wealth of future generations. But it does not seem to be a reason for not doing it at all. Samuelson, it should be noted, is not suggesting that the burdens should be equalized between the generations. The subsidies provided by future generations, he assumes, will be modest given their increased wealth. He leaves room for error in estimates about how wealthy they will be. Moreover, the policy can be adjusted if calculations drastically change, as Goodin notes. Present generations can be required to contribute more. Similarly, if we take out a long-term loan and then discover reasons for thinking that we are imposing unjust burdens on future generations, we can take steps to lessen this burden in conformity to the fair shares principle. Imposing debts on future people involves risks, and people have different opinions about what risks can be justified. But unless we think it wrong to engage in any risky course of action (which, as we shall see, is a requirement impossible to fulfil), uncertainty about the future does not seem to give us reason to reject all policies that require younger generations to subsidise older generations.

Kenneth Peter regards Jefferson's prohibition of intergenerational debt as a means of protecting the natural right to liberty of future citizens. 'Long-term debt violates natural law because one group of persons (the previous generation) removes some of the liberty of another (the next generation) without their consent' (2002: 375). Taking into account objections raised by Madison, Peter allows that incurring a public debt is permissible in some circumstances—but only when doing so is necessary to protect the life or liberty of future as well as present citizens. Defending free institutions against aggression would be an obvious example. But any potential for benefits must be weighed 'against a strong presumption that long-term debt is contrary to natural right' (380). Bruce Auerbach is somewhat less stringent, stipulating that debt can be incurred for projects that benefit future generations, but like Peter he is concerned about the way in which public debt can limit the freedom of future citizens (1995: 196ff). Neither allows a policy that forces younger generations to subsidise benefits that are wholly or mostly enjoyed by older generations—whatever the relative wealth of the generations.

There are several ways of interpreting this appeal to the freedom of future generations. The strongest is an objection against the very idea that resources can be extracted from a generation without its consent. When Peter stresses the separation between generations as a morally significant factor he seems to be supporting this view. The appeal to freedom can also be understood as a complaint about the way that long-term debt unduly restricts the freedom of future citizens to use their resources as they please. This is the criticism that Auerbach levels against the Reagan Administration in the United States, which drastically increased public debt. Or it could be understood in a more Jeffersonian way as an objection against taxation without representation—that is, an objection to policies that force compliance from those who are not in the position to participate in democratic decision-making.

'BENEFITTERS SHOULD PAY'

The idea that it is unjust to extract resources from members of young and future generations without their consent is sometimes appealed to by those who participate in the debates about policies for coping with demographic change. The Australian Government report, mentioned in Chapter 8, seems to adopt this view when it insists that governments should balance their budgets and declares that it would be inequitable for the current generation of tax payers to impose a higher tax burden on their successors. Justice, so conceived, requires that each generation pay for the benefits it receives, and it prohibits imposing costs on younger generations. A pension or social security scheme, according to this view, should not take the form extolled by Samuelson. It should not be a means by which wealthy younger generations transfer resources to poorer older generations. Rather it should take the form of a government-regulated insurance scheme that requires people to save for their own retirement, and participants should expect to get out of it more or less what they put in (plus the interest earned by their savings). They can reasonably complain if their expectations are not fulfilled (Thomson 1992).

The obvious objection to this conception of justice is that it flouts reasonable requirements of distributional justice. If it is accepted that members of a generational cohort can be called upon to subsidise each other according to relative advantages or wealth, then what is wrong with members of a wealthier generational cohort being required to subsidise the pensions and other benefits of members of an older generation? If cooperation is the basis for distributive justice among contemporaries (as Rawls believes), then surely it is equally the basis for justice among members of the generational cohorts who are cooperating to maintain intergenerational institutions and other goods.

On closer examination it becomes clear that a conception of justice that requires each cohort to pay for the benefits it receives is really a requirement that each individual should pay for himself or herself. Generational cohorts are, after all, nothing more than groups of individuals who share an approximate birth date, and what counts as a generational cohort is always open to redefinition. Baby-boomers are customarily regarded as belonging to the same cohort, but in many countries, more children were born in the first five years after World War II than in the following five years. So it seems that younger baby-boomers can reasonably complain that they as a cohort are contributing more than their fair share to an insurance scheme that gives the cohort of early baby-boomers more than their fair share. People born in 1947 might be able to complain that they are unfairly subsidising the pensions of people born in 1946; people born in June 1947 can say that they are unfairly subsidising the pensions of those born in July, and so on. By the same reasoning any individual should be entitled to complain if he is subsidising any other individual. So reduced, it becomes obvious that we are dealing with a libertarian view about justice—except that governments attracted to the user-pays philosophy often want to make it mandatory that individuals save for their own retirement.

Libertarianism, as we have seen, is not an attractive political philosophy for an intergenerational society, but it is also important to note that a user-pays scheme, which attempts to impose the costs of care on those who benefit, is not likely to succeed in this aim. A government which chooses to cut spending on the aged in order to save younger tax payers money is likely to impose other kinds of burdens on younger generations by forcing members of families, especially women, to take more responsibility for care. Even if people are required to save money for their own retirement, bad health, senility or, in many cases, poverty are likely to force many of them to fall back on their families, if indeed they have that option.

LIBERTY AND DEMOCRATIC RIGHTS

The Jeffersonian reason for thinking that intergenerational debts wrongly limit the freedom of future citizens appeals to their rights to participate in making decisions about the burdens imposed on them. His objection seems particularly compelling when citizens are forced to pay for policies that they regard as mistaken or wrong—for example, to pay for a war that they do not believe was just. But the objection does not depend on whether they agree or disagree with the reason for going into debt. The problem is that they never had an opportunity for consent or dissent. Thomas Pogge argues that democratic citizens ought not to be held responsible for the debts of a previous authoritarian regime over which they could exercise no control (2008: 159–60). Why then should present citizens have to pay the debts of their predecessors?

I argued in Chapter 6 that citizens as members of an intergenerational polity inherit responsibilities and entitlements from their predecessors. Their predecessors can make legitimate demands that they are required to fulfil. Present citizens are responsible for keeping commitments made by past generations and for making recompense for past injustices. The fact that they never had a chance to consent to these obligations is no reason to deny that they exist. This does not mean that citizens are never entitled to repudiate an inherited debt. They may have a justification to do so if paying the debt would impose unacceptable burdens on them or if those who lent their predecessors money knew that it would be used for purposes harmful to future generations. It would clearly be unjust for present generations to inflict an onerous debt on their successors or to engage in projects that will harm future citizens. But the democratic rights of citizens do not preclude intergenerational debts, and the democratic rights of citizens cannot prevail over a duty to fulfil requirements of justice. If Gaspart and Gosseries are right to maintain that justice can *require* intergenerational transfers, then an appeal to democratic rights ought not to stand in the way.

The complaint made by Auerbach that debt can unduly restrict the ability of citizens to make free decisions provides a good ground for criticising *some* acts that impose debts on future generations. If debts inherited from predecessors stand in the way of future citizens acting justly, maintaining institutions of justice or other things that they have inherited as an intergenerational good, then they are clearly unjust according to the fair shares principle. But a debt can also unjustly interfere with the freedom of future citizens in other ways. It can prevent them from embarking on individual or collective projects of their own, from making resources available to pursue collective goods, or simply from engaging in enjoyable or worthy activities. For members of a liberal democratic polity, the freedom to make such decisions is highly valued, and justice requires that the institutions and goods that we transfer to our successors ensure that their freedom to make democratic decisions is no less than our own. Debts that violate this principle are unjust. But obeying this requirement does not preclude transfers of resources from wealthy younger generations to less wealthy older generations. By making such a transfer we would be increasing our liberty at the expense of theirs, but if they are going to be better off than we are, then we are not bringing it about that their freedom will be less than ours.

COOPERATION AND FREE-RIDING

So far we have not found any reason in principle why it would be wrong to adopt policies that transfer resources from younger to older generations. We have not even found reasons to oppose the view of Gaspart and Gosseries that such transfers may be required by considerations of justice. But it is not hard to think of transfers that most of us would judge to be wrong even though they do not seem to violate the fair shares principle. Suppose that our offshore oil reserves, which we have so far not bothered to develop, have the potential to make our successors much richer than us. So we take out some long-term loans from the contemporary equivalent of the money lenders in Genoa and we spend the money on the fetes, festivals and fireworks displays that we enjoy so much (buying what we need mostly from foreign manufacturers), secure in the knowledge that even after paying our debt our successors will be no worse off than us. We allow public institutions to deteriorate on the grounds that our wealthy successors will be in a better position to pay for their upkeep. Our festive enjoyments may do economic harm to present people; our neglect of public institutions is likely to disadvantage those who now use them. The issue in question is whether we are imposing unjust costs on our successors—even if their wealth allows them to bear the burden without significant sacrifices.

Auerbach believes that a generation that behaves irresponsibly toward its successors is acting in a way that is destructive of its intergenerational community. If we fail to take into consideration the interests of future members, we make it less likely that they will value the traditions they inherit, fulfil our commitments or continue our projects. 'Future generations are likely to give us our due by reviling us and abandoning our institutions as unworthy of preservation' (1995: 225). He lays it down that we should define our intergenerational obligations in terms of a 'categorical imperative': 'We ought to act towards future generations in such a way that future generations are most likely to chose voluntarily to honour the commitments and build upon the moral traditions of their ancestors (225)'. His discussion makes it clear that following this rule is not simply a matter of prudence: that we should concern ourselves with the interests of future generations so that they will be more likely to maintain things that we happen to value. Given that we believe that our institutions are just, given that other intergenerational communities are depending on the commitments being kept, actions which predispose our successors to abandon these goods are morally irresponsible. Moreover, they involve an injustice to past generations who built for the future and wanted the things that they regarded as good to be available to future generations.

Auerbach's criticisms are directed at present generations whose irresponsibility is likely to cause serious harm to their successors. The people in my story are not committing such terrible wrongs. However, they are free-riding on the wealth of their successors and, in so doing, are showing a lack of concern for the maintenance of an intergenerational community. Their successors are likely to see little difference between them and a generation whose selfishness causes serious harm. If these successors are encouraged to follow in their footsteps and treat their own successors with a similar lack of regard, then the polity as an intergenerational community bound together by the project of maintaining institutions of justice and other things that its citizens regard as valuable will be undermined. The fair shares principle should be understood to encompass Auerbach's categorical imperative: we should do what is in our power to ensure that our successors are no less able and predisposed to maintain these things.

This requirement has implications for our intergenerational practices. It does not imply that intergenerational debts are forbidden, but it does require that we be careful about imposing them. In general it would be a good idea to do as Auerbach says: to incur debts only for objectives that will also benefit our successors, for the maintenance of an intergenerational project or in those cases where a practice, like the one described by Samuelson, is beneficial to each generation, and then to be alert for any factors that might cause the situation to change. This conservative policy has implications for how polities should deal with demographic change. If we think that younger generations will be wealthier then us, then it may not be unjust to force them to support a large cohort of elderly. But given uncertainties about the future and given the importance of demonstrating that we are responsible citizens of an intergenerational polity, it would be morally wise to take steps to alleviate the burden.

BENEFITING FUTURE GENERATIONS

The fair shares principle tells us to ensure that future generations will be no more burdened than us. It does not forbid us from engaging in actions that will make them better off—by increasing their wealth, taking on a larger share of the burden of reforming institutions or repairing environmental damage, or by transferring to them a larger share of the things that we regard as good. In this respect, it conforms to a common idea about our relationship with our successors: that it would be a good thing for us to make their lives better. Beckerman and Pasek think that this asymmetry in our conception of intergenerational justice shows how little we value equality between generations (2001: 50). The prospect that our successors may have fewer burdens, better lives or more freedom does not bother us. However, Gaspart and Gosseries point out that saving for future generations under conditions of reasonable affluence locks up resources that could be used to improve the well-being of our least well off contemporaries. How can that be just?

A distributive practice is not unjust if people—including members of less well-off groups—generally endorse it. Since most people care about the well-being of their descendants, the future of their projects and the flourishing of their communities, it is reasonable for them to endorse a policy of saving, or to accept extra burdens in order to allow their successors to enjoy more of the things that they value. Moreover, uncertainty about the future and the prudent desire to ensure that successors will have sufficient resources to meet any challenge that they might face makes it wise to save. The fair shares principle reflects these considerations.

A question remains about the limitations we should impose on moral theories for the sake of accommodating conditions in the real world. Should we accept the fair shares principle? Or should we instead accept an *equal* shares principle which requires, under conditions of reasonable affluence, that no generation should have a greater share of burdens or benefits than any other generation, but allows that, in practice, people will or should depart from this principle for prudential, altruistic or other reasons? Which we accept will make no difference to our practices and policies. However, there are philosophical reasons for preferring the fair shares principle. A moral theory is ideal in the sense that its prescriptions are not falsified by the fact that people do not always obey them. But in formulating prescriptive principles, a theory should take into account human propensities, including the interests that people are likely to have, and the difficulties they are likely to face when putting principles into practice. Its idealisations should not lose contact with reality. People generally have lifetime-transcending interests; they have to act in a world where the future—especially the more distant future—is uncertain. The fair shares principle better conforms to these facts about our interests and our situation.

GENERATIONAL SHARES AND POPULATION

I have argued that the fair shares principle provides the best understanding of how generations in a polity should share the burdens of maintaining institutions of justice and other goods. But attempts to apply it must take into account another problem of demography. Generational cohorts, as I have emphasised, are owed no duties in their own right. Our duties are to their members. We ought to act to ensure that the members of succeeding generations will bear no greater burdens than members of present generations. We do not necessarily fulfil our duties by passing on to our successors the same amount of wealth or other goods as we enjoy. If the birth rate increases and succeeding generations are larger but no wealthier, then they will bear heavier burdens. Having more children, in other words, can be a way of increasing the burdens imposed on future generations. Our reasoning about intergenerational justice must take population issues into account, and the making of people raises ethical problems that require a closer examination.

10 Creating Future Generations

The creation of people, or the failure to create them, is a factor that can make a crucial difference to the persistence of just relationships through the generations. Population growth might impose unfair burdens on succeeding generations by increasing pressure on the environment, using up vital resources or by putting a heavy demand on social resources. Population decline might result in smaller generational cohorts having to bear the burden of supporting larger generational cohorts in conditions where this burden is not offset by greater wealth. It is not necessary to agree with the fair shares principle to have a concern about population. If a population were to grow or decline to such an extent that future generations are no longer in a position to maintain institutions of justice or other things of value, then this would constitute a breakdown in relationships of justice, however we define it. Since the creation of people is something under our control, causing these harms would be an injustice to our successors. Like the irresponsible parents Stan and Janet (discussed in Chapter 2) we would do them wrong even though many of the people we bring into existence wouldn't have existed if we had done the right thing. A theory of intergenerational justice cannot avoid a discussion of population issues.

There is another reason why population growth or decline is a concern for anyone who theorises about justice. A theory of justice presumes that just relationships between contemporaries and the requirements of intergenerational justice can be made compatible. It aims to show that if we are just to our contemporaries we will not be unjust to our successors, and that by being just to our successors we will not be unjust to our contemporaries. We have seen that there are tensions between these two 'domains' of justice. Saving for future generations means that a society has less to distribute to its least well-off members. Bequest and inheritance, which I have argued that an intergenerational polity ought to support, seem at odds with equality of opportunity. But these tensions can be overcome, or at least resolved well enough in theory and practice, by recognising that citizens, including the least well off, have an interest in the well-being of their successors, and that inheritance rights can be recognised in a way that gives due weight to lifetime-transcending interests but does not seriously compromise equality of opportunity (which is, after all, also a concern of intergenerational justice). However, the ethical issues raised by population growth or decline point to a more intractable conflict between justice to contemporaries and the demands of intergenerational justice. Intergenerational justice may require that we impose controls on population—decreasing or increasing the number of people in the next generations. But the means of control are likely to be unjust to present people in one way or another.

CONTROLLING POPULATION GROWTH

Suppose that we have determined that a population of about ten million is all that can be sustained in our polity if future generations are to maintain institutions of justice and other goods that they value, including environmental goods. This is the view held by Tim Flannery about the sustainable population size of Australia, a country which now contains over 20 million people (1994: 371–4). It would, of course, be unthinkable for the government to cull the population or to force people to emigrate, so reducing the population size would have to be regarded as an intergenerational project, each generation doing its share to reduce the birth rate until the desired level is reached. But if the environmental problems are urgent (as Flannery believes), then the controls that each generation must impose on itself need to be stringent. The polity itself will have to make population reduction a priority. But the means of control that it is going to have to exercise is likely to be unjust to individuals who, according to the United Nations, have a right to make free decisions about procreation (United Nations 1994: Section 7.3). Hence, there is an irresolvable incompatibility between justice to contemporaries and intergenerational justice.

This argument can be challenged by denying that the problem or incompatibility really exists, denying the existence of a 'right to procreate' or by claiming that one of the requirements of justice takes precedence (Kates 2004: 62). Those who hold the latter position would deem it no injustice if the subordinate requirement has to give way to the superior principle. I will argue that none of these challenges is likely to succeed.

Some of those who think that there is no need to decide between right of procreation and justice for future generations do so because they believe that technological advances and economic growth will always be sufficient to offset the effects of population growth. Others believe that a population control policy is unnecessary because social developments, such as urbanisation, education of women, the higher cost of children, etc.—developments which have occurred in many countries—result in people having fewer children by choice (Sen 2001: Chapter 8). Indeed, as we have seen, the problem that concerns many governments is population decline, not population growth.

Neither of these positions seems convincing enough to persuade us to put the problem aside. It is difficult to believe that the earth will have sufficient resources to cater to a population that might be many times larger than the present world population, especially if people in poor as well as wealthy countries are to have a chance to satisfy their needs and live in a just society. And even if our successors are able to live a decent life in a crowded world, they are likely to lack many of the good things that we think people of all generations ought to be able to enjoy—especially the ability to enjoy nature. The decline in birth rate, which in any case has not occurred in all countries, may not be sufficient to achieve sustainability if environmentalists like Flannery are even partly right. The empirical issues are obviously complex. But since the central concerns of this study are moral and philosophical, I will not try to determine what views about a sustainable population are correct. For one reason or another, a polity may be fortunate enough to escape problems of population during part, or even all, of its existence. It may never have a need to introduce population control measures. But the difficulty for a theory of justice remains. Intergenerational justice seems to require that the population be controlled if the well-being of future generations is threatened and this is incompatible with a view of individual rights that says that such measures should not be adopted. The moral issue, even if it remains merely theoretical, needs discussion.

Some people think that the problem doesn't exist because they believe that there are effective means of limiting births that are not unjust to individuals. Preventing a person from having a child, or forcing her to have one, interferes in a drastic way with her freedom. But providing people with contraceptives and information actually enhances their ability to make a free choice. And if doing this is not enough, there are other methods that fall well short of the use of force. Propaganda about birth control does not deny people the ability to choose, and neither do incentive or disincentive schemes which either reward people for not having children or penalise them for doing so. These measures merely put pressure on people to change their behaviour or they alter the factors that people have to take into account when they choose. Let us accept that providing people with contraceptives and information is a good thing. Whether using techniques of persuasion or incentive schemes count as just depends on whether they unjustly constrain the ability of people to make truly free decisions or whether they unjustly affect the least well-off people of a society, whose choices are much more constrained by financial incentives or disincentives than are the choices of wealthier people. Wissenburg believes that a vigorous birth control campaign wrongly interferes with the ability of people to make up their own minds about procreation, and is thus incompatible with liberal views about justice (1998: 155). Those who hold a Rawlsian or some other egalitarian view of justice are likely to be concerned about a policy that puts greater constraints on the actions of the least well off. But how we make a judgment about these matters is likely to be affected by our reasons (or lack of them) for believing that individuals have a 'right to procreate'.

FREEDOM OF PROCREATION

There are two closely related ways of arguing that the freedom of individuals to make procreative decisions is fundamental and ought to be regarded as a right that cannot be abridged by an appeal to the general good. The first appeals to the profound effect that procreation has on the shape of a person's life, a woman's relation to her body and her connection with others; the second appeals to a person's lifetime-transcending interest in perpetuating something of herself or himself into the future or in being part of a generational continuum.

For most people having children is a profound experience that shapes their life, their identity and their relationships. They regard their children as central to the meaning of their lives. Their relationship with their children and the nature of the task of raising them predisposes them to take this view. The relationship between parent and child is one of the most demanding and intimate relationships that one individual can have with another. Moreover, children require care over a long period of time, a commitment that is likely to have a great effect on a person's life. Some people would prefer not to make this commitment or have other ideas about how to find meaning in life. But the importance of the decision for those who make it and the nature of the commitment are good reasons why people should not be forced to have children or be prevented from doing so. Making such a life-changing and personal decision ought to be left to those directly concerned.

A further reason of this kind for leaving decisions about having children up to individuals has to do with bodily integrity and the relationship of a woman to her body—particularly her sexuality. How a woman uses her body and expresses her sexuality is intimately related to her identity as a person. A violation of her sexuality—rape, for example—is a violation of her person that is experienced as different in kind from any violation of her property rights. Forced abortion is a comparable violation, particularly since a desired pregnancy involves an intimate relationship between a prospective mother and a being which she and others come to think of more and more as a person as the time for its birth approaches. Forcing a person to practice contraception, or to have a tubal ligation or vasectomy—though these interferences are not so serious—nevertheless count as violations of bodily integrity, and are not acceptable in a just society.

The second type of defence for a right of procreation appeals to the relationship of individuals to the future, including the future beyond their lifetime. Begetting children and forming their identity, says David Heyd, creates value by making the world a place in which value exists (1992: 212). The existence of future people who value themselves and things in the world assures the continued existence of values, and Heyd thinks that individuals have an interest in this continuation. 'Begetting children is a sort of self-expansion, an attempt to extend one's existence, a guarantee for a kind of continuity of the self beyond its individual-biological bounds' (213). He adds that there is great value for many people in regarding themselves as being part of a chain of generations, past as well as future. Procreation is participation in this continuum.

Heyd is appealing to what I have described as lifetime-transcending interests. The decision to have children is obviously productive of these interests—people generally care about the future fate of their children—and the decision is also often motivated, at least in part, by a desire to relate oneself to the future as well as the past. By having children, as Heyd says, people often regard themselves as participating in an intergenerational enterprise or contributing to a community or a family. People can, of course, participate in or contribute to such an enterprise in other ways. But having children is for many people the most satisfying and accessible means of participation.

These reasons for insisting that freedom to procreate is sufficiently important to be regarded as a right are reinforced by another consideration. In a liberal political society, government is supposed to exist for the people and not the people for the government. Laws and institutions should respect the needs and freely determined purposes of individuals. They should not dictate to individuals what their purposes ought, or ought not, to be. For the sake of protecting others, governments have to put some limits on the goals that individuals can pursue or the way they pursue them, but governments should be particularly loath to interfere with the pursuit of objectives that are highly personal, bound up with the identity of individuals and their religious or communal traditions or have to do with a woman's intimate relation to others and to her own body. Attempts to control procreation—at least those that involve forceful methods—would violate the understanding on which liberal government is based.

POPULATION AND MORAL DILEMMA

We have good reasons for condemning population control policies that involve forcible interference with procreative choices and behaviour. Concerns about privacy, bodily integrity and the limits of government do not so obviously rule out non-coercive policies—for example, the use of incentives to encourage small families or disincentives to discourage large families. These policies would constrain choice, but this in itself is not unjust. The right to procreation cannot require that people be unconstrained in choices about having children. However, constraints imposed by governments raise issues of justice when they prevent people from making a choice that is widely believed to be of great personal significance and when this constraint is experienced only by those who are less well off. Incentive and disincentive schemes constrain the choices of the poor much more drastically than the choices of the rich. The ability of the poor to make decisions about having children would be reduced, perhaps entirely undermined—at least so long as they want to be responsible parents. Moreover, nothing that a society can offer to those whose choices are limited by constraints counts as adequate compensation for the inability to have the children that they want.

The conclusion toward which we are heading is the one that many people have endorsed: that governments should not forcibly interfere with the ability of parents to make free choices about procreation, and they should also avoid population control measures that have unfair consequences. A government campaign that aims to encourage people to have fewer children through education or persuasion is probably not incompatible with freedom of procreation, despite the worries of Wissenburg about government propaganda. But more vigorous attempts to constrain choice are unjust for one reason or another.

If this conclusion is right, then a potential conflict exists between the requirements of intergenerational justice and justice to existing individuals. The problem that this creates for a theory of justice cannot be solved by contending that the welfare of future generations should prevail over an individual's freedom to procreate. Even if we decide that this is true, the injustice remains. The state of affairs created by the conflict is similar in many ways to the much-discussed clash between the desire to prevent harm to large numbers of people and the right of individuals not to be tortured. In a particular circumstance it might be judged that it is better to torture, but even if this is the right moral decision (and many people would dispute it), the rights of those who are tortured are being violated.

Not all methods of controlling population are equally bad. Daniel Callahan ranks them in an order of moral preference (1976: 34–5).[1] If education is not successful in curbing population growth, then the intervention that is least unjust, in his opinion, is an incentive scheme that rewards parents for having fewer children. Less preferable is a disincentive scheme that punishes people for having too many children and worst of all is a scheme that dictates whether a couple can have children and how many they can have. If it turns out that the only way of effectively controlling a growth in population that would have dire effects on future generations is by implementing the coercive policy, then members of a polity are faced with a difficult moral choice, and what they should do is not obvious.

This moral dilemma is an aspect of a wider difficulty that lurks in the background (and sometimes comes to the foreground) of discussions of intergenerational justice. From an intergenerational perspective, children born and raised are a social resource necessary for the continued existence of a just society and for the fulfilment of intergenerational requirements of justice. A polity has a vital interest in managing this resource and ensuring that it exists in the right quantity. But its production cannot be treated in the same way as the production of other resources that an intergenerational society needs. Even to describe children as 'social assets' or 'a resource' seems ethically incorrect.

When we take an intergenerational perspective it seems obvious that justice requires that society have some control over the production of children and that members of society should share the burdens of their production and education. Parents, especially mothers, who often make heavy financial and personal sacrifices to raise children, are making an important and necessary contribution to their society—a contribution for which they surely ought to be compensated.[2] However, from a perspective that takes seriously freedom of procreation and the entitlement of family members to raise children according to their values, it seems reasonable to insist that people should be able to make free choices about having and raising children, that they should bear the burden of their choices and that governments should hesitate to interfere. If a society were to compensate parents for all of the economic and social costs of having children, this would not only mean that parents might have more children than is compatible with justice to future generations. It would also take away responsibilities that are supposed to go along with the right to procreate. If individuals are free to procreate and society has to accept a large share of the responsibility for the consequences, then the push to circumscribe or even eliminate this freedom would be hard to resist—especially if the dangers of over-population are widely recognised.

The only practical solution is a compromise that allows the polity to influence choices about procreation and to insist on the fulfilment of standards of care as far as the raising of children is concerned. There is a good case for saying that a polity should provide some compensation to parents for having and raising children, but there is also a case for saying that compensation should fall far short of making up for their sacrifices. As in other matters concerning the family, any resolution of the problem has to adjudicate between competing claims and there is no way of providing a general principle that tells us what form the compromise should take.

DO WE HAVE A DUTY TO CREATE FUTURE GENERATIONS?

Environmentalists are worried about populations exceeding ecological limits. But there could be circumstances in which a population becomes too small. In some countries of the developed world the birth rate has become so low that citizens are not replacing themselves, and in response, some governments have introduced measures to encourage the birth of more children. Given the growth of world population and the large environmental impact of people in affluent societies, such policies can be criticised as short-sighted or even, in some contexts, racist. But these responses not only force citizens to consider whether and how the costs of making future citizens should be shared; they also raise the question of whether people can have a *duty* to procreate.

Suppose that a small, culturally distinct community living on an island is almost wiped out by a natural disaster, leaving a number of older people and a half a dozen young couples. If the young couples do not have children, the survivors are faced with the prospect that the traditions and institutions that they value, and that their predecessors sacrificed themselves to maintain, will cease to exist. From their point of view (using Heyd's way of speaking), they face the prospect of a future in which value—or at least the value they care about—has disappeared from the world. Are the young couples in this circumstance under an obligation to have children?

If the death of the community means that its values disappear from the world, then no one will be able to appreciate them in the future. But if no one is going to be deprived by the absence of these values, then what difference does this make? The rights of present community members are not being violated, nor are the rights of non-members, and it cannot be a duty to bring the unborn into existence. Feinberg argues that no one would have such duty even if the human race itself were threatened with extinction: 'My inclination then is to conclude that the suicide of our species would be deplorable, lamentable, and a deeply moving tragedy, but that it would violate no one's *rights*' (1980a: 220). The people of the imagined community may also lament the end of their community, but surely their regrets cannot override the right of individuals to decide that they do not want to procreate.

However, the rights of existing or future people are not the only matters to take into consideration. Since community members believe that it is important to pass on goods to their successors and to enable successors to inherit their projects and other things that they value, and since they think that they are entitled to impose obligations on their successors, then shouldn't they also regard themselves as having a duty to ensure that there are successors? It seems that the view of intergenerational justice that I am defending can give people a duty to procreate. If so, we have another reason to believe in the existence of an incompatibility between well-motivated views about individual rights and communal requirements in an intergenerational society.

However, it is important to recognise that the right of individuals to make their own decisions about procreation is not incompatible with them also having an obligation, in particular circumstances, to have children. Having a right means that others have a responsibility not to violate it (and perhaps other responsibilities as well). But there is nothing illogical, or even untoward, about believing that a person ought not, on a particular occasion, to exercise a right. You can have a right to do wrong, as Jeremy Waldron says, and since it is your duty to do right, in doing wrong you would be failing to fulfil a duty (1993: Chapter 3). Although this is morally bad, you are within your rights, and that means that no one is entitled to force you to do your duty.

For example, if a couple marries with the agreement that they will have children together, each of them acquires an obligation to fulfil their part of the agreement, and it would be wrong for one of the partners to refuse without a good reason. Having a right to procreation means that the wronged partner should not *force* the other to fulfil the obligation, but he or she can reasonably criticise the other for not doing so, and may be justified in seeking a separation. So if the young couples of the island community value their intergenerational communal institutions, if these institutions are indeed worthy of being valued and if they appreciate the efforts of their predecessors to provide things of value for succeeding generations and think that these things ought to be maintained, then the couples ought to acknowledge an obligation to procreate (unless they have overriding reasons for not doing so). The tension between recognition of individual rights and the interests of an intergenerational community exists because the community is not entitled to *require* that the couples reproduce or to use its means of enforcement to ensure that it happens. But it is reasonable to suppose that individuals who value their community and are in the position to have children will want to do so. The same point can be made about population reduction. A government ought not to use its powers to prevent people from having children; this would be a violation of their rights. But good citizens, recognising the need to limit population growth, ought to acknowledge a duty to contribute to the solution. Whether their sense of duty—so far as it exists—would solve the problem is another matter.

HUMAN SURVIVAL

Suppose that a comet hits the earth and very few human beings survive. However, the earth remains habitable and although conditions are now bad, future people could thrive and live good lives. Do the survivors have a duty to avoid the lamentable extinction of the human race? The reasons for thinking so are weaker then the reasons for believing that the young island couples have a duty to procreate. The survivors have no common community, no traditions to maintain; the good things that their former communities maintained have been destroyed.

If we hold that human life is intrinsically valuable, Bruce Auerbach says, then we should regard as morally problematic the demise of the human race. To procreate is a good thing, and it would be a particularly good thing for the few surviving humans (1995: 116). However, Auerbach shies away from making procreation a duty. To do so, he thinks, would be to buy into the utilitarian objective of maximising a good and all the problems associated with it. In particular, he objects to the way that this objective treats individuals as a means to an end. He concludes that procreation is a supererogatory act as far as morality is concerned. People have an imperfect duty to do good in their lives, and bringing children into the world and raising them well is one way of fulfilling this duty. The survivors of the comet might be persuaded that they can do good in their lives by having children. On the other hand, they might decide that the imperfect duty, so far as it exists, cannot demand of them the sacrifice and commitment involved in bearing and raising children under difficult, unsafe circumstances. Let us agree that this is so. Suppose, however, that these people make an agreement to set up an intergenerational polity. As a corollary of this agreement, it is reasonable to suppose that the parties to the agreement who are in the position to have and raise healthy children acquire an obligation, in the same way as do individuals who marry with the understanding that they will have children together.

Auerbach thinks that it is wrong to bring children into existence to serve an end, and if he is right, then the motivations of the islanders and the founders of the intergenerational polity look questionable. We should not procreate in order to have successors. But Auerbach's position rests on a confusion. Children are ends in themselves and ought to be raised and educated so that they can take their place in society as equal citizens and autonomous individuals. But children are produced in the first place because parents want to fulfil themselves, continue a family line, establish a connection with the future or for other personal, familial or communal reasons—as Heyd emphasises. Procreation, in one way or another, serves the interests of existing people or fulfils their sense of duty. But this is compatible with the insistence that children, once they are born (or as some people would say, once they are conceived) ought to be treated as ends in themselves.

PRODUCING QUALITY CHILDREN

Present generations not only determine the number of children who come into existence, they also influence what kind of individuals they become. Parents and societies do so in traditional ways by bringing them up and giving them an education. But as direct control over the selection or genetic constitution of embryos becomes more feasible, parents or societies have a greater potential to determine the biological nature of the next generations. There are methods available for detecting the existence of serious genetic abnormalities in foetuses, thus enabling a pregnancy to be terminated if the parents wish. It is now technically possible for parents to choose the sex of their child. In the future, according to some biotechnologists, they might be able to make choices about other characteristics of their offspring: height, body shape or even musical talent, intelligence and emotional traits.

These projections may be based on false ideas about the origin of desired traits, or they may depend on developments that are not technologically feasible or are too risky. But the very idea that the physical, intellectual and emotional characteristics of offspring could be influenced or determined by technological manipulation raises difficult ethical questions. Many of them are outside the scope of a theory of intergenerational justice. However, our increasing ability to select our successors and control their genetic constitution inevitably raises issues about the relationship between the generations. Some of these issues are intergenerational in the sense of being about the relationship between parents and children; others are intergenerational because they have to do with the ability of our successors to maintain the institutions and goods that we value. In what follows I will concentrate mainly on the latter concern.

Parents, care-givers and educators in a liberal society have a generational duty to ensure that children will be become free and equal citizens. If the use of genetic technology undermines the ability of children to become free and equal, then it violates their entitlements and jeopardises the very future of a liberal society. Jürgen Habermas thinks that genetic enhancement techniques pose this threat. If a genetic program makes a child into a certain kind of person, he claims, then she is not the sole author of her life. This means that she cannot speak for herself nor can she regard herself as ethically free (2003: 40–1). Moreover, a genetic program gives her the status of a made object—an extension of the will of others (53–4). The consequence is that the liberal assumption that individuals encounter each other as free and equal citizens will no longer hold in an age of genetic manipulation, thus undermining the liberal democratic polity and the institutions that we pass on to our successors (26).

Critics point out that Habermas's worries seem to be based on an overly deterministic idea of what genetic manipulation can accomplish (Agar 2004: 116–20). A child, however programmed, will have her own experiences and desires. She will develop a mind of her own and will have no difficulty making critical judgments about her parents' intentions. She does not have to use her skills and propensities to become the sort of person that they want her to be. She can rebel against her parents' attempt to determine her future by means of genetic technology just as she can rebel against their attempt to determine her future through education. Moreover, the nature of a child's genes is only one factor influencing her characteristics. Genetic programming cannot make her similar to the outcome of a manufacturing process in any way that would make her less worthy of respect than her fellows. But the problem with Habermas's position is not so much that it propounds a false idea about genetic determination, but that it puts forward an unreal conception of what it takes to be an autonomous person. None of us are the sole authors of our ethical lives. Our genetic constitution, the experiences of early childhood, the values that we imbibe from our parents and community—all of these factors beyond our control affect the way we feel, think and act. No one is in the position to criticise and reject all of the influences that have contributed to making her the kind of person that she is—nor would it make sense to do this (Harris 2007: 140).

However, there is a psychological truth embedded in Habermas's worries about parental influence on the future of their children. Parents have children for reasons that have to do with their interests, lives and relations to others. They may hope for a child that will fulfil their expectations, continue their projects or realise their goals. There is nothing wrong with having such desires. Nevertheless, they must also enable their children to become free and equal individuals—the independent subjects of a life who are entitled to choose their own destiny (Feinberg 1980b). For the sake of their child's autonomy, they must restrain their attempts to exercise control over her life and decisions—more and more so as she grows up.

So long as it is assumed that children will have predispositions and talents which are different from those of their parents, or different from what their parents could have predicted, it is not so difficult to regard them as independent beings, and not so difficult to resist the temptation to be controlling. The worry about genetic enhancement that Habermas misstates is that when parents have more control over the genetic constitution of their children, the temptation to try to take control of their lives will be harder to resist. People (not just parents) will be less inclined to regard children as independent beings; they will be less inclined to fulfil their responsibility to nurture and educate children so that they can make their own choices and live their own lives—and this will be so even if they have a false idea about what genetic manipulation can accomplish. If this is so, then liberal society has reason to be concerned about genetic enhancement projects, not so much for the sake of its institutions, but for the sake of the right of children to an open future.

GENETIC ENHANCEMENT AND INTERGENERATIONAL JUSTICE

Nevertheless, genetic technology could become a threat to the institutions and practices of an intergenerational polity in a number of ways. To perpetuate the just institutions and practices of a liberal society and ensure that future generations are not unjustly burdened it is necessary to maintain the conditions in which these institutions can exist and flourish. These conditions include a healthy social environment. If crime or social unrest increase significantly, or if class or race antagonisms escalate, maintaining just institutions will become much more burdensome, and perhaps might disappear altogether if citizens react to insecurity by limiting civil rights and individual liberty.

Genetic selection techniques—those actually existing or those that might become possible—could have this consequence. For example, sex selection, where it leads to gender imbalance of males over females, might result in an increase in crime and other more serious social disturbances. Or genetic enhancement and selection could result in a less just society by undermining mutual respect and trust. Suppose that parents will someday be able to ensure that their children will be intelligent and highly talented—at a price. Wealthy parents will be able to afford the genetic techniques; poorer parents will not. In a few generations, most of the rewarding and influential positions in the society are likely to belong to children of the wealthy. In succeeding generations we can expect that class divisions will become more pronounced. The poor will obtain fewer of the benefits of their society and will have little hope that things will be better for their children. Even if this situation does not lead to class warfare, we can expect that some of the prerequisites of a liberal society will be increasingly absent. The privileged 'upper class' will be predisposed to think of themselves as naturally superior to members of the 'lower class', and poor people are likely to find it increasingly difficult to be treated as equal participants in a common political enterprise. Society will become less just; perhaps just institutions will disappear.

The threats to just institutions arise because genetic manipulation could produce states of affairs that predispose parents, citizens and governments to act unjustly: to violate rights or to fail to treat others as self-determining individuals. 'Enhanced' children do not lose the ability to become self-determining individuals. The worry is that parents will fail to treat them as such. Similarly the 'unenhanced' people of the lower class deserve to be treated as equal citizens. The problem is that the class system produced by genetic engineering is likely to predispose upper-class citizens to treat them unjustly and gives them the power to do so. Perhaps parents and citizens are more inclined to act justly than this pessimistic predication supposes. Indeed, if we suppose that they inhabit Rawls's ideal world where everyone always satisfies the requirements of justice, then parents will never unjustly control the lives of their children and members of a society will never take away the rights of others or fail to ensure that the least well off get their due.

Suppose, however, that the members of the upper class in the society that I have imagined feel somewhat uneasy about the injustices that they are committing and are also worried that their lower-class subjects will someday revolt. They now have the genetic technology that can render the next generation of lower-class people into docile, stupid beings who are content to do menial tasks and are incapable of understanding abstract notions like 'freedom' and 'equality'. They use this technology, and when other people in the world complain about the injustice they have committed they are not at a loss for a reply. All judgments about justice or injustice, they say, assume that certain conditions are fulfilled. They refer to Hume's idea that a necessary condition for the application of requirements of justice is a rough equality of capacities and aptitudes (1975: 190–1). Or they claim that in order to have rights of citizenship people have to be able to claim them, and then point out that lower-class people are not interested in, or capable of, claiming citizenship rights. Or they simply argue that it would be as ridiculous to extend rights of citizenship to lower-class people as it would to chimpanzees or young children.

What the people of this imagined society have done is to undermine in a fundamental way the prerequisites of institutions of justice. They have made it impossible for liberal–democratic institutions of justice to be maintained, at least for all the people of the society.[3] The technology which could accomplish this result may never exist. But the imagined society, whether fanciful or not, can be used to raise a question about the requirements of intergenerational justice. If we could render the next generations incapable of being subjects of justice, according to our standards, then it seems that we have done nothing unjust. If requirements of justice do not apply to the future society in which these people exist, then it seems that present standards cannot be used to judge whether we have violated any principles of justice.

Two paradoxes that have been discussed in earlier chapters are embedded in this reasoning. The first is the second non-identity problem. By rendering their biological successors incapable of maintaining institutions of justice, the people of the imagined society will ensure that future people are not their political successors—and by doing so they have divested themselves of duties of intergenerational justice. The second paradox, briefly discussed in Chapter 2, is about a clash of generational perspectives. If people of succeeding generations do not subscribe to our ideas about justice, how can we legitimately claim that this is a bad thing?

The first paradox can be dealt with, I suggested, by an appeal to lifetime-transcending interests. The representative generation that makes the Rawlsian intergenerational social contract knows its members are likely to have such interests. It knows that members of every generation will want successors that are capable of carrying on their projects, maintaining their communities and fulfilling their legitimate lifetime-transcending demands. It will not accept an agreement that would allow any generation to render all, or even some, of its successors incapable of doing these things. Moreover, maintaining institutions of justice is assumed to be a lifetime-transcending concern of each generation of a political society, and so the representative generation will, above all, not accept a contract that makes it impossible for later generations to maintain it. The second paradox can be disarmed by pointing out that from our perspective—as people who have reason to accept certain principles about justice—we are justified in judging that it would be a morally bad thing if future generations are unwilling or unable to respect these principles, and thus we have a duty to make sure that they are capable of doing so, insofar as we can.

The discussion in Chapter 6 provides another way of dealing with these 'paradoxes'. Members of each generation have duties in respect to past as well as future generations. Each generation can demand of its successors, including more distant successors, that they remember and make an effort to appreciate its contributions and sacrifices. But if this intergenerational duty is accepted, then each generation must also acknowledge a duty to maintain for its successors the means that will enable them to fulfil it. If, for example, a generation, in an effort to break with the past, were to destroy all the records made by past generations and all the things that they regarded as good, then this would be an injustice—not only to the past generations who maintained these things for their successors, but to future generations who will not be able to obtain their inheritance or perform their duty of appreciation. It would be similarly unjust if this generation were to render their successors unable to understand or appreciate this inheritance.

GENETIC ENHANCEMENT AND SOCIAL PROGRESS

We ought not to allow genetic engineering to be used in a way that makes it difficult or burdensome for our successors to maintain institutions of justice or makes it impossible for them to appreciate the things that we value. But could we have a duty to lessen the burden by using genetic technology, should this be available, to make it easier for people in the next generations to be just? This might be achieved by eliminating from the next generations people with disabilities that predispose them to act unjustly: psychopaths, for example.[4] But with the right kind of technology, we might be able to take positive steps designed to increase the ability of members of the next generations to act justly: to bring it about that they will be more inclined than most present people to be reasonable, far-sighted, tolerant and cooperative. A population of people who have these characteristics should find it much easier to maintain institutions of justice and other good things.

The theory of intergenerational justice that I have been defending does not require members of generations to make it easier for future generations to maintain institutions of justice. However, if we have reason to believe that our society is about to encounter difficulties and that its institutions will be under threat, we might conclude that we can best do our duty to future generations by making them more constitutionally capable of maintaining a just society. Or we might decide that it is easier to do our duty in this way rather than by taking steps to avoid the threat. Or we might decide that we have a humanitarian duty, if not a duty of justice, to bring about better conditions for our descendants. Liberals have often dreamed of creating a better, more just world through education. Why wouldn't it be just as acceptable to bring it about by genetic engineering?

It would be wrong to pursue such a project by unjust means: by forcing people to have children of the 'right' kind, or by preventing them from having children who lack genetic improvements. And it might turn out to be a mistake to allow governments to wield, and possibly abuse, such great power over the constitution of future generations. But there are additional reasons for thinking that the project is misconceived. A world full of reasonable, intelligent people like John Stuart Mill might be a good thing in some ways, but limiting in others. By producing characteristics that are supposedly good for a liberal society or by eliminating characteristics that are supposedly not so good, we would perhaps eliminate capacities that are good for other reasons.

Would the products of liberal eugenics be loving and caring as well as reasonable, tolerant and socially cooperative? Feminists have often criticised liberals for valuing characteristics that have traditionally been associated with men in the public realm. The imagined program of liberal eugenics may turn out to be a way of making characteristics associated with masculinity more dominant in the population—perhaps to the detriment of activities essential for social life. Would products of liberal eugenics be prepared to sacrifice themselves for the sake of the survival of things that they value? A propensity to go to war for one's ideals is not generally a good thing, but it would also not be good if citizens were never prepared to make great sacrifices for their values and for the well-being of others. Would products of liberal eugenics be capable of a high level of artistic creativity? It could be the case that people with many different characteristics, including those with 'illiberal' propensities, are needed to maintain a just society and other things of value. This consideration is not a reason for rejecting altogether a program of liberal eugenics, but it indicates that some attractive proposals for achieving a social good through genetic engineering could turn out to be dangerous and counter-productive.

JUSTICE, RISK AND REMOTE GENERATIONS

The projects of genetic engineering could turn out to be bad for our successors, but is this a good enough reason not to embark on them? Harris warns us that playing safe is not always the least risky strategy, and adds that 'we should not withhold palpable benefits to future generations because they cannot consent to them or because they might regret or resent our legacy' (2007: 80). The worry, however, is not merely that our interventions may turn out to be harmful to individuals of future generations, but that we might destroy the relationship between generations by producing people who are not interested in, or capable of, maintaining the institutions and goods that we have reason to value. There is more at stake than Harris allows. But the problem of decision-making that he highlights remains. How should we decide whether a possible risk is a reason for not engaging in a project that will affect future generations? This is a difficult and controversial issue, but a theory of intergenerational justice must have something to say about it.

Another issue that a theory of intergenerational justice must face has to do with our responsibilities to remote future generations. As in the case of many of our present projects, the effects of genetic engineering, good or bad, will be visited not only on our immediate successors, but also on people of the more distant future. Some of these effects may only become truly harmful or beneficial in the more distant future. This not only underlines the problem of how we should make decisions; it also raises the basic ethical question of whether we ought to concern ourselves with what might happen to people in the distant future. One of the points that environmentalists often stress is that our increasingly powerful technology makes it ethically imperative to take a longer view than do traditional theories of intergenerational justice. In Chapter 11, I will consider whether the theory that I have been defending can meet this and other challenges posed by environmentalism.

11 Sustainability and Future Generations

Environmental problems make intergenerational justice a matter of urgency. They also provide a testing ground for any theory about justice between generations. If an idea of justice has nothing to say about the serious harm that could be caused to future people by our treatment of the environment, if problems or moral considerations highlighted by environmentalists are outside its scope, then we have reason to doubt its adequacy. In this chapter I will discuss whether the theory of intergenerational justice that I have outlined in the previous chapters of the book can meet these challenges, or if not, whether it can be amended or supplemented in a way that makes it more satisfactory.

Sustainability has become the key concept of environmental discourse concerning our responsibilities to future generations. Sustainability is a contested concept and there is considerable disagreement about what ought to be sustained and how we ought to sustain it (Jacobs 1999). Chapter 7 provided a particular answer to the question of what ought to be sustained. Citizens of a polity ought to sustain their just institutions, the ability to pursue historical projects and opportunities to appreciate and enjoy things that they and their predecessors regard as worthy of appreciation, along with the resources and environmental systems needed to maintain these institutions, projects and things of value. There are four main reasons why environmentalists might object to this conception of what sustainability requires. Some will say that it does not pay sufficient attention to the maintenance of environmental values—that it treats the natural environment in a shallow way as an instrumental means of preserving social institutions and human welfare. Others are likely to complain about the apparent inadequacies of a theory of intergenerational justice that concerns itself with relationships in a polity. Sustainability requires a concern not just for the well-being of our successors, but also for distant future generations—generations that might come into existence long after our polity has ceased to exist. A theory of justice for a political society does not seem like an adequate response to environmental problems that could have very long-term effects. A theory that concerns itself with justice in a particular polity also seems incapable of dealing with sustainability as a global concern about how humans can live within the environmental capacity of the planet. Environmentalists might also wonder how the risks and uncertainties that must be faced by any attempt to put an idea of sustainability into practice will be treated by my theory of intergenerational justice. In this chapter I will deal with the first, second and fourth challenges, leaving the third—the relation of intergenerational justice to global issues—for Chapter 12.

ECO-CENTRED VALUES

Suppose that members of a future polity can sustain their institutions and the things they value by substituting the products of technology for many natural materials and processes. Using nanotechnology and other devices, they build themselves a largely artificial environment and no longer need to worry about the degradation of natural environments or the using up of non-renewable resources. In Chapter 7 I argued that natural environments are likely to be among the things that members of a polity value as an inheritance for their successors. Citizens have reasons for resisting the substitution of artifices. But some environmentalists believe that a society that does away with natural environments, however unlikely this prospect may be, is not merely failing to provide valuable experiences for successors, but that it wrongly destroys something that is valuable in its own right.

Some who take this eco-centred perspective believe that preserving natural values is a concern of justice. Peter Wenz's pluralist 'concentric' theory of justice gives us duties of justice to animals and the environment (1988: 329–31).[1] Roderick Nash thinks that rights can and should be extended to things in nature (1990: 3–7). Whether concepts of rights or justice can be meaningfully extended to cover animals, trees or eco-systems may be open to doubt. But the important issue is not whether nature or natural things can be subjects of justice, but rather whether the preservation of nature for its own sake ought to be a central concern of political societies. Rawls says that justice is the first virtue of a political society. Eco-centred environmentalists can be understood as saying that it is not the only virtue. Societies ought to be just to their citizens and those outside their borders, and they also ought to preserve values in nature.

Whether the duty to preserve species and natural systems is part of a theory of justice or is regarded as a separate duty, it will have implications for any conception of justice. It will limit the freedom of individuals to pursue their ends. It will require that resources be devoted specifically to preserving natural value. Preserving natural value through the generations will have to be added to the objectives of a polity, alongside its human-centred concerns, and there is a potential for conflict between preserving nature and ensuring that future generations will not be unfairly burdened and will obtain things that we think they ought to value.

One of the difficulties with taking the preservation of natural values as a political objective is that eco-centred environmentalists are by no means in agreement about what ought to be valued in nature. Some environmentalists think that all living individuals have value (Taylor 1986: 13). Others think that environmental systems or species are valuable in their own right (Sylvan and Bennett 1994: 142–3). Some believe that the most valuable forms of nature are those that humans have interfered with the least (Elliot 1997a: 76–83). Others value a state of affairs in which humans have achieved a harmonious and sustainable relationship with nature.² Difficulties in defining what ought to be an object of concern are inevitable once we move beyond an ethical position that values for their own sake beings that have consciousness. Uncertainty about what to value compounds a further difficulty. Many people in existing polities do not hold an eco-centred philosophy. Nor are eco-centred environmentalists able to offer reasons why everyone should become eco-centric. Given that this is so, eco-centrism is best understood as an idea of the good that some people subscribe to. A liberal state cannot make the demands of eco-centrism a focus of its concerns without violating the requirement of neutrality.

However, a mass conversion to eco-centrism or a departure from liberal neutrality is not necessary in order to hold that a polity ought to protect natural values. Citizens should accept a duty to maintain things that they have reason to value so that future generations will also have the opportunity to appreciate them, and the objects of value that citizens are likely to want to preserve will include values in nature. Also included are likely to be particular activities or ways of relating to nature: for example, forms of contemplation or recreation that require closeness to nature or rural activities that preserve traditional landscapes and ways of life.

Those who value natural environments are likely to have a number of reasons for thinking that they ought to be sustained as a heritage for future generations. Some people value nature because they subscribe to eco-centric ways of valuing. Others value natural environments and things in nature because of their beauty, their uniqueness, their relation to the country's history or simply because they regard themselves as stewards of the land of their community or nation. People can value nature for human reasons without treating it as a mere instrument. They can believe that nature is worthy of attention and respect without thinking that it has value independently of human purposes. Not all citizens are going to be persuaded that nature is worthy of respect, but the preservation of a plurality of valued objects is not only compatible with liberal neutrality, but required by intergenerational justice. In the democratic process citizens may have to choose between preserving natural values and values of some other kind, but natural values will figure in their ideas about what they owe future generations. Eco-centred environmentalists may not be happy with this human-centred way of treating natural values, but I suggest that it is the best that they can expect in the context of a liberal polity, and for political purposes it will suffice.³

GENERATIONS DISTANT IN TIME

Nuclear wastes are a threat to human life and health and will remain so, in some cases, for thousands of years into the future. There is no existing technology for making nuclear wastes safe, so they are disposed of by being put into containers and kept in storage.[4] Let us assume that this method of dealing with wastes will protect our immediate successors from nuclear contamination. But containers eventually corrode and leak, and even the safest storage facilities can be subject to earthquakes or sabotage. Even our best practices will not necessarily protect more distant future generations from harm. Richard and Val Routley argue that accumulating nuclear wastes is morally comparable to the behaviour of someone who consigns a package containing a dangerous substance to a long-distance train when he knows that it is likely that the poison will leak out before the journey comes to an end (1982: 116–8). The fact that the people who are likely to be harmed by radioactive wastes may be living 500 or even 1000 or more years from now does not, in their eyes, make our actions any less wrong. If the Routleys are right, then a theory of justice that gives us obligations to those we count as our successors seems inadequate. Even if we assume that our successors include all future generations of our polity, the temporal scope of our duties is limited. Polities do not last indefinitely. Most, if not all, of those now existing will probably not be around in 1000 years' time.

The Routleys' condemnation of the practice of burying nuclear wastes is sidestepped by those who adopt the practice—common in economics—of discounting the future by assigning decreasing values to benefits and harms that will be incurred by people in succeeding generations. According to this procedure, harms that will be incurred by the next generation count less than present harms, and those that will occur only in the distant future do not count at all in our calculations of the benefits and costs of proposed policies. Many philosophers, including the Routleys, condemn this way of accounting because it seems to imply that future people count less than present people (Cowen and Parfit 1992). But many philosophers do, in effect, discount the future by assuming that our duties do not stretch all that far into the future. As we have seen, Rawls, who in *A Theory of Justice* gives heads of families the task of being 'deputies for a kind of everlasting moral agent or institution', only expects them to stretch their goodwill over a few generations and perhaps a bit beyond (1972: 128). Similarly, Passmore claims that our duties to future generations extend only to those whom we care about: to our children and grandchildren, but not much further (1974: 87–9). De-Shalit, as we have seen, says that we have duties to those whom we conceive to be members of our community, and communities, as he admits, have temporal limitations. From an environmentalist point of view these limitations seem obviously unacceptable. Does a theory of justice for an intergenerational polity have a way of dealing with this problem?

JUSTICE AND HUMANITARIAN DUTIES

The Routleys think that we owe duties to all human individuals wherever or whenever they exist. But the first non-identity problem makes problematic their analogy between distance in space and distance in time. Whether we and our successors become increasingly dependent on the use of nuclear power or, alternatively, develop other sources of energy may make a large difference to what industries come into being, where and how people live, and thus the composition of the population. Many of the people who in a distant future generation might be harmed by nuclear wastes would never have existed at all if we had not chosen the nuclear path. But it does not follow that we have no duties in respect to distant future generations. There are (at least) two ways of understanding how they can exist. The first is to insist that we have a humanitarian duty to ensure, so far as we can, that future people, whoever they turn out to be, do not suffer from harms like radiation poisoning. The second is to extend our conception of who counts as our successors.

Duties of justice are not the only duties that we possess. If by choosing a particular course of action we can avoid bringing about a state of affairs in which some future people suffer early and painful deaths, or if we can bring it about that people will live much better lives in the future, then, all things being equal, we ought to do so. A state of affairs in which some people suffer early and painful deaths is worse than one in which no one suffers this fate; a state of affairs in which people live good lives is a desirable objective. The identities of the individuals are not relevant to these judgments. Bringing about more desirable states of affairs is not a duty of intergenerational justice, at least as I conceive it. Being just to future generations is compatible with doing nothing to *improve* the living conditions of future people, to *increase* their lifespan or to *lessen* the incidents of suffering in future generations. Nevertheless, many of us do think that we have a duty to make things better for people of future generations. We can regard this as a humanitarian duty.

Humanitarian duties exist in conjunction with duties of justice. They can also extend beyond the boundaries of justice. Let us assume that we do not have duties of justice to people who will live in 500 or more years' time. But it is reasonable to think that we have humanitarian duties to future people whoever they turn out to be and whenever they come into existence. Humanitarianism so conceived is a form of consequentialism. We ought to act to bring into existence states of affairs that will be good for future people, whoever they are, and to avoid bringing into existence states of affairs that make people suffer.

Consequentialism as an approach to moral theory faces a number of difficulties, especially when it is applied to future generations. Does it require us to maximise a good like happiness by maximising the number of future people to the point where the lives of individuals are just short of miserable—a result that Parfit calls 'repugnant' (1984: 388)? Does it require us to make great sacrifices in order to maximise the good of numerous people in future generations? The theory of justice that I am defending gives us limited duties to our successors; adding a consequentialist requirement seems to expand our duties in both space and time to unbearable and implausible proportions.

Consequentialism can probably be tailored to avoid these counter-intuitive results. To avoid the repugnant conclusion we might build into our theory an indexical relationship among values that we wish to maximise. If we want to promote the value of autonomy as well as happiness in succeeding generations (as, indeed, our view of justice requires), then we can insist that no increase in the total amount of happiness can compensate for a reduction of autonomy in future populations. Tim Mulgan argues that a form of rule utilitarianism that includes indexicals is capable of dealing with most of the problems concerning duties to future people (2006: 79).[5] A theory of intergenerational justice might find a place in such an overarching framework. Or we might deal with the problem of over-demanding and implausible duties by being 'satisfisers' rather than maximisers. We might accept a duty to avoid obvious and serious harms to distant, as well as not-so-distant, future people and a duty to do some things that will make them better off—but not to do all we can to maximise well-being or to minimise suffering.

THE GENERATIONAL CONTINUUM

Some form of consequentialism can probably be found to do the work of giving us appropriate duties to distant future generations—but at the cost of theoretical awkwardness and uncertainties about the relationship between obligations of intergenerational justice and humanitarian duties. The second, preferable strategy for dealing with the problems we can create for distant future generations is to extend our obligations of justice into the more distant future by extending our conception of who counts as our successors. There is a tension between Rawls's description of the contractors as 'deputies for a kind of everlasting moral agent or institution' and his assumption that they will be concerned only with the next few generations of that agent or institution. We can understand this limitation as a pragmatic matter. Our powers only stretch so far. By drawing our attention to the ways in which our deeds can affect people in the far future, environmentalists give us reason to extend the boundaries of our concern, and thus the temporal scope of justice. If we are concerned about the well-being of our children and grandchildren, then we should also be concerned about their ability to ensure the well-being of their children and grandchildren, and we should recognise that their concern for these descendants will include a concern that the latter will be able to ensure the well-being of *their* children and grandchildren, and so on. What we can and should do for these more distant descendants is limited but at least we have a duty of justice not to undermine their ability to carry out their duties to their descendants.

In the course of time families die out and polities come to an end. But some of the environmental problems that we are creating, like the dangers associated with nuclear wastes, will last for thousands of years. So it seems that the above attempt to extend duties of justice into the more distant future, even if successful, will inevitably fall short of what is required. To see if we can meet this objection let us consider why a family line, or any other institutions that perpetuate themselves through the generations, can be described as 'everlasting'.

Polities, communities and families have temporal boundaries. But what matters, morally speaking, are not the contingencies which bring a community or political society to an end or cause a family to die out or to be incorporated into another family, but rather a continuity of relationships, and the responsibilities that go with them, from generation to generation. When we think of a family line as continuing indefinitely into the future, we are not supposing that people born in 1000 years' time will count as members of the same family. What perpetuates itself is not a family but intergenerational relationships of entitlement and obligation, and what is significant about these relationships is that they have no temporal boundary—no definite or foreseeable end point. They can be described as a 'generational continuum'.

A generational continuum need not be familial and it can transcend the limits of a polity in time or space and exist independently of it. Members of intergenerational communities of many kinds are participants in an intergenerational continuum. They see themselves as playing their part in perpetuating a tradition, an ideal, institutions or other things of value through the generations without a foreseeable end. People who participate in an artistic tradition, whether as lovers of art or as artists, regard themselves as belonging to a generational continuum that includes people of many different nationalities and which stretches into the past—perhaps for many generations—and which, they assume, will be continued by others indefinitely into the future. Scientists similarly are part of a generational continuum and see themselves as contributing to an endeavour that past generations pursued, and that will be continued indefinitely into the future.

Everything we value and want to perpetuate will someday come to an end—if not through some historical contingency, then through the extinction of the human race or the death of our planet. But we do not know when the end will come, and furthermore, we have reason to want the things or communities we value to be perpetuated indefinitely. Lukas Meyer (1997) thinks that a society should make it possible for people to pursue projects that only come to fruition sometime after their deaths. His point can be strengthened by taking into account the perspective of those who participate in a generational continuum. Few people can expect that their personal contribution to their profession, community or their service to an ideal will have a significant impact on people of distant generations. But this does not preclude a connection to the more distant future. By being a participant in a generational continuum a person can regard herself as making a contribution, however small, to a tradition, community or collective project that will perpetuate itself indefinitely through the generations. Even if she makes no contribution herself—if she merely appreciates the contributions of others—she is able to connect herself with something that has a historical legacy and a connection to the more distant future. Such lifetime-transcending interests, as I have argued, play an important role in people's lives. Polities should respect them, and in some cases, underwrite the ability of communities to perpetuate their ideals, projects and traditions.

But isn't it reasonable to suppose that people who live in 1000 years' time, if indeed any people exist at all, will not subscribe to our values or continue our traditions? This is the point made by Golding (discussed in Chapter 1) when he says that we do not have duties to people of the future who might, from our point of view, live degraded lives. The answer to this objection is simply that we ought not to assume that distant future people will *not* be our successors in respect to their values and aspirations. So we ought not to do things that would undermine the ability of these distant people to maintain things that are worth valuing.

Making use of the social contract idea as Rawls presents it in *Political Liberalism*, we can imagine that the contractors, who belong to a generation that does not know where it comes in a sequence of generations, recognise that they and, most likely, people of any generation have lifetime-transcending interests that depend on the indefinite perpetuation of a tradition, or community or family line. They will thus accept that requirements of justice stretch indefinitely into the future. They must do their fair share to ensure that every future generation is able to enjoy institutions of justice and other things of value. In the case of immediate successors this means engaging in policies that ensure that institutions, practices and traditions can be continued. In the case of distant generations it requires us to avoid activities that could undermine their ability to maintain things of value and pass them on to their successors.

It should be noted that this conception of the intergenerational contract transcends the boundaries of particular political formations. It requires us to maintain the conditions for the perpetuation of generational continuums. A particular political society may come to an end. It may split up into smaller units; it may be incorporated into a larger whole; it may change its form of government. But we must assume that people will continue to want to perpetuate the things that they value down through the generations and that generations will continue to be bound to each other in relationships of obligation and entitlement. We must assume that people of any generation will want to maintain in some form institutions and practices that enable the things they value to be perpetuated. Our ability to ensure that they can do so is limited. But at least we ought to avoid actions that could undermine the existence of these generational continuums.

DUTIES TO DISTANT PAST GENERATIONS

We ought to extend the scope of intergenerational justice into the distant future. Should we also extend its temporal scope into the distant past? Do we have duties to distant past generations? Feinberg says that our duties to Caesar, Nero and King Tut consist only of telling the truth about their lives—a responsibility which probably has to do more with the desirability of historical accuracy than avoiding harms to the dead (1974: 60). Why should we discount in this way the interests of the dead?

A theory of intergenerational justice provides an obvious answer. No connection exists between the lifetime-transcending interests possessed by Caesar or King Tut, whatever they were, and our present activities and concerns. They do not belong to our generational continuums, except in the sense that they participated in the march of history and had an influence on it—and this is no doubt behind Feinberg's insistence that we ought to tell the truth about them.

The existence of duties to members of past generations depends on them being part of our generational continuum, past members of our polity or members of another intergenerational community to which we belong. It depends on them being in the position to make demands on us that we are obliged to fulfil. As time passes and values and ways of life change there is bound to be a diminution in the salience of the demands that past generations could have made. Mrs White (of Chapter 5) could have reasonably demanded that her immediate successors remember what she contributed to her community. But it is less plausible to suppose that people living 200 years later would have the duty of remembering her. We have a stronger duty to appreciate the projects and values of our more immediate predecessors than our more distant predecessors. But this doesn't mean that we have no obligations to them at all. If our more distant predecessors made significant sacrifices for the sake of people of the future, then we have a duty to continue to remember and appreciate what they did.

Distance in time is, by itself, no barrier to the existence of obligations to people of the past. And since participants in a tradition or a community are predisposed to think that they are the heirs of a long line of predecessors, they are also predisposed to accept obligations to people who might have lived many generations ago. Nevertheless, there is an asymmetry between the indefinite temporal reach of our duties to future generations and the more limited scope of our duties to past generations. This asymmetry is explained by our different relationship to the past and future. We know what past people have done and how they are related to us (although there can be disputes about the nature of the relationship). We do not know how distant future people will be related to us. At the same time, we have values, institutions and projects that we believe ought to be perpetuated into the indefinite future. We may suspect that distant future people will find our values, aspirations and projects no more relevant to their lives than those of Caesar or King Tut are relevant to us. But from a moral point of view we have no option but to hope that our values and institutions will survive and to act accordingly.

RESPONSIBILITY AND UNCERTAINTY

Whether we conceive of our duties as being duties of justice or duties to humanity, it would be wrong, all things being equal, to engage in activities that will cause significant harm to distant generations. Does this mean that it is wrong for present people to store nuclear wastes that could leak and cause harm to people of distant generations? The answer depends on how we determine when 'all things are equal'. Among the factors that have to be taken into account are the costs, risks and benefits of nuclear power for all relevant generations compared to the costs, risks and benefits of alternatives; the likelihood that nuclear wastes will do harm; the attitude we should take toward the risks and how we think responsibilities and risks should be distributed between generations. All of these issues require considerable discussion and they raise questions about values as well as about facts. I have nothing to say about the first issue: the one at the centre of public discussion. But the question of how to deal with uncertainty and risk, in this and other cases, is a central issue for those who want to apply a theory of intergenerational justice—especially one that encompasses distant generations. Since decision-making procedures make moral assumptions and raise questions of value, a theory of intergenerational justice ought to indicate what guidelines should be accepted.

The Routleys suppose that nuclear wastes, like the poisonous substance on the train, will cause harm to innocent and unsuspecting people. The probability that the poisonous substance will leak and cause harm is likely to be calculable with a fair degree of accuracy. In the case of nuclear wastes, any attempt at calculating risk is plagued with uncertainty. Future generations may develop an inexpensive means of rendering nuclear wastes harmless. On the other hand, the problem may prove unsolvable or the expense prohibitive. The burial sites that we choose may keep them safe for millennia. On the other hand, they may be disturbed by geological events that we had no way of anticipating. If we choose not to take the risks and do not further develop nuclear power, then we are embarking on a path that could also have bad consequences for future generations by increasing the effects of global warming or by relying on the development of alternatives that may never prove adequate and which could cause other problems for present and future people. Given the uncertainties of the future, we are left with the question of what is the morally responsible choice to make.

The nuclear issue is not the only case where we are handicapped by lack of knowledge about the future. We lack reliable knowledge about the technology that our successors, even our more immediate successors, will have at their disposal. We do not know what political and economic events will affect their well-being. We do not even know how many of them there will be (or in the more distant future, whether there will be any). Even when we have well-founded beliefs about the future, our predictions may turn out to be wrong. And in many cases our evidence is far from reliable and we are forced to judge and act without any certainty of the consequences. Our lack of knowledge is, in many cases, serious and impossible to remedy, especially in respect to the more distant future. A thorough discussion of the problems of intergenerational decision-making is not possible in the confines of this study, but I will identify some of problems that ignorance, risk and uncertainty pose for the application of a theory of intergenerational justice and will provide rough guidelines for making decisions about what course of action is just.

Suppose that we have to choose between policies A and B. Making use of distinctions provided by Kristian Skagen Ekeli, we could be ignorant, knowledgeable or uncertain about their future consequences (2004). If we are ignorant about the harms that could result from either or both of these policies, then the risks that we run are unknown and provide us with no basis for choice. The same impediment to choice exists if we know that each policy entails risks but have no way of knowing which danger is more serious or more probable. If all of our intergenerational policies had to be made in these circumstances, we would not be able to apply to the future any theory of intergenerational justice.

We are knowledgeable if we are able to assign probabilities to the degree of harm that A and B could cause and to the likelihood that this harm will occur. Our evidence gives us a basis for making a choice, but it does not make choosing unproblematic. Let us assume that the harm that could result from choosing A would be severe, but that the probability of it occurring is small, whereas choice B would lead to a more probable occurrence of a lesser harm. The common sense of most people is likely to lead them to choose B rather than A, thus ensuring that the worst consequences are avoided. But people differ in their attitude towards risk, and it is not obvious at what point a high tolerance for risk becomes recklessness or a low tolerance is overly conservative.

Even if we have decided on our decision strategy, there are other issues of evaluation that are likely to arise. Sagoff points out that people evaluate risks differently depending on their circumstances (1991: 210–1). Voluntary risks, for example, are more acceptable to people than non-voluntary risks, and since the risks that we impose on future generations are not voluntary, it could be argued that it is morally less acceptable to put them at risk than to put ourselves at risk (if this is what choosing between A and B involves). On the other hand, a harm that will only manifest itself after a long period of time may be preferable to one that will manifest itself right away. In the former case, we, or our successors, might have time to avert or lessen the danger. What decisions should be made in the face of risks to present and future people is something that will probably have to be argued out on a case-by-case basis. But the existence of reliable evidence and well-supported calculations of probabilities provide a good starting point for deliberations.

In many cases, especially those that worry environmentalists, such evidence is not available. In choosing between A and B, let us say that we have determined that B is by far the more convenient and less expensive option, but there is some reason to believe that it could lead to catastrophic harm to future generations. However, the evidence is far from conclusive. It does not tell us whether such a catastrophe could occur at all, or if so, whether it is really very likely to happen. We can make no accurate assessment of probabilities to guide our choice and must make a decision under conditions of uncertainty. The first issue is whether inconclusive evidence should count at all. The basic moral idea of those who support a 'precautionary principle' is that inconclusive but reputable evidence that a course of action will result in catastrophic and irreversible harm should not be discounted. This position seems obviously right. Not to take into account evidence that harm could occur would be to act irresponsibly.

The second issue caused by uncertainty is *how* less-than-conclusive evidence should be counted. According to some versions of the precautionary principle any reason to believe that catastrophic, irreversible consequences could result from a course of action—or lack of conclusive evidence that these consequences will *not* occur—is reason enough to abstain from that action. As critics point out, this formulation is conceptually flawed (Manson 2002: 272–3). Both doing A and not doing A could, under imaginable circumstances, lead to catastrophic consequences. Further development and use of nuclear power could cause great harm to present and future generations, either because of contamination or by providing opportunities for weapons proliferation. But it is conceivable that failure to further develop nuclear power could lead to economic breakdown in some countries, and thus catastrophic consequences for present and future generations. Moreover, strong versions of the precautionary principle are likely to impose severe sacrifices on present people. We can't be sure that our successors will ever have adequate substitutes for non-renewable resources, for example, so it seems that we must drastically cut down on their use—even to the point of severe deprivation. For who knows how many generations might need them. But equally unsatisfactory is the proposal that we should respond to uncertainty with an optimistic assumption that the harm will not occur or that our successors will have the technological means to deal with it. The following guideline is meant to provide a path that avoids these two extremes:

Reputable evidence that a course of action A, proposed as a means of fulfilling requirements of justice to members of present or succeeding generations, puts more distant successors at risk of being seriously harmed gives us a *prima facie* duty to act in a way that makes it less likely that the harm will occur, even when there is no certainty that the harm will occur if we fail to act. However, if, according to evidence at least as reputable and certain, there is no alternative course of action which will not force present people, or their immediate successors, to accept unduly heavy burdens in order to fulfil requirements of justice, then we should accept course of action A with the proviso that we also accept a duty to search for, and to begin the process of developing, less costly ways of lessening the likelihood that our distant successors will suffer harm.

What counts as an unduly heavy burden is going to be a matter of controversy, but if the burden puts the future of just institutions and other intergenerational values at risk, then it is clearly too heavy. If it drastically decreases standards of living—particularly for the least well off—then there is also reason to believe that the burden is too heavy.

The fact that nuclear wastes pose a considerable threat to future generations gives citizens and governments a *prima facie* duty to discontinue storing them. But to determine whether, when all things are considered, we have a duty not to commission more nuclear reactors and to phase out the ones that exist, we have to assess whether doing so is likely to significantly increase burdens on present and succeeding generations. There is already good evidence that the conventional alternatives to nuclear power, which make use of coal or oil, pose a threat to succeeding generations because of the production of greenhouse gases. So we have to consider whether there exist, or could be developed, less harmful alternatives and whether the transition to the use of these alternatives can be made without serious economic and social disruption. It is, of course, necessary to consider other short- and long-term risks associated with nuclear power, like proliferation of nuclear weapons. But it might be the case that after considering all relevant factors, citizens of a polity are justified in deciding that, for the time being, nuclear power is less bad than other options. Given that citizens are imposing a risk on future generations, they have a duty to alleviate the threat by putting resources into developing alternatives and by engaging in research on methods that could make nuclear wastes safer.

DISCOUNTING THE FUTURE

If we adopt these guidelines, then we are permitted to initiate courses of action which could result in serious harm to more distant future generations. It allows us to impose risks on more distant future generations that would be unacceptable if they were imposed on present and more immediate future generations. Does this mean that we are discounting the future in a way that implies that members of distant future generations are less worthy of respect than present people and our immediate successors?

Critical to answering this objection are two factors: the time that elapses before the risk is likely to eventuate and the role that succeeding generations can play in alleviating the risk. If we bury nuclear wastes, centuries later they may leak and harm people. But many generations separate us from those who are harmed, and it is reasonable to consider what responsibilities the in-between generations might bear for alleviating the risk of harm. Perhaps it was reasonable for us to believe that our more immediate successors would have the technology to render the wastes harmless; perhaps we had established a system of protection for nuclear waste sites that we reasonably expected these successors to be able to maintain until a better solution was found. The alleviation of risk, in other words, could be regarded as an intergenerational responsibility—especially in those cases where succeeding generations share in the benefits of imposing the risk. The guidelines require that we make a contribution to the intergenerational task of alleviating risk by doing research on ways of rendering nuclear wastes harmless, by putting them in safe storage places and by developing and beginning the process of putting in place alternatives that pose fewer risks. Succeeding generations have a responsibility for carrying on these tasks.

If we imagine wrongs that are truly analogous to the action of the person who consigned a dangerous package to a train, then it becomes doubtful that we need a theory of intergenerational justice to condemn them. Let us suppose that contractors, who have the job of disposing of poisonous wastes, cut corners by burying them in a deserted place, although they know that sooner or later the wastes will leak out and cause harm to those who visit the site. They take their secret with them to the grave. Centuries later the poisons leak out and harm people. In this case, there are no intermediaries between the contractors who bury the wastes and the people who are harmed by them. We have no difficulty in blaming the contractors for causing harm for exactly the same reasons that we would blame the consigner for putting poisonous substances on the train. The nature of the wrong and our reasons for holding them responsible does not depend on whether the wastes leak out after two weeks or after two centuries. In such a case our moral intuitions tell us that it is no less of a wrong to do harm to people of the future than to people of the present. The contractors could not have excused themselves by saying that harm done to future people matters less. Time and the relationship between generations are irrelevant to the nature of the wrong or the assignment of responsibility. But this means that a theory about intergenerational duties is not needed to account for these wrongs.

In those more complicated and realistic cases where such a theory is needed, it is reasonable to suppose that responsibilities as well as benefits should be equitably distributed through the generations. This does not mean that we are justified in leaving all of our problems to be solved by future generations on the grounds that they will have the technology to deal with all the risks that we have imposed on them. This would be irresponsible as well as contrary to the very idea of relationships of intergenerational cooperation. But neither should we be expected to shoulder all of the burdens by ourselves. Becoming and remaining sustainable is an intergenerational responsibility.

It is also an international responsibility. In an age when the activities of polities and their citizens have global effects, a theory of intergenerational justice that confines itself to relationships among its past, present and future members is obviously inadequate. The very idea of sustainability, as most people understand it, requires us to concern ourselves with the well-being of all future people and not merely future generations of our polity. In Chapter 12, we will consider whether the theory that I have been developing can encompass duties to future generations who will not be members of our polity or of our generational continuums.

12 Intergenerational Global Justice

The account of intergenerational justice that I have been defending is founded on relationships of cooperation between generations in a polity. Since a polity is a bounded political association, typically a nation-state in a world of nation-states, such a theory faces an obvious challenge. If we pursue a policy that poses no danger to present people or to future members of our society, but which threatens the well-being of future generations in other polities or their ability to maintain what they value, then we are committing an injustice. An adequate theory of intergenerational justice needs to explain why it is unjust and to give an account of what counts as an injustice to future people who will be members of other polities. In this chapter I will offer three complimentary approaches to these issues. The first derives duties to future (and past) members of other polities from a duty to respect intergenerational relationships and the entitlements and obligations that these relationships create. It provides a conception of justice for an international world. The second takes into account the ways in which the people of the world interact with each other in a global society and form relationships that transcend borders. It considers whether we need to reconceive the requirements of justice in order to come to terms with these relationships. The third attempts to broaden our conception of who counts as our predecessors and successors by giving us reasons to identify ourselves as global citizens.

INTERGENERATIONAL JUSTICE AND FUTURE GENERATIONS

Let us assume, as do almost all contemporary moral and political theories, that every individual has an equal moral worth. We can also assume that people, wherever they are, have lifetime-transcending interests, and our respect for individuals ought to include a respect for the relationships and practices which enable them to make and fulfil legitimate lifetime-transcending demands and to pass on things that they value to their successors. We ought to respect the desire of citizens of other polities to maintain their intergenerational relationships and practices. We ought to appreciate the fact that members of other polities have duties of justice in respect to their predecessors and successors and we ought to act in a way that does not compromise their ability to fulfil their obligations or the ability of their successors to receive their rightful inheritance.

Our duties to members of other polities and our duty to respect their intergenerational relationships and practices also gives us duties to past and future members of their polities. Future citizens are the rightful inheritors of the traditions, practices and other things of value that their predecessors laboured to provide for them, including the institutions of their society. It is an injustice to act in a way that prevents people from obtaining their inheritance unless there are good reasons for regarding it as pernicious or illegitimate. The offence would be committed against those people, present and past, who provided the inheritance and against those who are the rightful inheritors. Moreover, a respect for members of other polities requires a respect for their desire to fulfil just requirements. So if our actions force them to impose unjust burdens on their young and unborn successors, then we commit injustices both to present and future members of their polity. If, for example, we were to deplete the resources of another country so that future generations are likely to live in poverty, we would be acting unjustly.

Making our intergenerational duties to people in other polities depend on a respect for their relations of entitlement and obligations may seem like a weak basis for duties of justice. What if their institutions are unjust or corrupt? What if their relationships are oppressive? What if present members of a polity show no concern for the well-being of their successors?

We are not relieved from our duty of respecting the intergenerational relationships of members of another polity, or from our duties to future members of that polity, by our perception that their institutions are unjust or that their society is corrupt or oppressive. What gives us duties to their successors is a proper regard for the lifetime-transcending interests of individuals and the practices that enable their legitimate lifetime-transcending demands to be fulfilled. Even if some of their institutions are unjust and their political leaders are corrupt, they are bound to have intergenerational practices and relationships—in families, communities and other organisations—that deserve respect. These relationships, as we have seen, transcend particular political traditions and institutions. Even if we think that all of their institutions and practices are corrupt or unjust, our respect for individuals should nevertheless encompass a respect for the fact that they are, and their successors will be, the possessors of lifetime-transcending interests and intergenerational obligations (whether they recognise and act on them or not). Moreover, in unjust states there are likely to be citizens who are fighting against oppression and injustice, or who are trying to maintain communities in the face of persecution. We should avoid actions that will make it more difficult for them and their successors to carry on a struggle to preserve or achieve things that they value.

Suppose that members of a polity are reasonably just to each other but are pursuing policies that will have bad effects on the ability of their successors to maintain just institutions. Let us say that they have built a toxic waste dump without due care and that the substances, while safely contained for the time being, are likely to leak out in future years. Since their actions suggest that they do not care about the well-being of their successors, why should we refrain from taking up their invitation to export our toxic wastes to their facility? If they are creating a threat for future generations because they know no better or because they cannot afford better facilities, then it would obviously be wrong of us to take advantage of them. But even if neither poverty nor ignorance is the reason for their behaviour, we nevertheless ought not to take advantage of their invitation. First of all, because they are not acting in their best interests or according to their obligations of justice. We should assume that they have lifetime-transcending interests and that they have reason to value intergenerational relationships and to want their successors to be able to maintain them. We can assume that they have duties to maintain just institutions and other things that they value for future generations. If we act contrary to their best interests, then we are unjustly taking advantage of them; if we ignore the fact that they have duties to their successors, then we are complicit in their injustice. Secondly, we should not take advantage of their invitation because we have duties to their successors. Respect for the members of an intergenerational polity includes respect for the ability of its future members to establish and maintain institutions of justice and other things that they regard as good. We should not do anything that stands in their way of recognising and fulfilling their obligations.

PRINCIPLES OF INTERNATIONAL INTERGENERATIONAL JUSTICE

We ought to respect the interests of others, including their lifetime-transcending interests, and we owe duties of justice to the members—past, present and future—of intergenerational polities and other intergenerational communities. Does this mean that we owe them assistance in establishing and maintaining institutions of justice, or do we merely have the duty of not preventing them from being just to their predecessors and successors? Are we entitled to regard our resources as the rightful inheritance of our successors, or do we have a duty of justice to share our wealth with citizens of impoverished polities so that they can provide their successors with a more substantial inheritance? Ought we to assist them in passing on things they value to their successors? These questions are at the heart of current debates about international and global justice and this study cannot deal with all of the issues at stake. I will concentrate on elaborating two basic principles that any theory of international justice ought to incorporate if it is to pay due respect to the existence of polities as intergenerational communities and to the lifetime-transcending interests of their members.

The first, and primary, principle is that polities, and other international agents, ought not to violate each other's entitlement, or the entitlement of communities within each other's borders, to maintain intergenerational relationships, practices and institutions which satisfy basic requirements of justice and to fulfil their intergenerational responsibilities within the framework of these relationships and institutions. A polity can violate this principle by an aggressive destruction of institutions or economic infrastructure, by interferences with culture or traditions, by destroying environmental resources or by causing them to be destroyed as the result of unfair agreements or by other forms of economic exploitation.

The second principle is a requirement of remedial justice. Polities and other international agents ought to make reparation for violations of the requirements of the first principle with the objective of bringing about a state of affairs in which both perpetrators and victims (or their successors) are no longer justified in regarding the violation as standing in the way of establishing or re-establishing just relationships. As we have seen, this requirement of reparative justice can give present citizens a duty to make reparations for the unjust deeds of their predecessors.

The principles are based on the assumption that members of polities ought to respect the intergenerational relationships of members of other polities and intergenerational communities unless they have reasons of justice not to do so, and thus ought to recognise their entitlement to maintain these relationships and fulfil the duties associated with them. To be worthy of respect, the intergenerational relationships of a polity or community do not have to be wholly just. Liberals must be prepared to respect non-liberal conceptions of what is right and to tolerate institutions and practices that are not perfectly just by anyone's standards. But there are limits to toleration. If citizens or leaders of a polity adopt policies that systematically impoverish the young and future generations, they fail to satisfy basic requirements of intergenerational justice and we should regard them as worthy of condemnation. Whether and when we would be justified in acting to prevent such injustice is a matter for debate, but it should be noted that serious injustice to future generations could be grounds for humanitarian intervention.

INHERITANCE AND THE DISTRIBUTION OF RESOURCES

The basic principles of intergenerational justice for an international society do not require that each political society or community have an equal ability to maintain the things that they value for future generations. The principles are compatible with states of affairs that force citizens of poorer polities to make greater sacrifices than citizens in richer polities to maintain their institutions and the things that they value. It is not wrong, according to the principles, if circumstances beyond their control force members of some polities to make hard choices about what they ought to maintain for future generations (although it would be wrong if these circumstances are the result of unfair dealing or other activities incompatible with mutual respect). The principles do not give people in wealthy countries an obligation to share their resources with those in poor countries so that they can maintain more of the things that they value or provide their successors with a better inheritance.

For cosmopolitans these principles are not sufficient. International justice, they believe, requires a more equitable distribution of resources between rich and poor polities or rich and poor populations.[1] From the perspective of intergenerational justice there is nothing to prevent us from adding to the previously mentioned principles a requirement of distributive justice. However, the position that I have been defending puts limits on what kind of distributive principle we can accept. Citizens are entitled to provide an inheritance for their successors and any principle which undermines this right would be unacceptable.

Suppose that our predecessors have, for many generations, laboured, saved and made sacrifices in order to develop a resource for future generations. Their efforts have borne fruit and we now enjoy material prosperity, as well as many other good things. People in neighbouring countries are not so fortunate. Their predecessors squandered their resources and, as a result, present citizens, though not poor, are much less prosperous than we are. Perhaps we should accept a duty to share some of our wealth with them. It is not their fault that their predecessors were so profligate. But we have no duty to divest ourselves of all of our inherited advantages to the point where our situation is no better than theirs. Our predecessors laboured for us; they wanted their successors to enjoy the fruits of their efforts. They were entitled to provide us with an inheritance and we are entitled to enjoy it. Any principle of international distributive justice must allow for a right of inheritance. Recognising this right would rule out ideas of international justice that some philosophers have defended. For example, it would rule out Darrel Moellendorf's rejection of measures that discriminate in favour of members of one's own nation (2002: 63).

Rawls defends the entitlement of peoples to retain for themselves wealth accumulated by past generations, partly because he thinks that inequalities between peoples do not have the negative consequences of inequalities among people of a society, and partly because he sees no reason why members of wealthier societies should subsidise those who have made different decisions about development and use of resources. Suppose, he says, that the people of one country choose to develop their resources while those of another opt to maintain their traditional way of life. 'Assuming, as we do, that both societies are liberal or decent, and their peoples free and responsible, and able to make their own decisions, should the industrializing country be taxed to give funds to the second?'(1999b: 116–7). Rawls thinks not, and Miller points out that doing so would give citizens a perverse incentive not to save for future generations (2007: 68–72).

The problem is that the people who make the decision are not the same as those who reap the result. Why should we accept a practice that can have bad consequences for those who had no opportunity to participate in making the decision? According to the position I defend, what is crucial is the entitlement of people to provide an inheritance for their successors and the right of successors to obtain it. In Chapter 5 I argued that an intergenerational polity ought to recognise and protect these entitlements. The same reasons that support entitlements of bequest and inheritance also support a collective right of inheritance for members of a polity. People, individually and collectively, have lifetime-transcending interests in their projects, their progeny and their desire to provide an inheritance for their successors ought to be respected by others. However, respect for a right of national inheritance does not preclude a conception of international justice that requires a polity to use some of its assets to assist disadvantaged polities. It does not rule out re-distribution of wealth.

Those who argue that distributive requirements ought to be part of a theory of international justice are often motivated by political and economic changes that bring into question traditional views about international ethics—changes that include the increasing interdependence of polities in a global economy and a world system that requires cooperative solutions to common problems (Beitz 1979). Whether these changes require a substantial alteration to views about justice is a matter of debate. But it is obvious that increasing interdependence makes fulfilment of the basic principles of international intergenerational justice more difficult and demanding. Polities, in their attempts to protect the well-being of citizens and maintain what they value, are increasingly likely to violate the first principle. Suppose, for example, that citizens of a wealthy democracy want to protect their agricultural sector in order to maintain a valued communal way of life or to preserve the beauty of traditional rural landscapes. They regard these things as a heritage that they want to preserve for succeeding generations—an apparently reasonable objective. But the tariffs they impose on foreign goods for the sake of protecting their rural communities seriously disadvantage people in some developing countries, so much so that many are impoverished and their governments are not able to accumulate the capital necessary to establish just institutions.

According to the first principle, an injustice has been committed and some form of compensation and amelioration is required. Perhaps the wealthy country will have to give up the idea of preserving its rural culture, at least in its present form. It also might compensate poor countries for imposing tariffs or protect some part of its rural industry, allowing poor countries to benefit enough so that their people can also maintain some of things they value. However, the principle does not require that wealthy countries do away with all restrictions or act in ways that ensure that poor countries will benefit as much from the global economy as they do. They do not forbid policies that have the effect of preventing other countries from being as wealthy as they are capable of being. Whether all restrictions on trade *should* be abolished, whether promoting free trade is the best way of bringing it about that all polities can establish just institutions (according to their conceptions) and preserve things that they value, is another issue beyond the scope of this discussion.

APPLICATION OF THE SECOND PRINCIPLE

A principle of international justice that requires wealthy polities or people to share some of their wealth with the poor is not necessarily incompatible with a respect for intergenerational relationships. But even without such a principle there is reason to believe that a conscientious application of the second principle—the principle that requires recompense for injustices—would result in transfers of resources from wealthier to poorer societies. Many injustices against the people of these poorer societies, as defined by the first principle, have been, or are being, committed by wealthy polities or other wealthy and powerful international agents. It is reasonable to believe that poverty is in many cases the result of these present or past injustices—at least in part. So if those agents who committed the injustices were prepared to abide by the second principle, this would undoubtedly result in a transfer of resources from the rich to the poor. Overcoming some of the difficulties that people in poor societies now suffer would be the obvious way of making up for past wrongs in a way that enables just relationships to be established and maintained.

It might be objected that agents in international society cannot be held responsible for many of the harms that they caused in the past, either because they were acting out of necessity or they were ignorant about the long-term harmful consequences of their actions. Those who invaded and exploited the territories of others were often driven by a need to protect their interests from competing powers. Industrialising nations were for a long time not aware of the problems they were creating for future generations within and outside of their borders by using up the greenhouse gas-absorbing capacity of the planet.

Moral culpability, as we have seen, is not a necessary condition for holding citizens responsible for reparation. When people's rights are violated we generally assume that the victims are entitled to make a claim—even in those cases where the agent who caused the harm was driven by necessity.[2] Though doubts arise in particular cases, I think that our common judgments favour the idea that we can be held responsible even for unwitting harms. Suppose that our predecessors, in the course of a state-sponsored scientific expedition, made contact with an island community which had been isolated for generations from the rest of humanity and inadvertently caused them to be infected with diseases which devastated their society—a blow from which they have never recovered. I think that most of us would agree that we have a special obligation to this community. The unwitting harms caused by our predecessors are not all that different from harms caused by predecessors who did not recognise the wrongness of slavery or who thought that indigenous people could be treated like animals.

How far our responsibilities for reparation for unwitting harm extend is a matter that requires more discussion, but for practical purposes the exact limits do not make much of a difference. The environmental and social harms that we are creating for people of other societies are no longer unwitting, and it could be argued that former ignorance was in many cases culpable. Wealthy polities and other international agents have a significant reparative debt.

GLOBAL INTERGENERATIONAL JUSTICE

International justice is justice in a world of polities. However, the global world that is coming into existence not only makes political societies increasingly interdependent. It also brings into existence or prominence other actors: multi-national corporations, federations, regulatory bodies, international pressure groups and other collectives that extend their influence over national boundaries. To incorporate these entities we can stipulate that the basic principles of international intergenerational justice also apply to them, thus making these principles global. However, some argue that a more radical reconception of justice is necessary in order to take global relationships into account.

Andrew Dobson believes that justice in a world where the actions and way of life of wealthy Westerners narrow the options of people in poor countries requires that each person do what he or she can to alleviate the harm (2003: Chapter 2). 'Post-cosmopolitan' citizenship, as he calls it, is not territorial; it gives us a responsibility for the effects of our behaviour on others—wherever they are—and this responsibility naturally extends to those others who will exist in the future.

One of the problems with Dobson's conception of justice in a global society is that it imposes a considerable amount of responsibility on individuals. The steps we could take to lessen our ecological footprint or to avoid products or activities that put a limitation on the options of others seem never-ending. Moreover, it is difficult to understand how justice can prescribe actions that will not do much at all to alleviate environmental and other harms. In global society most individuals have almost no effect on outcomes. Only people acting together as citizens of polities or as members of other organizations can bring about more just relationships.

However, if we stipulate that requirements of justice can only be imposed on agents who are in the position to bring it about that justice is done, then there is an obvious difficulty. Justice in the global world as it now exists seems impossible to achieve: the application of even minimal standards are likely to be frustrated by lack of cooperation, lack of regulation or the existing interests of powerful agents. Those who theorise about global justice, it seems, cannot be content with stating principles of justice. They have to say something about the institutions that could embody these principles and how a new global order could be brought into being.

This is a tall order, but some have attempted it. David Held argues for the establishment of democratic structures to govern relationships in world society (1995). Some call for the creation of a world-state or at least a federation in which a central power is capable of regulating economic affairs and promoting just relationships (Nielsen 1988). Thomas Pogge looks forward to the development of a world society in which states are no longer so important and polities of other kinds—regional, local and international—will share responsibilities and make connections between people who are now separated by national borders.

> Thus, persons should be citizens of, and govern themselves through, a number of political units of various sizes, without any one political unit being dominant and thus occupying the traditional role of state. And their political allegiance and loyalties should be widely dispersed over these units: neighborhood, town, country, province, state, region and world at large. People should be politically at home in all of them, without converging upon any one of them as the lodestar of their political identity (1992: 58).

Andrew Linklater similarly imagines an evolutionary moral and political development that results in people becoming citizens of interdependent trans-national associations (1998).

All of these conceptions are meant to enable us to picture a global society where people can cooperate to achieve common goals and where basic principles of justice can prevail. Indeed, such developments might provide the incentives and institutional basis for more demanding requirements of global justice. By bringing into existence new political associations, including associations that unite people across borders, the new global order would also provide forums for making decisions about what ought to be protected and maintained for future generations. And it would also change people's views about who counts as their political predecessors and successors. For example, in Pogge's world of overlapping political units, those who stand in the role of predecessors and successors would vary from context to context, and duties to these past and future people would depend on the intergenerational responsibilities of the various communities.

What counts as a desirable political outcome of globalisation and how this outcome can be brought into being are matters on which there is little hope of reaching a consensus. As far as global society is concerned, we are not in the position of Rawlsian citizens who can confidently embark on the intergenerational project of constructing just institutions. However, this does not mean that we have no obligations. Citizens, through their political representatives, have a duty of justice to promote forms of cooperation that will make global society more just. They ought to act with the hope that their efforts will eventually bring about a world in which more effective and just relations of cooperation will exist.

GLOBAL CITIZENS

A world-state is not a foreseeable outcome of present developments, and many people believe that it would be undesirable. Nevertheless, some individuals conceive of themselves as belonging to a global society with responsibilities in respect to all of its present and future members. They are, according to an increasingly popular term, *global* or *world citizens*. Dobson, as we have seen, believes that citizenship involves taking responsibility for the impact that one has on the life chances of others—including those outside our borders. According to Robin Attfield, 'the role of people aware of global problems and of their own responsibility for ameliorating them can best be understood as one of global citizenship' (1999: 196).

If we think that citizenship and the obligations of citizens require appropriate institutions, or at least universally accepted relationships of cooperation, then 'global citizenship' is a misnomer. But whether we use the term or not, the idea that people of the world form a common society in which all people have entitlements and obligations of justice in respect to each other is a morally positive view to take—even if this society does not yet exist. Those who regard themselves as global citizens are anticipating this morally desirable outcome and accepting a humanitarian responsibility for bringing it about. In doing so, they make it more likely. The global society that global citizens anticipate is one in which all the world's people are participants in just, cooperative relationships—whether these relationships are backed up by the institutions of a world-state, a democratic federation or the network of associations advocated by Pogge and Linklater. It is also a global society in which all future people count as the successors of present generations.

There are two developments that make plausible the idea that we should perceive ourselves to be global citizens in a prospective intergenerational global society. The first is the perception that the whole of humanity is united by a common history and common interests; and the second is the need to deal with crises and challenges that threaten the interests—including the intergenerational concerns—of all the people of the world.

The idea that humankind has a history in which all peoples, motivated by similar interests, have played a role is encouraged by investigations into the natural history of our species as well as an awareness of the ways in which peoples came into existence and interacted with each other during the course of migrations, conquests and the building of societies. From this wider perspective our predecessors are not merely our ancestors or political forebears, but those who we can regard as making a contribution to our culture or to the creation of a human culture that exists in many forms but has common elements; and our successors are those who inherit the products of human endeavour and will continue the history of the humanity. Education and increasing contact with other cultures could make this way of thinking more widespread.

The perception that we must cooperate to solve problems that threaten the well-being of all present and future people contributes more obviously to the idea that there are intergenerational duties shared by all human beings. The idea of sustainability is, by its nature, a global concept. Rich and poor, developing as well as developed countries must play a role if global environmental problems are to be solved. Maintaining resources that everyone depends on—for example, the planet's capacity to absorb greenhouse gases—must be regarded as a common responsibility and thus as a task that ought to be shared. Where common responsibilities exist, questions of justice become relevant. Each relevant group or polity should do its fair share to maintain a good necessary for the well-being of the successors of all. In the absence of universally acceptable institutions and practices capable of determining fair shares and ensuring that duties are performed, this idea of intergenerational responsibility is utopian. But its existence as an ideal can motivate people and their leaders to make an effort to bring such institutions into existence, or at least to work more justly within the imperfect ones that exist.

PROSPECTS FOR INTERGENERATIONAL JUSTICE

In this study I have presented a theory of intergenerational justice with a number of notable features. It is founded on a conception of individuals as selves with interests and desires that transcend their lifetimes. It encompasses duties to past, as well as future, generations. It regards intergenerational justice as being about relationships between existing people, as well as relationships between present and unborn (or dead) generations. It makes intergenerational relationships and their requirements central to the concerns of political societies.

I have shown how this theory can meet some of the challenges that it faces: challenges posed by environmentalists as well as by those concerned about the well-being of people distant from us in time or space. But there is another challenge which seems much more difficult to meet: namely to establish that such a theory is capable of motivating actions and decision-making. All theories of justice presented by philosophers and other political theorists face a similar difficulty. They might appeal, as Rawls does, to common sense ideas of fairness or to what reasonable, well-motivated individuals should accept. But in practice people are often not reasonable or well motivated. And inevitably they are influenced in their moral and political reasoning by their situation in society, their communal affiliations and their ideas of the good.

However, theories of intergenerational justice face a special difficulty. Intergenerational justice is not a topic that generally excites much interest. As we have seen, even moral and political philosophers treat it as a marginal issue, when they treat it at all. Environmentalists have brought intergenerational issues into the public arena, but the failure of citizens and governments to treat these concerns with the seriousness that they deserve or to initiate the policies that seem to be required suggests a widespread lack of interest or motivation. If citizens were truly concerned about the well-being of their children and grandchildren, the future of their communities or the ability of their successors to value what we regard as good, then surely they and the governments that represent them would be doing more to avoid the worst effects of global warming, the breakdown of ecological systems and the extinction of species. They and their governments would be doing much more to curb nuclear proliferation, to reduce armaments and to develop better institutional means for dealing with global problems.

For the theory I am defending this apparent lack of interest and the failure of governments, even in democratic polities, to take adequate steps to deal with problems that are likely to have dire consequences for future generations pose a theoretical, and not merely a practical, problem. I argue that people have lifetime-transcending interests that are important to their lives. Yet they do not act as if they are much concerned with the future beyond their lifetimes or even the conditions that they will experience later in their lives. So it might be argued that citizens are not capable of rational pursuit of their own interests—a view that would bring into question the ability of democratic governments to deal with existing problems—or that their lifetime-transcending interests are not so important after all, or that other interests not taken into account are far more important.

MOTIVATION AND FUTURE GENERATIONS

A failure of individuals or governments to adopt adequate measures to prevent injustice to future generations could be due to psychological or social factors, or both. Personal experience, as well as psychological data, tell us that individuals tend to be more strongly motivated by immediate costs and benefits compared to costs and benefits that might occur in the future—so much so that they may be disinclined to make even small sacrifices in order to avoid greater future costs. Added to their predisposition to discount the future is a tendency, more pronounced in some people, to avoid thinking about what will happen when they are old or after they are dead. Nevertheless, an overvaluing of present costs and benefits is something that can be countered by rational reflection and public discussion. Individuals can learn how to be more prudent, far-sighted and morally responsible. A democratic polity should be able to encourage these qualities in its debates about public issues.

Norman S. Care (1982) believes that the problem is more serious. What stands in the way of being motivated to make sacrifices for the sake of future generations, he believes, is that the factors and relationships that motivate ethical behaviour when we are dealing with existing people are not present in the case of more remote future generations (1982; 1987: Chapter 5). The problem with unborn generations is not only that they are faceless and impersonal to present people. There is also no mutual cooperation between us and them and no exchanges that might motivate us to accept a duty. There is no reciprocity of the kind that would cement community bonds.

In this study I have attempted to show that cooperative relationships entailing the existence of intergenerational obligations exist between the generations. Face-to-face contact or direct interactions are not necessary to cement relationships or motivate behaviour. Care, it is true, is concerned not so much with our motivations to be just to our more immediate successors, but rather with our lack of concern for people who might be living 50 generations from now—those people who could be harmed by our radioactive wastes, for example. But even these distant people are connected to us through a continuum of relationships of entitlement and obligation. Although we may not be accustomed to the idea that we can have duties to people of the distant future, the existence of a generational continuum and our desire to perpetuate our communities and ideals into the indefinite future, can be sources of motivation. Most of our efforts, so far as future generations are concerned, are properly invested in ensuring that our more immediate successors will not bear heavy burdens in order to maintain the institutions and other things that we regard as good and pass them on to *their* successors. If we fulfil our duties to our more immediate successors in a way that ensures that they can also fulfil *their* intergenerational duties and that their successors will be able to do the same, and so on into the indefinite future—that is, if we act according to the guideline discussed in Chapter 11—we will have also fulfilled our duties to more distant generations. Most people are already predisposed to believe that they have duties to posterity. Why should it be so difficult for them to expand their notion of who posterity includes?

Another obstacle for a theory of intergenerational justice is persuading people that they have responsibilities in respect to the past that include obligations of reparation for the injustices of their predecessors. One of the difficulties here is that members of a community, though predisposed to commemorate their predecessors for their accomplishments and sacrifices, do not like to think that they also committed injustices. Resistance to admitting that this is so is increased by the belief (whether true or not) that these predecessors were acting in good faith according to their own moral conventions. A further difficulty is that present citizens fear that admitting responsibility would result in enormous costs for them and their families; that it would result in them losing much of what they inherited from past generations. The account of reparative responsibilities that I have offered shows that these reasons for refusing to accept responsibilities for the past are not sound. A conception of reparative responsibility that focuses on the repair of communal relationships would not countenance measures that ignore the situations and interests of existing people. And by admitting that wrongs were committed in the past, we are not implying that past people were wicked or irresponsible. We make judgments about justice—past, present and future—from our own point of view and are justified in acting accordingly. We do not have to suppose that past people were being intentionally unjust, and even if they were, their bad actions were often accompanied by worthy deeds. People of every generation do both actions that are noble and actions that are base. A more sophisticated understanding of history would help to break down the resistance to admitting the existence of historical injustices.

SOCIETY AND RESPONSIBILITY

Many people believe that what stands in the way of the realization of an intergenerationally just polity are attitudes or ways of life that are common in contemporary societies. Care himself thinks that a lack of concern for others, including future people, is encouraged by an emphasis on self-realisation in education and competitiveness in economic life (1982: 212). Arendt, as we have seen in Chapter 4, believes that people of a consumer capitalist society are not much interested in perpetuating values or projects into the future. Nevertheless, the upsurge of concern about sustainability suggests that the delights of consumer capitalism do not prevent people from developing a sense of responsibility for future generations. This sense of responsibility can be augmented, as Dobson believes, by an education in responsible citizenship (2003: Chapter 5).

Other social and political factors undoubtedly influence the motivation, or lack thereof, of citizens and leaders. People who are on the verge of starvation cannot afford to make sacrifices for the sake of future generations. Immediate necessities outweigh the prospect, however serious and imminent, of future harms. Although people in liberal democracies are not in this perilous situation, they may nevertheless persuade themselves that they have no choice—for the sake of their livelihood, their business or their political career—but to continue on a course that threatens future generations. The sacrifices that they would have to make seem too vast; the consequences of making them seem too uncertain. Added to this is the difficulty of achieving international cooperation to deal with problems that threaten present and future generations. Faced with problems that seem to them insurmountable or too difficult or costly to solve, it is not surprising that many people respond by refusing to think about what the future holds or simply by hoping that technological innovation or the free market will save the world.

There are political solutions to these problems. In a democracy, citizens can debate, discuss and decide on appropriate forms of action. They can commit themselves to making sacrifices—as has been done by people of past generations. Governments can make and carry out effective policies and act together to deal with global problems; industrialists can be required to turn their minds to developing safer and more sustainable processes. How these desirable and morally imperative results can be brought into existence is a matter far beyond the competence of a philosopher. But it is important to recognise that there is no intrinsic opposition of interests between present and future generations. Present people have lifetime-transcending interests, and thus reasons to be concerned about the future beyond their lifetimes. These interests may not prevent them from failing to give due concern to the fact that their successors will also have such interests, but the gap between the interests of present people and the needs of future generations is not so great as many people assume. If my position is right, then the problem for democracy is not so much that the interests of future generations are not represented, but that the lifetime-transcending interests of citizens have not been properly addressed, discussed and acted on. What political and social changes would bring this about is another topic beyond the scope of this study. But education for citizenship that Dobson recommends, as well as more opportunities to deliberate, more involvement of citizens in discussions and decision-making, are measures that are likely to improve the chances that the interests of all generations will be properly appreciated and acted on, and that the intergenerational polity will not vanish from the earth.

Notes

NOTES TO CHAPTER 1

1. For a discussion of Jefferson's views on intergenerational responsibilities and a comparison with the views of Abraham Lincoln, see Weiner (2005: Chapter 3).
2. The 'non-identity problem' has been discussed by many philosophers, most notably in Schwartz (1978), Kavka (1982) and Parfit (1984).

NOTES TO CHAPTER 2

1. For a description of approaches to the non-identity problem, see Edward A. Page (2006: Chapter 6) and Lukas Meyer (2008: Section 3).
2. See Melinda A. Roberts (1998).
3. Alan Carter (2001: 438) claims that Rawls fails to overcome the non-identity problem but does not take into account the caring relationship that motivates the agreement in the original position and the duties that result.
4. Tim Mulgan (2006: 45) thinks that this will be so if we take the interests of children into account.
5. The second formulation avoids the problem noted by Avner de-Shalit (1995: 110–1) that the existence of some of the members of future generations who are supposed to participate will be determined by the decisions made in the original position.
6. This idea of the intergenerational contract seems to lead to a paradox inspired by Jefferson's insistence on generational freedom. If we think that each generation ought to be free to determine their own conception of justice, then it seems that we are also endorsing their right to order their polity according to their principles, whatever they are. But this means that we are forced to acknowledge their right to choose and live according to principles that we would regard as unjust. There are two ways of dealing with this 'paradox'. We could insist that future generations do not have a right to accept principles that we regard as wrong (though there is nothing we can do about it except to give them a good education), or, more plausibly, we could simply accept that they have a right to determine their own view of justice, even though their ideas might be wrong.
7. See Margaret Gilbert's account of how plural subjects are formed and how individuals who make them up acquire obligations (1989: 408ff).
8. Jane English, who first suggested that Rawls could jettison the appeal to the concerns of fathers of families if he made use of the resources of ideal theory, does not recommend this proposal. The ideal world, she says, is not relevant

to our situation in the real world, where compliance is a problem. 'For this reason, it seems wiser to base our solution to the saving problem on considerations other than those of ideal theory' (1977: 98).
9. There are accounts of how to avoid the non-identity problem which might be able answer these questions: for example, one that gives us a responsibility not to bring a person into an existence that will be below a specified threshold of well-being (see McMahan 1998). But such accounts do not fit into a framework that prescribes a distribution of costs and benefits between generations who cooperate to produce and maintain institutions of justice.

NOTES TO CHAPTER 3

1. There is also the problem, much discussed in the literature, about whether we have duties of reciprocity or gratitude for benefits that we did not ask for or receive voluntarily (Nozick 1974: 95ff). Obviously, this would rule out intergenerational duties of reciprocity or gratitude from the start.
2. Miller allows that people who have been persecuted or discriminated against have no reason to value their nation.
3. *Communitarianism* is a term that has sometimes been used to describe the views of those who stress the role of identification with others or with a group or culture in the development of the self and its acceptance of obligations. Primary theorists identified as 'communitarian' include Michael Sandel (1998), Alasdair MacIntyre (1981 and 1998) and Charles Taylor (1989).
4. Robert Elliot (1997b) interprets de-Shalit as an ideal utilitarian who aims to maximise certain social values.

NOTES TO CHAPTER 4

1. I am referring to the popular notion of stoicism. When stoicism became popular in ancient Rome, endorsed by emperors as well as slaves, it was a worldly philosophy centering on the cultivation of civic virtues.

NOTES TO CHAPTER 5

1. This problem is evident in John O'Neill's 1993a discussion. He points out the ways in which a scientist's reputation can be affected by what happens after his death. But none of the vicissitudes that he describes, though they could be judged greatly harmful or beneficial to the dead, seem to give us duties. For example, we do nothing wrong if we refute the theories, and thus diminish the reputation, of a dead scientist.
2. Tim Mulgan (1999) argues that citizens of a polity cannot be neutral about the status of the dead. If we believe that the dead can be harmed or benefited by what we do, then their interests must count in our political deliberations—if we don't believe this, then we will count only the interests of present and future people. If my argument in the following section is correct, then this difference of opinion about the status of the dead need not lead to a difference of opinion concerning intergenerational duties—including duties to past generations.
3. This interpretation defuses an objection that Feinberg makes to Partridge's contractual justification of duties in respect to the dead: 'It is absurd to think that once the promisee has died, the status of a broken promise made to him while he was alive suddenly ceased to be that of a serious injustice to a

victim, and becomes instead a mere diffuse public harm' (1984: 95). We can continue to think that an injustice was done to a person now dead—without having to suppose that it causes him harm.
4. Nelson P. Lande (1990) argues that we have a duty of justice to rehabilitate those who have been falsely maligned in the past. (He has in mind the early Bolshevik leaders who were falsely accused by Stalin of crimes.) His account of why this duty exists depends on the claim that the dead have rights, but it can be less problematically defended by an appeal to lifetime-transcending interests and what they enable us to legitimately demand on our behalf or the behalf of others.
5. Inheritance can also be criticised for its social inefficiency, as D.W. Haslett does (1986).
6. For a more detailed discussion, see Thompson (2001).
7. See Thompson (2000: 2–13).

NOTES TO CHAPTER 6

1. In Thompson (2003) I discuss in more detail some of the views presented in this chapter.
2. This version of Boxill's argument seems to follow from his Lockean starting point. In other places, he makes reparation depend on present-day African Americans being harmed by the legacy of slavery (2003: 65).
3. Ridge appeals to the generally accepted convention that citizens are responsible for the agency of their political society, including its past deeds (45–6). Though it is true that many people accept this convention, it would be more satisfactory if we could explain why they ought to accept it.

NOTES TO CHAPTER 7

1. Capital, says Rawls (1999a: 256) does not merely consist of factories and machines, 'but also the knowledge and culture, as well as the techniques and skills, that make possible just institutions and the fair value of liberty'.
2. Some theorists prefer to drop the requirement of neutrality. John O'Neill (1993b: Chapter 6) argues that liberalism, properly understood, makes the pursuit of the good life central to politics, but he also allows that citizens—through their government—can support a plurality of goods.
3. Annette Baier (1981: 176) argues that if a generation runs down or destroys valuable assets that its predecessors built for future generations, then it has wronged these predecessors as well as its successors.

NOTES TO CHAPTER 8

1. For a discussion of the distinction between age groups and generational cohorts, see Norman Daniels (1988: 12–3).
2. Jeffrey Blustein (1977: 440) supports a similar conclusion.

NOTES TO CHAPTER 10

1. See also Michael D. Bayles (1976: 51).
2. Rolf George (1987) argues that the economic disadvantages to parents are so great that 'it would be palpably absurd to have children, and not many

people would have them: in the last cohorts we would find only the children of the religious and the careless' (3).
3. For fictional examples of societies where liberal democratic institutions are no longer possible, see H. G. Wells (1964) and Aldous Huxley (1955).
4. Hardy Jones argues that, provided that genetic controls are feasible and reliable, 'we should exercise them so as to produce individuals who will respect others' rights and to avoid the production of persons who will violate rights' (1976: 37).

NOTES TO CHAPTER 11

1. Animals ought to be respected, and their welfare is a concern to citizens of a polity. However, I do not think that we have intergenerational duties to animals—apart from the duty to maintain institutions that ensure that animals are treated well. It would not wrong presently existing animals if we bring it about that their species becomes extinct, so long as this does not cause individual animals pain and suffering.
2. This view could be attributed to Leopold (1949).
3. For a similar strategic approach to environmental valuing, see Bryan G. Norton (1989).
4. For a discussion of these and other ethical problems posed by the nuclear industry, see Kristin Shrader-Frechette (1995: 477–93).
5. Mulgan's theory is complicated by the problems caused by partial compliance.

NOTES TO CHAPTER 12

1. Such cosmopolitans include Charles R. Beitz (1979), Darrel Moellendorf (2002) and Charles Jones (1999).
2. Joel Feinberg (1978: 102) argues that a backpacker who uses someone's property in order to save his life is not culpable but owes compensation to the owner.

Bibliography

Abdel-Nour, F. (2003) 'National responsibility', *Political Theory*, Vol. 31: 693–719.
Ackerman, B. A. (1980) *Social Justice in the Liberal State*, New Haven, CT: Yale University Press.
Agar, N. (2004) *Liberal Eugenics: In Defence of Human Enhancement*, London: Blackwell.
Anderson, B. (1983) *Imagined Communities: Reflections on the Origin and Spread of Nationalism*, London: Verso.
Arendt, H. (1958) *The Human Condition*, Chicago: University of Chicago Press.
Aristotle (1980) *Nichomachean Ethics*, D. Ross (trans.) Oxford: Oxford University Press.
Attfield, R. (1999) *The Ethics of the Global Environment*, Edinburgh: Edinburgh University Press.
Auerbach, B.E. (1995) *Unto the Thousandth Generation: Conceptualizing Intergenerational Justice*, New York: P. Lang.
Baier, A. (1981) 'The rights of past and future persons', in E. Partridge (ed.) *Responsibilities to Future Generations*, Buffalo, NY: Prometheus Books.
———. (1985) 'Cartesian persons', in *Postures of the Mind*, Minneapolis: University of Minnesota Press.
Ball, T. (1985) 'The incoherence of intergenerational justice', *Inquiry*, Vol. 28: 321–327.
Barry, B. (1978) 'Circumstances of justice and future generations', in R. I. Sikora and B. Barry (eds.) *Obligations to Future Generations*, Philadelphia: Temple University Press.
———. (1979) 'Justice as reciprocity', in E. Kamenka and A. Erh-Soon Tay (eds.) *Justice*, London: Edward Arnold.
———. (1999) 'Sustainability and intergenerational justice', in A. Dobson (ed.) *Fairness and Futurity: Essays on Environmental Sustainability and Social Justice*, Oxford: Oxford University Press.
Bayles, M. D. (1976) 'Limits to a right to procreate', in M. D. Bayles (ed.) *Ethics and Population*, Cambridge, MA: Schenkman Publishing.
Becker, L. C. (1986) *Reciprocity*, London: Routledge.
Beckerman, W. and Pasek, J. (2001) *Justice, Posterity, and the Environment*, Oxford: Oxford University Press.
Beitz, C. R. (1979) *Political Theory and International Relations*, Princeton, NJ: Princeton University Press.
Blustein, J. (1977) 'On the duties of parents and children,' *Southern Journal of Philosophy*, Vol. 15: 427–441.
Boxill, B. R. (2003) 'A Lockean argument for black reparations,' *The Journal of Ethics*, Vol. 7: 63–91.

Buchanan, A. (1990) 'Justice as reciprocity versus subject-centred justice', *Philosophy and Public Affairs*, Vol. 19: 227–252.
——. (1991) *Secession: The Morality of Political Divorce from Fort Sumter to Lithuania and Quebec*, Boulder, CO: Westview Press.
Burke, E. (1968) *Reflections on the Revolution in France*, London: Penguin.
Callahan, D. (1976) 'Ethics and population limitation', in M. D. Bayles (ed.) *Ethics and Population*, Cambridge, MA: Schenkman Publishing.
——. (1980) 'What obligations do we have to future generations?', in E. Partridge (ed.) *Responsibilities to Future Generations*, Buffalo, NY: Prometheus Books.
Callahan, J. (1987) 'On harming the dead', *Ethics*, Vol. 97: 341–352.
Care, N. S. (1982) 'Future generations, public policy, and the motivation problem', *Environmental Ethics*, Vol. 4: 195–213.
——. (1987) *On Sharing Fate*, Philadelphia: Temple University Press.
Carter, A. (2001) 'Can we harm future people?', *Environmental Values*, Vol. 10: 429–454.
Commonwealth of Australia (2002) *Intergenerational Report*, 2002–03 Budget Paper 5. Online. Available HTTP: <http://www.budget.gov.au/2002–03/bp5/html/index.html> (accessed 23 September 2008).
Daniels, N. (1988) *Am I My Parents' Keeper: An Essay on Justice Between the Young and the Old*, Oxford: Oxford University Press.
De George, R. T. (1981) 'The environment, rights and future generations', in E. Partridge (ed.) *Responsibilities to Future Generations*, Buffalo, NY: Prometheus Books.
de-Shalit, A. (1995) *Why Posterity Matters: Environmental Policies and Future Generations*, London: Routledge.
Dobson, A. (2003) *Citizenship and the Environment*, Oxford: Oxford University Press.
Dworkin, R. (1986a) 'Can a liberal state support art?', in Dworkin, *A Matter of Principle*, Oxford: Clarendon Press.
——. (1986b) 'Liberalism', in *A Matter of Principle*, Oxford: Clarendon Press.
Ekeli, K.S. (2004) 'Environmental risks, uncertainty and intergenerational ethics', *Environmental Values*, Vol. 13: 421–428.
Elliot, R. (1997a) *Faking Nature: The Ethics of Environmental Restoration*, New York: Routledge.
——. (1997b) 'Contingency, community and intergenerational justice', in N. Fotion and J. C. Heller (eds.) *Contingent Future Persons: On the Ethics of Deciding Who Will Live, or Not, in the Future*, Dordrecht, The Netherlands: Kluwer.
English, J. (1977) 'Justice between generations', *Philosophical Studies*, Vol. 31: 91–104.
Feinberg, J. (1974) 'The rights of animals and unborn generations', in W. T. Blackstone (ed.) *Philosophy and Environmental Crisis*, Athens: University of Georgia Press.
——. (1978) 'Voluntary euthanasia and the inalienable right to life', *Philosophy and Public Affairs*, Vol. 7: 93–123.
——. (1980a) 'Is there a right to be born?', in *Rights, Justice and the Bounds of Liberty: Essays in Social Philosophy*, Princeton: Princeton University Press.
——. (1980b), 'The child's right to an open future', in W. Aiken and H. LaFollette (eds.) *Whose Child? Children's Rights, Parental Authority and State Power*, Totowa, NJ: Rowman and Littlefield.
——. (1984) *Harm to Others*, Vol. 1 of *The Moral Limits of the Law*, Oxford: Oxford University Press.

Feldman, F. (2004) *Pleasure and the Good Life: Concerning the Nature, Varieties and Plausibility of Hedonism*, Oxford: Oxford University Press.

Flanagan, O. (1996) 'Identity and reflection', in *Self Expressions: Mind, Morals, and the Meaning of Life*, New York: Oxford University Press.

Flannery, T. F. (1994) *The Future Eaters: An Ecological History of the Australasian Lands and People*, Port Melbourne, Australia: Reed Books.

Gaita, R. (1999) 'Guilt, shame and community', in *A Common Humanity: Thinking About Love and Truth and Justice*, Melbourne, Australia: Text Publishing.

Gaspart, F. and Gosseries, A. (2007) 'Are generational savings unjust?', *Politics, Philosophy and Economics*, Vol. 6: 193–217.

George, R. (1987) 'Who should bear the cost of children?', *Public Affairs Quarterly*, Vol. 1: 1–42.

Gilbert, M. (1989) *On Social Facts*, London: Routledge.

Golding, M.P. (1972) 'Obligations to future generations', *The Monist*, Vol. 56: 85–99.

Goodin, R. E. (1999) 'Treating likes alike: intergenerationally and internationally', *Policy Sciences*, Vol. 32: 189–206.

Green, R. M. (1981) 'Intergenerational distributive justice and environmental responsibility', in E. Partridge (ed.) *Responsibilities to Future Generations*, Buffalo, NY: Prometheus Books.

Grey, W. (1999) 'Epicurus and the harm of death', *Australasian Journal of Philosophy*, Vol. 77: 358–364.

Habermas, J. (2003) *The Future of Human Nature*, Cambridge, England: Polity.

Harris, J. (2007) *Enhancing Evolution: The Ethical Case for Making Better People*, Princeton: Princeton University Press.

Haslett, D.W. (1986) 'Is inheritance justified?', *Philosophy and Public Affairs*, Vol. 15: 122–155.

Held, D. (1995) *Democracy and the Global Order: From the Modern State to Cosmopolitan Governance*, Cambridge, England: Polity Press.

Heyd, D. (1992) *Genethics: Moral Issues in the Creation of People*, Berkeley: University of California Press.

Holmes, S. (1988) 'Precommitment and the paradox of democracy', in J. Elster and R. Slagstad (eds.) *Constitutionalism and Democracy*, Cambridge, England: Cambridge University Press.

Hubin, D. C. (1976) 'Justice and future generations', *Philosophy and Public Affairs*, Vol. 6: 70–83.

Human Rights and Equal Opportunities Commission [HREOC] (1997) *Report of the National Inquiry into the Separation of Aboriginal and Torres Strait Islander Children from Their Families*, Canberra, Australia: Human Rights and Equal Opportunity Commission.

Hume, D. (1975) *An Enquiry Concerning Human Understanding*, L.A. Selby-Bigge (ed.) 3rd Edn, Oxford: Clarendon Press.

Huxley, A. (1955) *Brave New World*, Harmondsworth, England: Penguin.

Jacobs, M. (1999) 'Sustainable development as a contested concept', in A. Dobson (ed.) *Fairness and Futurity*, Oxford: Oxford University Press.

Jecker, N. S. (1989) 'Are filial duties unfounded?', *American Philosophical Quarterly*, Vol. 26: 73–80

Jefferson, T. (1907) *The Writings of Thomas Jefferson*, Vol. 7, A. E. Bergh (ed.) Washington, DC: Thomas Jefferson Memorial Association.

———. (1984) 'Letter to James Madison, Paris, 6 September 1789', in M. Peterson (ed.) *Thomas Jefferson: Writings*, New York: Literary Classics.

Jones, C. (1999) *Global Justice: Defending Cosmopolitanism*, New York: Oxford University Press.

Jones, H. (1976) 'Genetic endowment and obligations to future generations', *Social Theory and Practice*, Vol. 4: 29–46.
Kates, C. A. (2004) 'Reproductive liberty and overpopulation', *Environmental Values*, Vol. 13: 51–79.
Kavka, G. (1982) 'The paradox of future individuals', *Philosophy and Public Affairs*, Vol. 11: 93–122.
Kumar, R. (2003) 'Who can be wronged?', *Philosophy and Public Affairs*, Vol. 31: 99–120.
Lamont, J. (1998) 'A solution to the puzzle of when death harms its victims', *Australasian Journal of Philosophy*, Vol. 76: 198–212.
Lande, N. P. (1990) 'Posthumous rehabilitation and the dust-bin of history', *Public Affairs Quarterly*, Vol. 4: 267–286.
Laslett, P. (1992) 'Is there a generational contract?', in P. Laslett and J. S. Fishkin (eds.) *Justice between Age Groups and Generations*, New Haven, CT: Yale University Press.
Laslett, P. and Fishkin, J. S. (1992) 'Processional justice', in P. Laslett and J. S. Fishkin (eds.) *Justice between Age Groups and Generations*, New Haven, CT: Yale University Press.
Leopold, A. (1949) 'The land ethic', *A Sand County Almanac With Other Essays*, Oxford: Oxford University Press.
Levine, A. (1998) 'Just social security', *Public Affairs Quarterly*, Vol. 12: 307–332.
Lincoln, A. (1863) *Gettysburg Address*. Online. Available HTTP: <http://libertyonline.hypermall.com/Lincoln/gettysburg.html> (accessed 26 September 2008).
Linklater, A. (1998) *The Transformation of the Political Community: Ethical Foundations of the Post-Westphalian Era*, New York: Columbia University Press.
Lomasky, L. E. (1987) *Persons, Rights, and the Moral Community*, New York: Oxford University Press.
MacIntyre, A. (1981) *After Virtue: A Study in Moral Theory*, London: Duckworth.
———. (1998) *Whose Justice? Which Rationality?*, South Bend, IN: University of Notre Dame Press.
Macklin, R. (1981) 'Can future generations correctly be said to have rights?', in E. Partridge (ed.) *Responsibilities to Future Generations*, Buffalo, NY: Prometheus Books.
Manson, N. A. (2002) 'Formulating the precautionary principle', *Environmental Ethics*, Vol. 24: 263–274.
McMahan, J. (1997) 'The limits of national partiality', in R. McKim and J. McMahan (eds.) *The Morality of Nationalism*, Oxford: Oxford University Press.
———. (1998) 'Wrongful life: paradoxes in the morality of causing people to exist', in J. Coleman (ed.) *Rational Commitment and Social Justice: Essays for Gregory Kavka*, Cambridge: Cambridge University Press.
Meyer, L. (1997) 'More than they have a right to: future people and our future oriented projects', in N. Fotion and J. C. Heller (eds.) *Contingent Future Persons: On the Ethics of Deciding Who Will Live, or Not, in the Future*, Dordrecht, The Netherlands: Kluwer.
———. (2008) 'Intergenerational justice', in *Stanford Encyclopedia of Philosophy*. Online. Available HTTP: <http://plato.stanford.edu/entries/justice-intergenerational/#ResNonIdePro> (accessed 28 September 2008).
Miller, D. (1999) 'Social justice and environmental goods', in A. Dobson (ed.) *Fairness and Futurity: Essays on Environmental Sustainability and Social Justice*, Oxford: Oxford University Press.
———. (2007) *National Responsibility and Global Justice*. Oxford: Oxford University Press.
Moellendorf, D. (2002) *Cosmopolitan Justice*, Boulder, CO: Westview Press.

Mulgan T. (1999) 'The place of the dead in liberal political philosophy', *Journal of Political Philosophy*, Vol. 7: 52–70.
———. (2006) *Future People*, Oxford: Oxford University Press.
Mumford, C.J. (1996) *Race and Reparations: A Black Perspective for the 21st Century*, Trenton, NJ: Africa World Press.
Naess, A. (1973) 'The shallow and the deep, long-range ecology movement: a summary', *Inquiry*, Vol. 16: 95–100.
Nagel, T. (1979) 'Death', in Nagel, *Mortal Questions*, Cambridge: Cambridge University Press.
Nash, R. (1990) *The Rights of Nature: A History of Environmental Ethics*, Leichardt, Australia: Primavera Press.
Nielsen, K. (1988) 'World government, security, and global justice', in S. Luper-Foy (ed.) *Problems of International Justice*, Boulder, CO: Westview Press.
Norton, B. G. (1989) 'The cultural approach to conservation biology', in D. Western and M.C. Pearl (eds.) *Conservation for the Twenty-first Century*, Oxford: Oxford University Press.
Nozick, R. (1974) *Anarchy, State and Utopia*, Oxford: Blackwell.
———. (1989) *The Examined Life: Philosophical Meditations*, New York: Simon and Schuster.
O'Neill, J. (1993a) 'Future generations: present harms', *Philosophy*, Vol. 68: 35–51.
———. (1993b) *Ecology, Policy and Politics: Human Well-Being and the Natural World*, London: Routledge.
Paden, R. (1997) 'Rawls's just savings principle and the sense of justice', *Social Theory and Practice*, Vol. 23: 27–52.
Page, E. A. (2006) *Climate Change, Justice and Future Generations*, Cheltenham, UK: Edward Elgar.
Paine, T. (1971) 'The rights of man' [1791], in H. Collins (ed.) *The Rights of Man*, Harmondsworth, England: Penguin.
Parfit, D. (1976), 'On doing the best for our children', in M.D. Bayles (ed.) *Ethics and Population*, Cambridge, MA: Schenkman Publishing.
———. (1984) *Reasons and Persons*, Oxford: Oxford University Press.
Parfit, D. and Cowen, T. (1992) 'Against the social discount rate', in P. Laslett and J. Fishkin, (eds.) *Justice Between Age Groups and the Generations*, New Haven, CT: Yale University Press.
Partridge, E. (1981a) 'Posthumous interests and posthumous respect', *Ethics*, Vol. 91: 243–264.
———. (1981b) 'Why care about the future?', in E. Partridge (ed.) *Responsibilities to Future Generations*, Buffalo, NY: Prometheus Books.
———. (2001) 'Future generations', in D. Jamieson (ed.) *A Companion to Environmental Philosophy*, Oxford: Blackwell.
Passmore, J. (1974) *Man's Responsibility for Nature*, London: Duckworth.
Peter, K. B. (2002) 'Jefferson and the independence of generations', *Environmental Ethics*, Vol. 24: 371–387.
Pitcher, G. (1984) 'The misfortunes of the dead', *American Philosophical Quarterly*, Vol. 21: 183–188.
Pogge, T. (1992) 'Cosmopolitanism and sovereignty', *Ethics*, Vol. 103: 48–75.
———. (2008) *World Poverty and Human Rights*, 2nd Ed., Cambridge, England: Polity.
Posner, R. A. (1995) *Aging and Old Age*, Chicago: University of Chicago Press.
Post, S. (1990) 'Women and elderly parents: moral controversy in an aging society', *Hypatia*, Vol. 5: 83–89.
Rawls, J. (1972) *A Theory of Justice*, Oxford: Oxford University Press.
———. (1996) *Political Liberalism*, New York: Columbia University Press.

———. (1999a) *A Theory of Justice*, Revised Edition, Cambridge, MA: Harvard University Press.
———. (1999b) *The Law of Peoples*, Cambridge, MA: Harvard University Press.
Richards, D.A.J. (1983) 'Contractarian theory, international justice and energy policy', in D. MacLean and P. Brown (eds.) *Energy and the Future*, Totowa, NJ: Rowman and Littlefield.
Ridge, M. (2003) 'Giving the dead their due', *Ethics*, Vol. 114: 38–59.
Roberts, M. A. (1998) *Child versus Childmaker*, Lanham, MD: Rowman and Littlefield.
Routley, R. and Routley, V. (1982) 'The nuclear train to the future', T. Regan and D. VanDeVeer (eds.) *And Justice for All: New Introductory Essays in Ethics and Public Policy*, Totowa, NJ: Rowman and Littlefield.
Sagoff, M. (1991) 'Technological risk: a budget of distinctions', in D. Cooper and J. Palmer (eds.) *The Environment in Question*, London: Routledge.
Sandel, M. (1998) *Liberalism and the Limits of Justice*, 2nd Edition, Cambridge: Cambridge University Press.
Scanlon, T. (1998) *What We Owe to Each Other*, Cambridge, MA: Belknap Press.
Schwartz, T. (1978) 'Obligations to posterity', in R.K. Sikora and B. Barry (eds.) *Obligations to Future Generations*, Philadelphia: Temple University Press.
Sen, A. (2001) *Development as Freedom*, Oxford: Oxford University Press.
Shrader-Frechette, K. (1995) 'Ethical dilemmas and radioactive wastes: a survey of the issues', in A. Brennan (ed.) *The Ethics of the Environment*, Aldershot, England: Dartmouth Publishing Group.
Smolkin, D. (1994) 'The non-identity problem and the appeal to future people's rights', *Southern Journal of Philosophy*, Vol. 32: 315–329.
Sylvan, R. and Bennett, D. (1994) *The Greening of Ethics*, Cambridge, England: White Horse Press.
Tamir, Y. (1993) *Liberal Nationalism*, Princeton: Princeton University Press.
Taylor, C. (1989) *Sources of the Self: the Making of the Modern Identity*, Cambridge: Cambridge University Press.
Taylor, P. (1986) *Respect for Nature: A Theory of Environmental Ethics*, Princeton: Princeton University Press.
Thompson, J. (2000) 'Injustice and the removal of Aboriginal children', *Australian Journal of Professional and Applied Ethics*, Vol. 2: 114–135.
———. (2001) 'Historical injustice and reparation: justifying claims of descendants', *Ethics*, Vol. 112: 114–135.
———. (2003) *Taking Responsibility for the Past*, Cambridge, England: Polity.
———. (2008) 'Apology, justice and respect: A critical defense of political apology', in M. Gibney (ed.), *The Age of Apology: Facing Up to the Past*, Philadelphia: University of Philadelphia Press.
Thomson, D. (1992) 'Generations, justice, and the future of collective action', in P. Laslett and J.S. Fishkin (eds.) *Justice Between Age Groups and Generations*, New Haven, CT: Yale University Press.
———. (1991) *Selfish Generations? The Ageing of New Zealand's Welfare State*, Wellington, NZ: Bridget Williams Books.
Turnbull, C. M. (1972) *The Mountain People*, New York: Simon and Schuster.
United Nations (1994) *International Conference on Population and Development*. Online. Available HTTP: <http://www.un.org/popin/icpd2.htm> (accessed 26 September 2008).
Waldron, J. (1992) 'Superseding historical injustice', *Ethics*, Vol. 103: 4–28.
———. (1993) 'A right to do wrong', in Waldron, *Collected Papers 1981–1991*, Cambridge: Cambridge University Press.

Weiner, B.A. (2005) *Sins of Parents: The Politics of National Apologies in the United States*, Philadelphia: Temple University Press.
Wellman, C. (1995) *Real Rights*, New York: Oxford University Press.
Wells, H.G. (1964) *The Time Machine*, New York: Airmont.
Wenz, P. S. (1988) *Environmental Justice*, New York: State University of New York Press.
Wicclair, M. (1990) 'Caring for frail, elderly parents: past parental sacrifices and the obligations of adult children', *Social Theory and Practice*, Vol. 16: 163–190.
Wissenburg, M. L. (1998) *Green Liberalism: The Free and Green Society*, London: UCL Press.
Wolf, S. (1997) 'Happiness and meaning: two aspects of the good life', *Social Philosophy and Policy*, Vol. 14: 207–225.
World Bank (1994) *Averting the Old Age Crisis*, Oxford: Oxford University Press.
World Commission on Environment and Development (1987) *Our Common Future*, Oxford: Oxford University Press.

Index

A
Abdel-Nour, Farid, 75
Aborigines, 71, 80
Ackerman, Bruce, 69–70, 93, 118
age groups, 106–107
Anderson, Benedict, 4
animals, 90, 146, 178n11:1
apologies, 74, 77, 78, 80, 83
Aristotle, 57–8, 62
Attfield, Robin, 169
Auerbach, Bruce, 122, 124, 125–126, 136–137

B
baby-boomers, 2, 123
Baier, Annette, 4–5, 177n7:3
Ball, Terence, 22, 36, 88
Barry, Brian, 20, 23–4, 30, 90, 110
Becker, Lawrence, 30–2
Beckerman, Wilfred and Pasek, Joanna, 9, 91, 116, 117–119, 126
Boxill, Bernard, 74, 76, 80, 83, 177n6:2
Burke, Edmund, 7–8, 11, 28, 29–30, 84

C
Callahan, Daniel, 108, 109, 133
Care, Norman S., 172, 173
Civil War, 5, 33, 83
collective responsibility, 3–4, 6–7, 50, 54, 55, 74, 77–78, 111
communitarianism, 7, 34, 37, 45, 46, 85, 176n3:3
consequentialism, 10, 136, 149–150
cosmopolitanism, 13, 145, 164, 167, 178n12:1

D
De George, Richard T., 8
dead, the: commemorating, 2, 4, 29, 31, 66–67, 86, 97–100, 153–154; harming and benefiting, 8, 56–59, 61–62, 68, 77, 153, 176n5:1; promises to, 53, 55, 56, 57, 59–62, 63, 64; rights of, 3–4, 8, 53
democracy, 1, 6–7, 74, 85, 86, 92, 98, 122, 124, 138, 140–141, 147, 165, 168, 169, 171–172, 173–174
demographic change, 12, 104, 107, 112, 116–117, 122, 126, 127
de-Shalit, Avner, 34–40, 45, 52, 67, 148, 175n2:5, 176n3:4
diachronic approach to justice 2–4, 7–8, 11, 29, 73, 101–102, 106, 128
difference principle, 11, 106, 113, 117, 119, 126–127, 130
discounting the future, 148, 157–159
Dobson, Andrew, 94–95, 167, 169, 173, 174
Dworkin, Ronald, 93

E
eco-centrism, 145, 146–147
ecology. *See* environment
Ekeli, Kristian Skagen, 155
English, Jane, 113, 175n2:8
environment: as heritage, 32–33, 86, 92, 93–5, 129, 146–7; as source of problems: 4, 9, 10, 24, 31, 90, 92, 119, 121, 126, 128, 145, 151, 155–158, 163, 166–168, 170
equality: between generations, 11–12, 109, 113–114, 116–119, 126–127; of individuals, 9–10, 20, 22, 70, 72, 82, 91–92, 128, 130, 138–139, 140–141, 157–158, 160; of polities, 163–164
eugenics. *See* genetic enhancement

F
fair shares principle, 12, 112, 170, 114, 116–121, 124, 125–127, 128

Families: entitlements of, 17, 18, 72, 77, 80–84, 87, 111–112, 134, 161; and generational cohorts, 103, 109, 111–112, and the intergenerational social contract, 19–21, 22–23, 24–25, 37, 39, 53, 105, 148, 175n2:8; responsibilities of, 3, 16, 20, 21, 63–64, 66–68, 73, 101, 103, 104–105, 106–107, 109, 123; as a source of identity, 4–5, 7, 10, 33–4, 69–70, 132, 152; women and, 21, 47, 101, 104–105, 123, 134
Feinberg, Joel, 10, 56–7, 59–60, 65, 135, 139, 153, 176n5:3, 178n12:2
Feldman, Fred, 49
feminism, 105, 106, 143
filial duties, 108–109
Flanagan, Owen, 47
Flannery, Tim, 129, 130
free-riding, 125–126

G

Gaita, Raimond, 75
Gaspart, Frédéric and Gosseries, Alex, 113–115, 119, 121, 124–125, 126
generational cohorts: defined, 103–104; distributions among, 102–103, 108–111, 113–114,121, 122–123, 126
generational continuum, 1, 84, 131–2, 150–153, 159, 172
genetic enhancement, 11, 137–140, 142–143
genocide, 81
global citizenship, 160, 167, 169–170
global society, 160, 167–169, 170
global warming, 9, 42, 154–155, 157, 166, 170, 171
Golding, M.P., 10, 18, 46, 47, 152
Goodin, Robert, 116–7, 118, 119, 121
gratitude: to parents, 108–109, 111; to past generations, 30–32, 55, 78, 176n3:1
greenhouse gases. See global warming

H

Habermas, Jürgen, 138–9
Harris, John, 138, 143
Haslett, D.W., 70–1, 177n5:5
hedonism, 49, 50
Held, David, 168
Heyd, David, 131–132, 135, 137
history: and intergenerational projects, 85–86, 91–92, 114–115, 145, 169; interpretation of, 97–98, 173; as source of entitlements and obligations, 2, 3, 7, 73–78, 80–83, 99–100, 163, 166–167; as source of identity 1, 4–5, 31–33, 44, 147, 152
Hubin, D. Clayton, 20
human survival, 135, 136–137
Huxley, Aldous, 46–47, 178n10:3

I

indigenous people 1, 71, 76–77, 80, 167
inheritance: of capital, 11, 22, 85, 88–89, 90, 113, 164–165, 177n7:1; of communal heritage, 7, 31, 69, 71–73, 75, 77, 85–86, 93–96, 97, 141–142, 165; of debt, 2, 7, 33, 63–64, 74, 78, 112, 117, 120–122, 123–126, 167; of institutions, 23, 85–86, 88–89, 91, 92, 97, 100, 161; of property, 60, 68–71,73, 75–7, 87, 93, 128
intergenerational partnership, 7, 29–30, 34–36

J

Jecker, Nancy, 108, 111
Jefferson, Thomas, 6–8, 11, 12, 25, 30, 74, 85, 88–89, 98–99, 120, 121–122, 123–124, 175nn1:1; 2:6
just savings principle, 19, 23, 85, 88, 113–16, 165

K

Kumar, Rahul, 15–16, 18

L

Laslett, Peter, 90, 102, 110–11
Levine, Andrew, 106–7, 109–10, 116
liberal values 43, 63–65, 66, 69, 70–72, 85, 92, 93–95, 124, 132, 138–139, 140–141, 147, 163, 177n7:2
libertarianism, 70, 75–76, 104–105, 123
lifetime-transcending interests: defined, 5, 40, 42–43; and intergenerational justice, 40, 43–44, 50–54, 73; and meaningful lives, 44–46, 50, 76–77; and obligations, 53–54, 58–59, 61–63, 67, 86, 75
Lincoln, Abraham, 29–31, 85–86, 96, 99, 175n1:1
Linklater, Andrew, 168, 169
Lomasky, Loren, 45–46, 68–69

M

MacIntyre, Alasdair, 7, 75, 176n3:3
Macklin, Ruth, 8
Madison, James, 88, 121
McMahan, Jeff, 31, 176n2:9
Meyer, Lukas, 44, 151, 175²:1
Miller, David, 32–34, 44, 77–78, 90, 93–94, 164–165, 176n3:2
Mollendorf, Darrel, 164, 178n12:1
mysticism, 49–50

N

Nagel, Thomas, 56, 65
Nash, Roderick, 146
nation, 1, 4, 6, 7, 11, 28–29, 31–34, 44, 74–75, 77–78, 90, 120, 147, 160, 164, 176n3:2
national debt, 12, 33, 76–78, 112, 120–122, 123–126, 167
neutrality, 69–70, 92–95, 97–98, 118, 147, 176n5:2, 177n7:2
non-identity, 9, 10, 13–15, 17–18, 19, 23, 25–26, 33, 51, 141, 149, 175nn1:1–3
Nozick, Robert, 45–6, 75–76
nuclear wastes, 10, 148–149, 151, 154–155, 156, 157–158

P

Paden, Roger, 25, 89–90
Page, Edward A., 31–32, 175n2:1
Paine, Thomas, 6–8, 30, 74
Parfit, Derek, 15, 175n2:1
Partridge, Ernest, 35, 37, 44–45, 46–48, 49, 50–51, 60, 176n5:3
Passmore, John, 18
Peter, Kenneth, 12, 121–122
Pitcher, George, 56–58, 59, 68
Pogge, Thomas, 124, 168, 169
polities: defined, 1; and identity through time, 5, 83, 152–153; as intergenerational agents, 5, 73–74, 77–80, 160; in relation to each other, 79–80, 160–164, 166
population control, 10–11, 129, 132–134
Posner, Richard, 108
posthumous reputation, 40, 48, 55, 58, 65–66, 177n5:1
precautionary principle, 156–157
procreation rights, 129–133, 134
procreative duties, 134–135, 137

R

Rawls, John, 2, 8, 11–12, 18–30, 37, 39, 40, 51, 53, 62, 72, 85, 87–89, 91, 93, 97, 113–118, 123, 130, 140, 146, 148, 150–151, 152, 164–165, 169, 170, 175n1:3, 177n7:1
reciprocity, 29, 30–33, 78, 108–110, 172, 176n3:1
rectification. *See* reparations
reparations, 5–6, 73–77, 79, 80–84, 97, 163, 166–167, 172, 177n6:1–3
Ridge, Michael, 77, 177n6:3
Routley, Val and Richard, 148–149, 154

S

Sagoff, Mark 155–156
Scanlon, Thomas, 15, 22, 61
scepticism about intergenerational justice, 22, 29, 36, 140–141
secession, 86, 99–100
slavery, 5, 74, 76–77, 80–81, 82–83, 99, 167, 177n6:2
social contract, 3–4, 5–8, 19–21, 22–27, 28, 36–37, 51–54, 60–61, 79, 88, 93, 105, 110, 118, 141, 150, 152–153, 175n2:3–6
stoicism, 49–50, 176n4:1
sustainability, 4, 87, 89–90, 116, 129–130, 145–146, 159, 170, 173
synchronic approach to justice 2–4, 7–8, 11, 29, 73–74, 87, 101–102, 106, 108, 128

T

Tamir, Yael, 4
Taylor, Charles, 46, 47, 176n3:3
treaties, 69, 73–74, 79–80, 84, 85
Treaty of Waitangi, 84
Turnbull, Colin, 47

U

uncertainty about future, 121, 126–127, 145–146, 154–157
utilitarianism. *See* consequentialism

V

veil of ignorance, 19, 22–23, 26, 28, 29, 51, 52, 72, 114

W

Waldron, Jeremy, 76–77, 82, 135,
Wellman, Carl, 8
Wenz, Peter, 146
Wicclair, Mark, 108–109, 111
Wissenburg, Marcel, 90, 130, 133
Wolf, Susan, 45

About the Author

Janna Thompson is an Associate Professor at La Trobe University in Melbourne, Australia. She is the author of *Taking Responsibility for the Past* and other writings on historical obligations, environmental ethics, and global and intergenerational justice.